Pardner of the Wind

THE AUTHOR

The first person to attempt a systematic study and collection of cowboy songs and range ballads, N. Howard ("Jack") Thorp, himself a cowboy, cattleman, and top rider, at the turn of the century was making horseback trips of hundreds of miles through half a dozen cow-country states, spending his time mostly in cow camps, at chuck wagons, or in line camps, picking up a whole song here and part of one there, and writing a good many songs himself to add to the cowboys' repertoire. One of his ballads, "Little Joe the Wrangler," is perhaps the most widely known of all rangeland songs. Jack is here seen aboard Lark, a Texas steel dust, a favorite horse of his later years.

Story of the Southwestern Cowboy

PARDNER OF THE WIND

By

N. HOWARD (JACK) THORP

in collaboration with
NEIL M. CLARK

"*Just let me live as I've begun*
And give me work that's open to the sky;
Make me a pardner of the wind and sun
And I won't ask a life that's soft or high. . . . ."

A COWBOY'S PRAYER

UNIVERSITY OF NEBRASKA PRESS · Lincoln and London

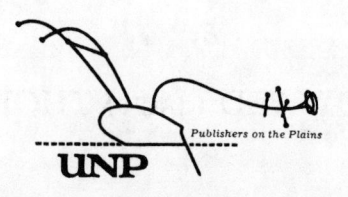

Publishers on the Plains

UNP

Copyright 1941 by The Caxton Printers, Ltd.
Caldwell, Idaho
Renewal copyright 1972 by Neil M. Clark

First Bison Book printing: 1977

Most recent printing indicated by first digit below:
1   2   3   4   5   6   7   8   9   10

Library of Congress Cataloging in Publication Data

Thorp, Nathan Howard, 1867–1940.
  Pardner of the wind.

  Reprint of the ed. published by Caxton Printers, Caldwell, Idaho.

  1. Thorp, Nathan Howard, 1867–1940. 2. Cowboys—Southwest, New—Biography. 3. Southwest, New—History. 4. Frontier and pioneer life—Southwest, New. I. Clark, Neil McCullough, 1890– joint author. II. Title.
F786.T47   978'.02'0922 [B]   77-7243
ISBN 0–8032–0938–X
ISBN 0–8032–5875–5 pbk.

SALUTE!

Jack, you were eager to see this book of yours in print, but you couldn't wait for it at the last. There came a call from the other side of the range and you had to go. Gold strikes, you used to say, always get richer the farther away from them you are; and you knew that maybe a man's big hopes for heaven are only another kind of gold strike. But I like to think —yes! I like to think that you are still riding over yonder in the big valley of the sunset; that the smell of sage and horseflesh and hot leather are still in your nostrils, the pounding of cattle hooves in your ears, and big mountain-bounded horizons all around you. Give you matches in your pocket, flour and bacon in your saddlebags, your old banjo for company, and a soogan to wrap yourself up in under the stars, and you'll make out for the journey across those misty lonesome flats, however far it be. Wherever you are and whatever you think of it all now, this is the book we planned. It would have been a better book if you could have stayed to see the last stages through. But "Blarney," helped me wonderfully; she and I have done as well as we could. All the best of it, of course, is yours, for it was you who had the living of it.

—N. M. C.

CONTENTS

ILLUSTRATIONS

Pardner of the Wind

INTRODUCTION

I
N ONE of the stories in his privately-printed book, *Tales of the Chuck Wagon*, Jack Thorp puts in cowboy language just why it is that more bed-rock true stories are not written about the old West of cowboy and cattleman. Jess Hill, tall puncher from the Sacramento Mountains, rides in to join the round-up wagon. He finds the boys who are sitting around in idleness because it is raining too hard to do any work, trying to keep dry under a bed-tarp stretched out like a tent. After a day of slick trails and grief with a pack horse that was down more than once in boggy ground, Jess speaks his mind in this fashion:

"Punchin' cows in these mountains ain't like it is in a book I read before I left the ranch, where all the cute waddie had ter do was ride slick fat horses, sleep on a geese-hair bed, set the boss' daughter en afterwards marry her, en she the prettiest girl in the West. I wonder why some sure-enough cowhand don't write the truth about it, heh?"

And this was the answer Jess got:

"If we fellers that were raised in a saddle would a' wrote those books we wouldn't a' been raised in the saddle, and those fellers who do write the books haven't been raised in the saddle, and that's the reason they can write 'em. They was raised in an office. En say, Jess, wouldn't you and I look fine settin' here under this bed-sheet tryin' to write a story about one of them offices in a big city, huh?"

Nathan Howard (Jack) Thorp was a "sure-enough cow-hand" and cattleman, from the grassroots under his boots to the top of his wide-brimmed hat. For much the greater part of his life—for fifty years and more—he rode the range, lived the life, made his living out of cattle, and was an integral part of the cowboy scene. But it was far from unimportant, in reckoning the total accomplishment of his life, that he was born in a very different environment, and lived in it long enough to be able to appraise objectively the life of the range as he found and took part in it. It also was far from unimportant that he possessed a highly literate and cultured mind, and that it was given to him to understand that what he saw would presently pass, and that it was his privilege as well as his responsibility as far as he had the capacity to do so, to make some record of the life he saw and lived. Jack did not have a very great literary gift. His published works are limited to his pioneer booklet, *Songs of the Cowboys*, containing just twenty songs of the range, and put out in red paper covers by Jack himself in 1908; the bigger book of the same title published by Houghton Mifflin Company in 1921; *Tales of the Chuck Wagon*, privately printed by Jack in 1926; and fugitive pieces in the *New Mexico Magazine*, *The Cattleman*, and some other papers and magazines. A few times in his later years, when the money would have been welcome, he tried to dress up some of his writings in the so-called wild-west style demanded by the pulp magazines, but he had no success with it—he couldn't get far enough away from the facts into fantasy.

Jack had little or none of the fictional skill of Eugene Manlove Rhodes—the two were contemporaries and fellow ranchers for a while in the San Andrés Mountains, but his skill with a horse was greater than Gene's, and in the cattle industry he was the caliber of man who could, and did, serve as State Cattle Inspector. And when Mexico was in revolution, he was the caliber of man who could, and did, go deep into Chihuahua with a cook and one cowhand, bringing back to the States a herd of cattle that had belonged to the recently murdered President Madero.

Adventure, indeed, always had a bright face for him, and he was working as foreman for a gumbo camp in Texas when he and his partner (a lad named Buxton) heard of the Klondike gold rush. That was in 1897, and Jack was thirty. The two men, when they added up their joint assets, found that they had about two thousand dollars saved up, and they resolved to head for Alaska and make their everlasting fortunes. They got as far as Seattle together, and there learned that the steamship companies wouldn't accept passengers unless they could prove that they had enough cash for the fare up and back, and a year's keep besides—it was figured that the minimum sum was eighteen hundred dollars per person. Since it was obvious that both of them couldn't go, they retired to a hotel room and played freeze-out poker for the money. Buxton won, and went to Alaska; Jack never heard of him again.

He himself sailed from Seattle to Peru with a party of engineers engaged by some railroad outfit which went broke shortly after Thorp reached South America. The stranded engineers hocked their instruments in order to live, and Jack, determined to get back to the States by hook or crook, haunted the steamship docks to see what might turn up. One day a steamer came in, bound for San Francisco. It had six Negro stokers. While the ship was in port, one of them died. Thorp, who was a powerful man, offered to take the dead man's place in pay for his passage. The offer was accepted—"I was the sixth nigger!" The members of the stoker crew, he told me, would work in the stokehold for fifteen minutes, then come up for five minutes to be hosed down with cold water. When he left Peru, Jack weighed two hundred pounds; when he got to San Francisco, he weighed one hundred and twenty.

This was only an interlude. He was always a man of action, but his special field of intellectual interest was the singing cowboy, and he was the pioneer collector of cowboy songs. Almost from the time when he first came to the West, he began to pick them up here and there and copy them in his notebook, although nobody else was doing such a thing with any idea of publication, nor did anybody else seem to think that those songs might have any value or interest. Jack not only gathered songs first-hand, but also wrote many letters to people he knew in other states, asking them to send him any cowboy songs they might know or hear. When he finally had a sheaf of authentic cowboy verse, with the language carefully pruned to be printable, he could not find any publisher interested in risking money on it; so he became his own publisher. Jack had quite a gift for balladry himself, and the number of songs that he wrote was considerable; the best known, by all odds, being "Little Joe the Wrangler," a song which, like many other range ballads, was woven around an actual incident of the trail, witnessed by the singer. Jack often told how he wrote that famous song on paper bags beside the campfire, and sang it first to his partners on the trail drive; and how the song made its first public appearance elsewhere in Uncle Johnny Root's saloon at Weed, New Mexico. Since then, it has been sung and heard on the radio and phonograph records and in cow camps, millions of times.

Thorp's early background was the East—the East of New York and Newport. He was born on June 10, 1867, the third and youngest son of a wealthy New York lawyer. He was sent to St. Paul's School at Concord, New Hampshire, where he used to sing in the boys' choir, with a little white robe around him. When the family was in residence in the summer home at Newport, Jack spent most of his spare time on the water. His first acquaintance with the West and his love for Western horses came when his older brother, Charles, set up in business with a cattle ranch in Nebraska, and Jack went out to spend some of his summers there. It was at this ranch, located near the town of Stanton, that he did his first bronc riding. He had already learned to ride in the East, but only on the flat or the hunting saddle, for polo or fox hunting. Jack, together with his cousin, Frank Underhill, Theodore Roosevelt, and Roosevelt's brother-in-law, constituted a polo team that played at Meadowbrook and elsewhere.

While Jack was still in his 'teens, his father, through obligations assumed in behalf of a partner in a big real estate transaction, lost all of his money. Jack therefore had to pass up college, and he headed West to take care of himself; and from then on, the West was his real home. For a few years he combined business and the kind of pleasure he had been familiar with, by buying likely Western ponies, which he shipped east and trained for polo on Sandy Point Farm, near Newport, which he operated jointly with Underhill. He usually made enough on the ponies he sold, to finance a season's polo for himself. But after his mother's death, in 1894, he rarely cared to go East again.

Jack had practical training as a civil engineer, and his first regular employment in New Mexico was as superintendent of the Enterprise Mining Company, in the silver mines at Kingston —now a ghost town. It was a raw and undeveloped country in the late eighties, and the silver from the mine was freighted out on burros to El Paso. Within a year or so after Jack's arrival, silver was demonetized, and it became unprofitable to operate the mines; so Jack now took his first flyer in the cattle business. He bought about two hundred head of longhorns, and ran them in the San Andrés Mountains under the Slash SW (/SW) brand. He made a little money on them, but soon went to work for one of the big outfits of the region, the Bar W, which in those days ran from ten to fifteen thousand head in one of the greatest producing open-range areas the country has ever known. Barbed wire had not as yet come into use, and when Bar W cattle drifted south along the Carrizozo flats, they could get a long way from home. Part of Jack's job was to keep an eye on them and head them north. His first year with the Bar W he worked as a plain cowhand, the next year as an outside man. In the latter capacity, he rode the range on horses not bearing the Bar W brand, to look at other herds and strays and see if he could spot any "burnt" cattle. In subsequent years he engaged in various ranch enterprises of his own, sometimes with partners; some of the enterprises being more, some less successful. Jack was married, in 1903, to Annette Hesch, whose father was a sheepman with a ranch near Palma, New Mexico. Mrs. Thorp declares that the only sheepman and cattleman she ever knew who could get along were her father and her husband. To Jack and Jack's friends, his wife was always "Blarney"—her father was an Austrian, but her mother was born in the city of Cork. Jack was a powerful man physically, standing two inches over six feet, weighing from two hundred to two hundred and fifteen pounds, and all of it muscle. His speech was humorous and picturesque, with the imaginative exaggeration characteristic of men of the range. He seldom talked seriously or much about himself and his personal history, and when directly questioned, if he felt that the occasion warranted, he was likely to give a fillip of fiction to his replies. Alice Corbin Henderson has recorded that once when he was asked how long he had been in the West, Jack ducked his head toward some ancient cedars growing on the hillside. "See those?"

His listener nodded.

"Well, I planted 'em."

Nor could he tolerate bores and fawners; though always kindly, the barbs on his wit could puncture the stuffing in stuffed shirts. At a gathering of writers who were called together in connection with the Coronado Cuarto Centennial, a flittery woman well past sixty fluttered up to Jack and introduced herself, saying, "Oh, Mr. Thorp, I understand you're quite a cowboy. You know, I'm quite a cowgirl. We must just have a long, long talk."

"Lady," said Jack, shying off as fast as he decently could, "You've got me all wrong. I never was on my horse in my life till two years ago—an' he throwed me."

"I never was with Jack Thorp as much as I wish I had been with him."—I quote from a letter from J. Frank Dobie, author of several classic books on the Southwest—"but our chemicals seemed to mix. I went out to his little place at Alameda one afternoon, having left Albuquerque with the intention of getting to Santa Fe that night. When the sun was about down I said I had to go, but Jack said no I had better wait. I waited and we had supper and then kept on talking until away after midnight. I did manage to get to Santa Fe the next afternoon. All Jack needed was a good listener. He never seemed to run out and yet his stories always had pertinence and were based on character more than on anything else. He had a wonderful memory. I mentioned to him the Lost Adams Diggins, long-horns, and bear stories, and he at once drew up from his well narratives both illuminating and interesting. He sent me a story about an old-timer getting down in a pit and fighting a grizzly bear. That is as good a bear story as I ever read. His sense of humor, his sweetness of nature, and his adequate use of observation made his memory a useful and delightful agent."

It is proper to tell how the present book was produced. It is, in the fullest sense of the word, a collaboration, and a great deal of the actual writing was done by Jack himself. He had many unpublished manuscripts in his files to which he gave me free access, and he wrote others especially for this book. Some of his manuscripts were narratives of personal experiences and observations, others were stories that he had picked up from acquaintances and friends, and still others were serious attempts to make an accurate record and appraisal of Southwestern range life and practices. My primary function, therefore, was to organize and edit, and write when I had to, after asking him endless questions and taking notes. Whenever I could do so, I used Jack's own direct and pungent words. We had many a long session in his home or mine, and I like to think now that perhaps those talks gave him as much pleasure as they did me.

In the last years of his life, when the cattle business did not prosper, and fortune in other ways did not favor him, Jack must have worried some, I think, but he never lost his cheerful spirit and quick humor. He proudly made out with what he had, and told with hearty approval of the old puncher who, riding by on the way from Texas, stopped for a bed and a meal or two at Jack's house. Asked why he was quitting Texas, the puncher replied, "Jack, a man can live better in New Mexico jest a triflin', than he can in Texas workin' hard!" Jack himself had a deep and enduring love for the West, and he put his feeling for it into one of his songs, the first and last lines of which went as follows:

Oh, come en ride the Western range along with Blue en me;
Forget your cares and worries—just play you're young en free. . . . .
Wear old clothes, hunt, fish, en idle; do exactly as you please,
Forget set rules en schedules—with a good horse between your knees.

The last letter I had from him, written on April 29, 1940, was wholly characteristic. He said in part:

The last two weeks I have practically spent in bed, a doctor flitting in the background. Just what the ailment may be has not been determined. It does not seem to be described in the *materia medica*, & I may take out a patent on it, pushing it as the latest '40 fad. There are two old sayings in the West which hold good—"He who drinks of the waters of the Hassayampa never again may speak the truth"; and "when an old cowhand quits his saddle, he quickly goes to pot." If you care for the use of a saddle this summer, I have a good one here you will be welcome to. Drop in and see the old wreck when you are in town, & if I can get all four feet working again, will come out.

A hurry call came for me to go to Chicago, and I never did get to see him again. On the evening of June 4 he died suddenly while sitting up, talking. When Jack Thorp went, a veritable part of the Old West went, too.

NEIL M. CLARK

(Thanks are due to the editors of *The Atlantic Monthly* and *The Cattleman* for permission to reprint certain material that appeared in somewhat different form in the columns of those magazines.)

BANJO IN THE COW CAMPS

*"Now boys I'll tell you a story
of a horse I owned long, long ago."*

I

WORDS and banjo-strumming floated soft and clear on the night. I reined up in the brush to listen. It was pitch dark where I was, Pecos River behind me, Roswell down that-a-way quite a piece, and somebody's chuck wagon just ahead, drawn up for the night in flat sand-dune country rich in grama grass and tabosa. The campfire flickered and fell. I knew there would be maybe half a dozen men sprawled around it, their day's riding done, supper over, and a banjo-pickin' cowboy to tell a story under the stars: a story in verse, about their own country and kind, in their lingo, home-grown and maybe as thorny as cactus. This one I was hearing now was about "a little steel dust the color of rust," the fastest cutting-horse in Texas—name of Dodgin' Joe. It was a new song to me. As the final words died away, I rode into the light of the campfire.

A young man's impulse sent me out on the road collecting cowboy songs almost fifty years ago—an interest which, as cowboy and cattleman, I never lost. And it was more than thirty years ago, in the year 1908, that I made a dicker with a printer in Estancia, New Mexico, to print two thousand copies of the first little book of cowboy songs ever published. I paid the printer six cents per copy. The book was printed on rough stock and bound in red paper. There were fifty pages, twenty-four songs.

I advertised in some Kansas papers that published patent sheets, and sold a good many of the books at fifty cents apiece.

They were fragile, and most of the copies probably were torn to pieces or lost long ago, the few that are left fetch twenty-five dollars or so from collectors.

Few people know of the difficulties encountered in gathering those first songs. Today you can find scores of cowboy ballads in song books accessible anywhere, and Tin-pan Alley manufactures new ones fresh every hour. In the nineties, with the exception of about a dozen, cowboy songs were not generally known. The only ones I could find I gathered, a verse here and a verse there, on horseback trips that lasted months and took me hundreds of miles through half a dozen cow-country states, most of the time being spent in cow camps, at chuck wagons and line camps.

Songs of the range had a special appeal for me. I was a singin' cowboy myself, by adoption, with a little mandolin-banjo that went where I went, and the songs I heard some cowboys sing were an authentic feature of the land and life that made it seem good to me. Sometimes on the trail or in camp I would think up a song of my own.

On this evening I'm telling about, in March of '89, my first song hunt proper started. I had been looking for a couple of stray Bar W horses, and I was tired after a forty-five-mile ride. About to unpack and make a solitary camp, I spied fire in the distance. "What's the use of campin' by yourself?" I thought. So I rode in to the camp which Nigger Add and his men had pitched at the tail of their chuck wagon.

Cowmen from Toyah, Texas, to Las Vegas, New Mexico, knew Add, and most of them at different times had worked on round-ups with him. He was the L F D outfit's range boss, and worked South Texas colored hands almost entirely. Black though he was, Add was one of the best hands on the Pecos River, well liked, and in due time hero of a cowboy song himself.[1]

I hobbled out my horses and rustled a plate and cup from the chuck box; coffee and a pot of stew were kept hot all night at such camps. Having eaten my fill, I inquired who had been singing just before I came in. Heads nodded at a colored boy known as 'Lasses. He owned up. I asked if he would mind singing the song again. He did it for me. But he only knew two verses, that's all. And none of the other hands in camp knew more. That was one of the difficulties encountered in the earliest effort to assemble the unprinted verse of the range. None of the cowboys who could sing ever remembered an entire song. I would pick up a verse or two here, another verse or two there.

After 'Lasses finished, I sang a song and so did several others. Somebody knew a couple of verses of "Sam Bass"—not the whole thing. The other songs they knew were about cotton patches, like one which celebrated a colored girl named Mamie. She picked her weight of cotton in the morning, 'twas said, then, with her feet under a bush and her head in the sun, went fast asleep. Cotton-picking songs were fine if you liked them, but they weren't what I was after. By the light of the fire I copied in my notebook the two verses of "Dodgin' Joe" which 'Lasses knew. Then I spread my tarp, wrapped my soogan around me, and, with feet to the fire, fought off sleep for a while because a big idea was buzzing in my head. Here I was, I told myself, workin' for wages for the Bar W. Nothing on my mind. Not much in my pocket: three dollars or so, and no more comin', for I always kept my money all drawed up:

> The cowboy's life is a dreary life, though his mind it is no load,
> And he always spends his money like he found it in the road.

Nigger Add had told me the two horses I was looking for were safe in the L F D horse pasture; no need to worry more about them. I was handy with horses, and in cow country somebody was always wantin' horses broke; they paid wages for it. My saddle horse, Gray Dog, and my pack horse, Ample, were my own property. Right here on my own range I had ridden into Add's camp and heard part of a cowboy song brand new to me.

"If there's one here," I thought, "there must be plenty more off my own range that I never heard."

So I made up my mind to keep driftin'.

Next morning when the mule star went to bed and the morning star got up, I had breakfast and started.[2] No trouble to say good-by to my job. When I got near the first post office a week or so later, I dropped a letter in the box telling my boss where his two strays were, and adding that one of his cowhands was a stray now too, and he should expect me back when he saw my dust arrivin'.

"Add," I said, "how far is it to the next water?"

"Keep this draw ten or twelve miles, Jack," he told me. "You'll see some cow trails comin' in. Head due east and you'll strike a dry lake." .

I was on my way!

A couple of hours after leaving the chuck wagon I reached Comanche Springs and there found two V T men watering a bunch of saddle horses. The rest of the day I saw no one. Just me, a couple of horses, a little rough country, a lot of rolling prairie; and at night, near the northeast end of Mescalero Valley, a lone camp and a dry one. I hobbled my horses, laid out my bed in a chamiso flat where the brush was three to four feet high, ate a snack, and made a fire to be sociable and show the folks I was rich and had matches in my pocket.

II

Maybe cowboy singing was an answer to loneliness. Maybe it was just another way of expressing good fellowship. Maybe it was several things. Something happened in the day's work, funny or sad, and somebody with a knack for words made a jingle of it; if it was liked, others learned it and passed it on. A ballad like "The Old Chisholm Trail," with its catching *come ti yi youpy* refrain, seems to have just grown. It was sung from the Canadian line to Mexico, and there were thousands of verses; nobody ever collected them all. Every cowboy knew a few, and if he had a little whiskey in him, or was heading for town with wages in his pocket, he might make up a few. These weren't "cultured" songs. Sometimes the rhymes didn't match very well. Often the language was rough and had to be heavily expurgated for publication. But ballad-making and song-singing were living parts of cowboy life.

I have never attempted any highbrow explanations of cowboy balladry. Not long ago in a newspaper I read a piece about

the "singin' families" of East Tennessee who by word of mouth
keep alive scores of ballads they have never seen in a book. It
was that way on the range. Singing songs, and making them too
(homely, everyday songs, not highbrow stuff), seems as natural
to human beings as washing herself is to a cat. And the faculty
gets more practice when people are cut off in isolated groups.

The little notebook diary of my first trip, which I still have,
is a vivid reminder of things I saw and did while on the trail of
these ballads. That period in our history has passed and will not
return. The way men lived, the country itself, the method of
earning a livelihood, peculiar characters and incidents—these
were the cowboys' background and the material for their songs.

It was a big country and an empty one, remember. Cowboys liked it or they wouldn't have been there.

> To the hot place with your city
> Where they herd like frightened rats
> On a range so badly crowded
> There ain't room to cuss a cat.

An old-timer, impressed by the size and empty character of
Texas and New Mexico, remarked that it was a circumstance
if you met one cowboy in a day's ride, and a happenin' if you
met two. So big and so empty, the country put a premium on
neighborliness in a way not always understood by outsiders.

I had been gone only a few days and was in a rather desolate
area twenty miles west of Ringgold, Texas, when I spied what
I judged to be a movers' wagon. You could generally tell 'em
ten miles off. They were early versions of modern *Grapes of
Wrath* families. The wagon was likely to have from two to
four horses hitched to it, a few head of stock drifting alongside,
a water keg on one side, bedding piled high, and anywhere from
six to twenty-five kids. Often the old woman was driving and
the old man asleep inside. Movers were horizon-hunters, a
foresign of the passing of the range. But in '89 there was still
plenty of room for them to move around in, and move they did,
often without any clear idea of where to—like a lot of the people
in automobiles today. When this particular wagon came up, the
man who was driving stopped and spat, said "Howdy!" and

asked if I reckoned he was headed right for Henrietta. We
"augered" a bit. I asked where he was bound for.

"Well, I'm goin' over here a right smart piece," he said—and
I knew that he didn't know, himself. He was just headin' for
the sunset, because he heard it callin' an' had to go.

Presently the wagon sheet was raised. A towheaded girl of
about sixteen looked out. She had a snuff stick in her mouth and
not fifteen cents worth of clothes on her back—just an old
Mother Hubbard.

She cocked a disillusioned eye at a landscape in which there
was no visible habitation, and said, "Mister, what do you do for
sassiety around here?"

I just couldn't answer that. However, cowboys made the
most of "sassiety" when and where they found it, and hospitality
was universal:

> For this is the law of the Western range,
> When a stranger hails in sight—
> "Jest tie up your hoss in the old corral,
> En 'light, stranger, 'light!

Three or four days after crossing the *Llano Estacado* (so flat,
as Uncle Johnny Martin once said, that you could see the water
in the bottom of a forty-foot well ten miles away), I was
heading for the town of Tokio, up Red River way. I had started
my travels toward Red River because an old cowman had once
told me that they did nothing much in that district but sing,
cuss, and go to camp meetin'. Some miles short of Tokio I
caught sight of a little ranch house and headed for it. The
owner was busy slaughtering a beef. I turned to and helped
him. We soon had the carcass cleaned and hung up. The
rancher showed me the gate to his horse pasture; the grass looked
fine and I decided to stay all night. Even if the owner had been
away, I should have been welcome to go in and help myself to a
meal and feed my horses. No doors were locked. All they
asked was that you leave other things alone. If you wanted to,
you might wash up the dishes you dirtied.

As we entered the house, I saw a banjo hanging on the wall.
"You play?"

The rancher said he did. So I went to my pack and got my mandolin-banjo.

We ate a hearty supper. I pushed back and started up a song. My host was soon singing too. Little square room with a light in it, lonely cabin miles from any neighbor. Fire in the stove, dishes dirty, bellies full. Banjos makin' melody. "Sassiety" enough for one night for a couple of horny cowhands. I don't know how many songs we sang that night. The coyotes must have gathered outside and laid off howlin' to listen.

Cowboy songs were always sung by one person, never by a group. I never did hear a cowboy with a real good voice; if he had one to start with, he always lost it bawling at cattle, or sleeping out in the open, or tellin' the judge he didn't steal that horse. Some of the cowboy actors and radio cowboys nowadays, of course, have very beautiful voices.

The cowboy hardly ever knew what tune he was singing his song to; just some old, old tune that he had heard and known as a boy. Very often the old familiar airs were used. Both "Little Joe the Wrangler" and "Little Adobe Casa" were sung to the air of "Little Old Log Cabin in the Lane." "Sky High" was sung to the tune of "Solomon Isaacs"; "Overland Stage" to the air of "Son of a Gambo-leer." "The Little Cowgirl" was sung to the tune of "Turkey in the Straw"; the people of Texas didn't know the national anthem, but they all knew "Turkey in the Straw."

Two of the songs we sang that night, I know, were important for me. One was "Sam Bass." This famous song, if you don't remember, has to do with a cowboy turned train robber and outlaw, and betrayed by one of his pals. It is supposed to have been written by John Denton of Gainesville, Texas, about 1879. It goes like this:

> Sam Bass was born in Indiana, it was his native home,
> And at the age of seventeen young Sam began to roam.
> Sam first came out to Texas a cowboy for to be—
> A kinder-hearted fellow you seldom ever see.
>
> Sam used to deal in race-stock, one called the Denton mare;
> He matched her in scrub races and took her to the fair.

Sam used to coin the money, and spent it just as free;
He always drank good whiskey wherever he might be.

Sam left the Collins ranch, in the merry month of May,
With a herd of Texas cattle the Black Hills for to see;
Sold out in Custer City, and then got on a spree—
A harder set of cowboys you seldom ever see.

And so on. I first heard some of it sung at a dance hall in Sidney, Nebraska, and one of the boys in Nigger Add's camp had sung a couple of verses. My host this evening sang five verses, three

SAM BASS

of which I had not heard. Into the notebook they went. When I published my first little book, nearly twenty years later, I had found three more verses, making eight which appeared in the first printed version. But there were more. I printed eleven in my bigger book in 1921. This will indicate how songs grow. Versions were likely to vary from singer to singer. Verses were added, eliminated, altered, and otherwise "improved" as they went the rounds. In my first version of "Sam Bass" it was "Jonis" who was due to get a scorching "when Gabriel blows his horn"; in the later version it was "Jim Murphy." Take into account that many of the songs had to be dry-cleaned for unprintable words before they went to press, and you get some notion of the chore a song collector had who was only a cowboy himself.

The second song important for me that night was "The Death of Jesse James." Two verses of it, just two. I got several additional verses some days later in the bunkhouse of the Craul and Jacobs' cow spread west of Ringgold. And in Ringgold itself I got two more from an old cowpuncher, who I had been told was "dripping" with songs. I have noticed that the farther you are from a gold strike, the richer it is. This old cowpuncher, and two other people in Ringgold who had been recommended to me as great singers, knew between them "My Bonnie Lies Over the Ocean," "Clementine," several revival songs, two French love songs, and the two final verses of "The Death of Jesse James." A song-hunter had to pick up his gold in small hunks where he found it.

III

A lot of singing on the range had nothing to do with cowboy songs as such. In different camps I encountered railroad, mountain, river, and granger songs, as well as sticky-sweet sentimental ballads like "Mollie Lou, Sweet Mollie Mine," and "My Little Georgie May." Cowboys weren't always singin' about "little dogies" or "give me a home where the buffalo roam," and when they sang river songs, it was generally something about running logs down a mountain stream. Railroad songs celebrated head-on collisions, or told how a brave conductor saved a train. Granger songs usually had something to do with a yoke of oxen, old Buck and Spot, and a boy who was tired of driving them to a plow and so quit home. These were a part of the singing West too, but I was mainly interested in songs that had all the elements of the range—the cow range, and its special codes and points of view.

It is generally thought that cowboys did a lot of singing around the herd at night to quiet them on the bed ground. I have been asked about this, and I'll say that I have stood my share of night watches in fifty years, and I seldom heard any singing of that kind. What you would hear as you passed your

partner on guard, would be a kind of low hum or whistle, and
you wouldn't know what it was. Just some old hymn tune,
like as not—something to kill time and not bad enough to make
the herd want to get up and run.

Cowboy songs, as I have said, were quite often sung to old
familiar airs. Failing these, there was a kind of standard monotonous tune used over and over that even uneducated fingers
could pick out on the banjo. A young friend who has listened
to me hum it, says the tune looks like this in printed notes:

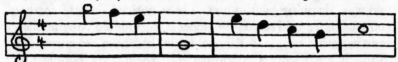

One of my own songs, "On the Dodge," went to a more or
less monotonous melody like this:

Things that cowboys liked, things they hated, incidents of the here, and reflections on the hereafter—these were the chief themes of their songs. Their ways were rough, but they knew gold from glitter when they saw it. They judged a man not by his boasts, but by what he could and did do when the time came for action. They played hard practical jokes, but the best of them could "take it" when their jokes backfired. No theme of cowboy balladry illustrates these characteristics better than the one incorporated in "The Educated Feller," "Cowboys Victimized," "The Zebra Dun," and others built around the same essential situation. I can best explain by telling what happened to me one day.

I had camped for the night in a motte of *bois d'arc*, and towards morning raised out of my camp bed at the sound of approaching horses. Presently, as good daylight came, I saw the lead horse of a big bunch approaching, and at some distance two men driving them. I pulled on my boots and threw sticks on the coals of my last night's fire, put on the coffee pot, and as the two waddies came abreast, called out, "Come and get it!" They turned their remuda loose to graze, and got down out of their saddles.

"How!" said one.

"How!" I replied. "Had anything to eat lately?"

"No. We was just aiming to unpack en git us a snack."

"No need. I got the fixin's right here."

As we were eating, I noticed their horses were in the G W brand, and asked if they owned them. No, they said, they were working for old man Waggoner north of the river in Paul's Valley.

"Any chance of a job with him?" I asked.

One of the waddies was sandy-haired and had a world of freckles, with a skin that would burn and peel, burn and peel, but wouldn't tan. Cowboys generally had a word for everything, and a sure word for a person "complectioned" like this, was Speckles. "The old man," said Speckles, "has a bunch er broncs he wants broken. That is, if a man can ride."

"Well," I replied, "where I come from most everyone can ride a little. When a horse comes into a *remuda* with a saddle

and no man in it, the man who should have been in it is liable
to get his time. New Mexico wagon bosses are terrible fussy
that way."

"You're from New Mexico?" asked Speckles.

I sided these boys all morning. They were studying some
about me, I judged. Had I just talked big to show off? Or could
I ride? We pulled up for noon, and Speckles told me I better
catch up a fresh horse out of their bunch; he suggested I put
my twine on a certain big roan. I had no need of a fresh horse.
They knew it, and I knew they knew it. That was their idea of
a tryout; and I was willing. I noticed that Cinnamon, as they
called the big roan, had no saddle marks on his back and no
cinch marks on his belly, indicating that he hadn't been ridden
for a long time, if ever; but I said nothing. I roped and saddled
him.

"Now I better tell you about that horse," Speckles began.

"Never mind," I said, "he'll tell me about himself when I
get in the saddle."

I cheeked him and went aboard. If a horse don't like the feel
of a saddle, or if you tighten his cinch strap too tight, he's goin'
to say somethin' if it's in him. Many of the horses you see in big
rodeos are reasonably gentle and won't buck unless cinched very
tight. And no horse can buck if his head is out straight; he
must get it between his legs before he can really take you to
church with him. Sure enough, Cinnamon swallowed his head.
After two or three jumps, however, I batted him between the
ears with my quirt and he broke in two—that is, quit pitchin'
and went to runnin'. I checked him up in a few hundred yards
and rode back with one leg around the horn of the saddle.
Showin' off? Sure. Why not! I had ridden their bad horse,
hadn't I? For the balance of the day, Cinnamon acted the real
gent.

Well, we three camped together that night. I started singin'
a song. When I finished it, the second waddy, Tom, perhaps
having in mind the little spisode with Cinnamon, sang a couple
of verses of "The Educated Feller." Later during the trip I got
the whole of it for my notebook. It's as typical of the range as

"HOTEL" FOR HORSE AND MAN

Campyards providing shelter for a man and his horse at a cheap rate were common in Western cow towns. When hunting for cowboy songs, Jack Thorp often put up at them. Here he is, asking his way from the keeper of such a yard. The horse he is riding, a buckskin with black legs and black tail named "Glassy," was stolen from him a little later and never found.

THE PUNCHER POET

By Phil LeNoir

Jest onct, I was a temper'mental, sentimental poet.
Grew a mane like Colonel Cody's fur to show it.
I'd write pomes in my dreams
Then I'd sing 'em to the teams.
    Yup!
A sentimental, ornamental poet.

Wrote a pome onct about ol' Bloody Bill,
Told about the many humans he had killed,
Took him through his entire life,
Showed his love and showed his strife,
Then I hung up like a lunger on a hill.

I was near the happy ending of my tale,
Had ol' Billy ketched an' in the county jail.
When them words plum petered out,
Wouldn't flow, wouldn't spout.
Then I roared an' hit the temper'mental trail.

I went to pawin' an' a-clawin' fur them words,
Skeered the wife an' sent her roostin' with the birds
But they wouldn't come alive
Though I raved till half-past five,
Then I quit the house an' joined the loco herd.

Now I only hear one temper'mental call—
It's the rumble of the cattle's organ-bawl,
    As fur the little tale
    Bloody Bill is still in jail,
Which was a damn good place to leave him a'ter all.

(Poetry: A Magazine of Verse)

DRAWING BY WILL JAMES

WRITIN' COWBOY

When Jack Thorp was writing his ballad about Billy the Kid, he found himself bogged belly-deep over a rhyme that wouldn't come, and he told his troubles to his friend, Phil LeNoir. Phil wrote this poem about the incident, and Will James made the illustration for it.

JEAN BEAUMONDY
Girl champion trick roper of the world at the time this snapshot was made (about 1911). Miss Beaumondy also is credited with authoring the song, "Fightin' Mad," which describes the feelings of a cowpuncher who was offered a soft drink when he wanted redeye. Jean learned the art of roping almost in the cradle, being taught by native cowhands of Old Mexico on her father's ranch near the border.

"THE LAW"

Judge Roy Bean, famous character of Langtry, Texas, was one of the men visited by Jack Thorp in his search for cowboy songs. The Judge told him the incident that Jack made into his ballad, "The Pecos River Queen." This snapshot shows what was left of Judge Bean's "courthouse" and saloon in 1928, when Jack revisited Langtry with Mrs. Thorp.

ants in chuck wagon biscuits. The story, of course, is about a
stranger at the ranch who looked so green and talked so big that

> .... he made the boys all sick,
> And they began to look around just how to play a trick.

The stranger had put his money into clothes out of sight,
and a little derby hat, and he said he would like to borrow a nice
fat saddle horse: "Please, mister, could I ride one of them?" So
Shorty roped the Zebra Dun, wildest outlaw on the place, and
the stranger climbed aboard. Old Dunny, of course, quit the
earth, "his hind feet perpendicular, his front ones in the bits."
But

> The stranger sat upon him and curled his black mustache,
> Just like a summer boarder waiting for his hash.

The cowboy moral being that "every educated feller ain't a
plumb greenhorn." Nobody relished the humor of being taken
in this way more than the cowboys themselves. A good rider
was their idea of a man who couldn't be all bad.

Who wrote the cowboy songs? The authorship of many of
them is doubtful or unknown. Often the authors, if they
hailed from the range direct, didn't bother or care to acknowl-
edge authorship. Thus "The Camp-Fire Has Gone Out," which
I heard when I was ranching in the San Andrés Mountains, was
written, I believe, by Gene Rhodes; but, so far as I know, Gene
himself never said so.

"Hell in Texas" is a popular ballad describing a supposed
deal between the Lord and the Devil by which the latter acquired some land so bad that the Lord couldn't use it, but
perfectly suited to the Devil's needs for a little hell on earth: he
"put thorns on the cactus and horns on the toads .... poisoned
the feet of the centipede," and did more of the same—and
called it Texas. At one time or another I picked up five versions
of this song, each supposed to be by a different author. Some
of them say the place the Devil got hold of was Texas, others
say New Mexico, depending on the writer's partisanship.

There was "Fightin' Mad," too, a ballad about a cowboy

who was offered ginger ale to drink. This I got from Jean
Beaumondy at the annual Colorado Springs Roundup. Jean
was then the champion trick girl roper of the world—she's still
good, according to accounts of a movie film in which she did
her stuff less than a year ago.

"Did you write the song, Jean?" I asked her.

"Oh, I was around when it was written," she said. And
that's all I ever could get out of her.

Sometimes a song lost its author and even changed its name
as it passed from mouth to mouth. Henry Herbert Knibbs
once brought me a cowboy song from southern Arizona, known
there under the title "High-Chin Bob." Actually the song
was written by Charles Badger Clark, Jr., and the original version appeared in his book, *Sun and Saddle Leather,* under the
title, "The Glory Trail." A song of mine called "Nigger 'Lasses"
had this four-line refrain:

> Oh, dere ain't no horse what can't be rode,
> Dat's what de white folks say!
> En dere ain't a man what can't be throwed,
> *Oh, Mah!*
>   I finds it jest dat way!

J. Frank Dobie once heard this song at Eagle Pass, Texas, sung by
a darky singer, and Frank asked him where he got it. The singer
said, "Ah don' know, sah. A man named Mister Jack he wrote
it—ah dunno."

Authorship wasn't reckoned very important—nothing to
fight over. But when you did discover a song's author, sometimes it was a surprise. The second night after I threw in with
Speckles and Tom, we penned the horses on the outskirts of
Gainesville and later hunted up a pasture to put them in for
the night. While we were cooking supper a great tall ganglin'
swamp angel moseyed into camp looking hungrier than a dieting
deb. A swamp angel was a fellow raised down in the swampy
lands, maybe Louisiana or Arkansas. They all had chills and
fever, 90 per cent of them chewed snuff sticks, and they generally looked like walking matches. This one seemed to be a
fair sample of the breed. Seeing my little banjo lying on my

bedroll, he asked if any of us could sing. No, we said, but sometimes we opened our mouths and noise came out.

"Want me ter sing you a song?" he asked.

"Sure!" we said. So he picked up my banjo. And what a
banjo-picker he was! He sang "Bucking Bronco"—sang the
whole song of five verses. What's more, he knew the author's
name. Belle Starr, he said, wrote it.

I had met Belle several times in Dallas and Fort Worth.
Now, I was told, she had a ranch at Younger's Bend. Belle was
one of the most famous of the women outlaws of the Southwest.
A beautiful brunette, well educated, she wore guns and had a
bunch of desperadoes working for her. She was running a
holdout stable in Dallas, where stolen horses were fenced. But
the horses came from the Indian Territory, which made it all
right; nobody in Texas would bother her. All the cowpunchers
went there to put up their horses when they came to town.
Belle sang in the church choir, played the piano, and was a
"sassiety" lady in those days. That she was also a song writer
was news and quite a surprise to me. But Belle was an original,
a product of the times and the region; and her end, when it
came, was tragically in keeping with her life. Returning from
a trip to Fort Smith, she was two miles from her ranch at
Younger's Bend when she was shot in the back by one of her
tenants with whom she had quarreled, a man wanted in
Florida on a murder charge but afraid to meet Belle face to face.

"Bucking Bronco" went like this, after it was expurgated:

> My love is a rider, wild broncos he breaks,
> Though he's promised to quit it, just for my sake.
> He ties up one foot, the saddle puts on,
> With a swing and a jump he is mounted and gone.
>
> The first time I met him, 'twas early one spring,
> Riding a bronco, a high-headed thing.
> He tipped me a wink as he gayly did go,
> For he wished me to look at his bucking bronco.
>
> The next time I saw him, 'twas late in the fall,
> Swinging the girls at Tomlinson's ball:
> He laughed and he talked as we danced to and fro,
> Promised never to ride on another bronco.

He made me some presents, among them a ring;
The return that I made him was a far better thing;
'Twas a young maiden's heart, I'd have you all know
He'd won it by riding his bucking bronco.

Now, all you young maidens, where'er you reside,
Beware of the cowboy who swings the rawhide,
He'll court you and pet you and leave you and go
In the spring up the trail on his bucking bronco.

I broke out some fifty head of broncs for old man Waggoner in Paul's Valley, picking up what songs I could; and when I felt I had enough cash ahead to last a spell, I saddled up Gray Dog, packed Ample, and started drifting and song hunting again, south this time towards Dallas, Austin, San Antonio, and points farther south and west.

IV

Cowboy songs did not always reach me through cowboys. I took them where I found them, from all sorts and kinds of people. Walking up Main Street in Fort Worth one morning, I heard the air of "My Old Kentucky Home" through the doors of the Silver Dollar saloon. I went in and found a girl singing a cowboy song for a drink. Her audience soon left and she sat at a table with me. She knew only one song, but it was a good one for the notebook—"Buster Goes A-Courtin'."

In Dallas I camped in a pecan grove outside the fair grounds near a group of Irish gypsies who drew crowds by fomenting horse races, and here I picked up "My Pet Horse," and "Riden Jane"—not quite cowboy songs, but good enough to go into the notebook.[3] "Buckskin Joe" I first heard in the public square of Waco.

I had arrived in Waco after plowing through some of the worst gumbo mud I ever saw. I went to a campyard and put up my horses. Campyards for horsemen were common in the Western towns then, as tourist camps for motorists are now, and as caravanserais were in ancient cities of the Far East. Campyards were very crude—a yard, generally with box stalls on two sides, and a shed and a high fence around. In the shed

you could make your bedroll down. Generally there was a stove
in it, where you could cook if you wanted to. It was a great
hangout for horse traders. The common charge was twenty-
five cents a night for man and horse, and twenty-five cents
more if you required grain and hay for your horses. Having
found a place for my bedroll in such a campyard in Waco, I
tucked my banjo under my arm and went uptown to get supper.
I was starting through the door of a chili joint, when a man
grabbed me by the arm.

"Want a job?" he almost shouted. "Can you sing?"

A cowboy could generally skirt the truth when he had to,
and I answered yes to both questions. The man explained that
Professor Scott, Wizard Oil King, needed a man like me. His
banjo-picker was drunk, and his show was due to open on the
public square in a few minutes. Would I come? I downed a
bowl of chili in a hurry, and went.

Professor Scott's show was given from the rear end of a
large van backed up to the sidewalk. The Professor himself was
tall and impressive, long-haired, and maybe forty-five years old.
He wore a scarlet coat and a huge sombrero. He sold patent
medicines put out by big companies—Spanish Oil, Wizard Oil,
pills—and of course he was a great talker. He could make a pea
do tricks under three shells, and if people weren't buying reme-
dies for their ailments, he would take their money that way.
Occasionally he would fondle a pet Gila monster that he carried
around with him (its venom, of course, was removed, though
the audience didn't know that), and explain that among other
mysterious powers he had a strange influence over dumb animals. He employed cappers, picked locally, who pretended to
be members of the audience and walked up when volunteers
were invited to take sample doses of his medicines.

"Sit down there!" he would say, placing them in a prominent
place after spooning them full of oil or pills. He would go on
to something else, and when a proper time had elapsed, would
ask them how they felt. They would mumble unintelligibly.
"Open your mouths!" The professor would reach in and pull
out something long, rubbery, and black, and throw it down on
the floor. "That's your trouble!" he'd say; and the cappers

would immediately go off with every appearance of experiencing great relief. "You don't have to wait till next week for this to take effect," the professor would point out to his goggling audience. "Who'll be first?"

Between sales and tricks I entertained the crowd with songs. I was paid five dollars for the two-hour performance, and afterwards was urged to travel with the show. I declined. But I got what suited me better than a medicine-show job, namely, a notebook version of "Buckskin Joe." The professor recited this barroom surprise story ballad with oratorical flourishes that would have astonished Shakespeare.

South of Waco one night, I rode in the dark. It was a night for riding! I saw a city on fire below the edge of the world, and presently the moon popped up and made the whole state of Texas bright so you could read a newspaper. A campfire flickered, and I rode in where three men were camped. They were dressed no differently than other mounted Texans—no uniforms, no brass. They invited me to get down and camp. I unpacked, unsaddled, hobbled out my horses. Seeing my banjo, they asked me to play. I did. One of the three responded with a song, a new one to me. That there was such a song I knew, but this was my first hearing of it. "The Texas Rangers" it was, and it was a ranger who sang it. These three were part of Captain Hughes' famous force, on their way to Fort McKavett, they told me, to investigate a report of trouble between sheepmen and cattlemen.

Followers of many trades were found in the cow country, many of them with songs on their lips. From San Antonio I headed into mesquite and cactus country where the rivers that run down to the Rio Grande are named Frio, Nueces, Devil's, Pecos. I reached Devil's River four miles south of the town of Juno, and found a strange assemblage of wagons, all manned by Mexicans. They invited me to get down and try a cup of coffee.

Their wagons, I noticed, were loaded with square five-gallon oil cans, some empty, some full. My curiosity had to be satisfied, so one of the men took me across the road and showed me what they were up to. The Devil's River district is noted for caves and sink holes, caused by the undercutting of water.

These men had rigged a windlass over a natural shaft or "cueva," as they called it. I saw hundreds and hundreds of honeybees streaming out of the shaft. The honey hunters, for that's what they were, threw lighted pitch-pine knots down the shaft to smoke them out. Then two of the men, protected by thick clothes, mosquito-netting helmets, and thick gloves, were lowered into the cave. I was glad it was they and not me, for a bee will kick me in the face every time. They shoveled the honey, comb and all, into those five-gallon cans, and it was a rich harvest. When heated and strained, they told me, it made the best honey in the world.

At this camp one of the younger Mexicans sang four verses of a song, in Spanish, called *El Rio Rey*, "The River King." It was a ballad of a *palomino* stud that roamed the range uncaught, untamed. I never found anybody who knew more of the original than the four verses sung for me by this Mexican. But some months afterward I was lying in my bedroll at two or three in the morning, and words to complete the song suddenly came to me. I slid out of my bed, got my little notebook out of my chaps pocket, and wrote four new verses in English. I translated the four from Spanish, and in that way completed the ballad. Such was the bastard ancestry of some cowboy songs.

Roy Bean wasn't much of a singer, but he was a cow country character, and "The Pecos River Queen" grew out of an incident he told me. Self-elected justice of the peace and owner of the Jersey Lily Saloon in the little town of Langtry, not far west of where the Pecos cuts deep through rock to meet the Rio Grande, Roy has gone down in history, legend, and motion pictures, as "the law west of the Pecos." He was a man of medium height, about five feet ten, weighing around a hundred and sixty-five pounds, and he had a mustache and a beard. He married a Mexican woman and they had a lot of half-breed children. His erratic home-grown legal decisions made him famous. For example, when a dead man was found under the bridge, Roy appointed himself coroner and found a pearl-handled revolver and forty dollars on the corpse. He confiscated the revolver because, he said, it was against the law to carry a gun in Texas; he fined the corpse forty dollars for the offense (which "the law" pocketed) ; and he ordered the dead man buried at the county's expense. Another time, a man whom Roy didn't like was brought before him for a petty offense, and Roy bundled him off to Austin in charge of a deputy, with papers committing him to the penitentiary for ninety-nine years.

The Judge owned a pet bear which he had raised from a cub, and once when the cowboys were having a dance, Roy, drunker than $700, ordered every cowboy present to dance with the bear—and enforced the edict. The bear was then chained to the center pole of the tent, but grew tired and walked off, pole and all, nearly smothering everybody to death when the tent top came down on their heads.

When the railroad was being built past Langtry, a high-happy cowboy caught a coolie track laborer by the cue, and hooked the cue over the horn of his saddle. The Chinaman died, either of fright or a broken neck. The cowboy was arrested and brought before Judge Bean, who looked solemnly through his law book and brought in a verdict. It was murder, he said, to kill a white man, and actionable if you killed a Mexican, a nigger, or even an Indian; but the book said nothing about Chinese coolies.

"Cowboy," he said sternly to the prisoner at the bar, "feel in your pockets and see if you can't dig up enough cash to set up the drinks."

I rode down to Langtry to visit Roy and his near neighbor, Bill Ike Babb, who ran the Langtry store. Roy mentioned, among other things, the Comstock railroad trestle near by, supposed to be the highest in the West. A girl named Patty Moorhead, he said, had ridden her horse across it. Patty was as pretty and full of fire as they come, even in Texas, and in the song I wrote I made her the queen of the river. I took the liberty of introducing a cowpuncher lover who was afraid to follow her across the trestle as she bade him do—"so she's still without a mate."

It was at Toyah, near the New Mexico line, from another cow country character, "Sally" White, that I got four verses of "The Great Round-Up":

There, according to the Word,
The angel cowboy of the Lord
Will cut the human herd.

"Sally" was no girl despite his name, but was so called from his
fondness for singing a song with that title. No, Mr. White was
no girl. I remember the night he got drunk in Pecos town. They
had a law against wearing six-shooters within the city limits.
"Sally" tied his gun to the end of his rope, thus in his opinion
complying with the law, and went all over town dragging the
rope and yelling, "Don't step on my tail, boys! Open the door
an' let me an' my tail through!" His song, author unknown,
ends with:

No maverick or slick will be tallied,
In the great book of life in his home,
For he knows all the brands and the earmarks
That down through the ages have come.
But along with the tailings and sleepers
The strays must turn from the gate;
No road brand to gain them admission,
But the awful sad cry of "too late."

Yet I trust, in the last great roundup,
When the rider shall cut the big herd,
That the cowboys shall be represented
In the earmark and brand of the Lord;
To be shipped to the bright mystic regions
Over there in green pastures to lie,
And led by the crystal still waters,
In that home of the sweet by and by.

V

Cowboy songs, as I have said, were full of the vernacular of
the range, and it wasn't always parlor talk. I vividly remember
sitting in the ranch house on Crow Flat with old Jim Brownfield during the latter stages of my trip, and hearing him give
the entire range version of "The Top Hand." The theme—
ridicule of a cowboy too big for his boots—was a scorcher in
itself, and the words of the song would have burned the reader's

eyeballs if printed as Jim sang it. I expurgated it and had to change even the title, and the song has appeared exactly as I rendered it in all books of cowboy songs published since.

> While you're all so frisky, I'll sing a little song:
> Think a horn of whiskey will help the thing along,
> It's all about the Top Hand when he's busted flat,
> Bumming round town, in his Mexicana hat.
> He'd laid up all winter and his pocket-book is flat.
> His clothes are all tatters, but he don't mind that. . . . .
>
> When you ship the cattle he's bound to go along
> To keep the boss from drinking and to see that nothing's wrong;
> Wherever he goes, catch on to his game,
> He likes to be called with a handle to his name;
> He's always primping with a pocket looking-glass;
> From the top to the bottom he's a holy jackass.

The same is true of Belle Starr's "The Bucking Bronco" and many others.

In fact, I have found that cowboy songs have their adventures after they get into print as well as before. I closed my first little paper-covered book with a ballad I wrote myself, called "Speckles." There were eight verses as I wrote it, but the printer lost part of the copy and printed only six. Some time later a very learned professor brought out a big book of cowboy songs which he claimed to have collected with great labor, and he printed my abbreviated "Speckles" (without credit), but changed the name to "Freckles" and called it a fragment that he had picked up.

Another song of mine also had a rather checkered history. In 1898, nearly ten years after the trip I am writing about, I helped trail a herd of O cattle from Chimney Lake, New Mexico, to Higgins, Texas. There were eight of us in the crew. One night I sat by the campfire with a stub of pencil and an old paper bag and wrote the story of little Joe, the horse wrangler, a Texas stray who had left home, he told us, and struck out for himself because his daddy had married again and his new ma beat him. The boss "sorter liked the little stray somehow," and took him on as a hand. One night in a thunderstorm everybody

turned out to check a stampede. The cattle ran a ways, but
were headed, and when they were milling and kind of quieted
down, one of the hands was missing—our little Texas stray.
He was found next morning in a wash twenty feet deep, under
his horse, Rocket:

> Little Joe, the wrangler, will never wrangle more;
>   His days with the "remuda"—they are done.
> 'Twas a year ago last April he joined the outfit here,
>   A little "Texas stray" and all alone.
>
> We'd driven to Red River and the weather had been fine;
>   We were camped down on the south side in a bend,
> When a norther commenced blowing and we doubled up our guards,
>   For it took all hands to hold the cattle then.
>
> Little Joe, the wrangler, was called out with the rest,
>   And scarcely had the kid got to the herd,
> When the cattle they stampeded; like a hailstorm, long they flew,
>   And all of us were riding for the lead.
>
> 'Tween the streaks of lightning we could see a horse far out ahead—
>   'Twas little Joe, the wrangler, in the lead;
> He was riding "Old Blue Rocket" with his slicker 'bove his head,
>   Trying to check the leaders in their speed.
>
> At last we got them milling and kinder quieted down,
>   And the extra guard back to the camp did go;
> But one of them was missin', and we all knew at a glance
>   'Twas our little Texas stray—poor Wrangler Joe.
>
> Next morning just at sunup we found where Rocket fell,
>   Down in a washout twenty feet below;
> Beneath his horse, mashed to a pulp, his spurs had rung the knell
>   For our little Texas stray—poor Wrangler Joe.

I sang the song to the men who were with me on that trail
trip. After our return, I sang it for the first time in any man's
hearing—save on that trip—in Uncle Johnny Root's store and
saloon at Weed, New Mexico. From that time on it was passed
along by word of mouth. I led off my first little book with it,
but didn't sign it; none of the songs in that book were signed,
though five of the twenty-four were my own compositions. In

the course of time "Little Joe, the Wrangler" became one of the
most widely sung and best liked of cowboy songs. I have no idea
how often it has been sung over the radio in the last few years.
I do know that it has been put on phonograph records and more
than 375,000 of them have been sold—and the author of the
song not richer by a penny for having written it.

> Never a cent in our pockets,
> But what did a cow-puncher care?[4]

VI

A morning in March, 1890, just a year after I started out,
found me back on my home range not far from the place where
I had encountered Nigger Add and his chuck-wagon camp. I
had but twenty-five miles more to go to the old Carrizozo
ranch, better known as the Bar W. I reflected on the miles I
had ridden (more than fifteen hundred of them), the handful
of songs I had collected, the nights and days I had passed in
cow country new to me, the hands I had shaken, the men "good"
and "bad" I had come to know.

I had spent some time with "Old Perk," who once dug a pit
to trap predacious bears, and when his pet dog fell into the pit
while it was occupied by a big trapped silvertip, Old Perk
followed feet first with no weapon but a butcher knife to save
his dog. A braver deed, wholly without audience, it would be
hard to find. Old Perk killed the bear and saved the dog, but
received terrible scars which he wore to the end of his life. He
was so sensitive about his appearance that he would never come
to town except for necessary food and then only after dark.

I had eaten and bunked, too, with a man who made his home
in a cave in the Guadalupes. He was "wanted," whether for
murder or horse stealing I did not know, and he certainly rode
horses with too many different brands to be honest; but he was
as likable a man as you could meet.

Cowboys didn't judge too harshly. The best of them would
do to ride with anywhere, and the worst weren't all bad. "Show
me a perfect man and I'll show you Christ" was their tolerant
attitude. With such men I had lived and would live, and the

time did not seem to me ill spent. Next spring, I thought as I jogged along, I'll go again, this time through western New Mexico, and on through Arizona, Utah, Colorado, Wyoming.

You would ride those ranges in vain today to find men who ride and make songs and sing them in the old free larruping spirit and under like conditions.

What's become of the punchers
We rode with long ago?
The hundreds and hundreds of cowboys
We all of us used to know?

But the country and the life as it was survive authentically in the balladry, crude though it may have been, that grew out of the very lives the cowboys led and the troubles they had, and our literature is richer for it.

Late afternoon brought sight of the cottonwoods around Carrizozo Springs and the old Bar W. Ample, the pack horse, had been raised there. He recognized home, and passed me at a fast trot. Gray Dog too commenced fishin' at the bit. Hi, boss! want an old hand for the roundup? Our dust is arrivin'.

SPANISH THUNDERBOLTS

Well, old horse, you're buried, en your troubles, they are done,
But I often sit en think of what we did,
En recall the many scrapes we had, en used to think it fun,
Es we rode along the Rio Grande.
              Good-by, old kid!

I

SINGIN' was amusement for the cowboy's times of ease, but what really mattered in the cow country was ridin'. The horse was the main thing in a cowboy's life. Cattle in the days when I first came West were no-good old Spanish stock; but there were some good horses in the country and that was what we all looked at and were interested in. One cow outfit had a duke and two English lords workin' for 'em, but a title on a cow spread was worth whatever the owner of it could make himself worth as a man and a rider—no more. A good cow horse, however, was supper and breakfast, wife and sweetheart, pal, means of conveyance, the main tool and brains of the cow business, and sometimes life itself. "I've bought 'em by the thousand, I've owned 'em everywhere." The ones that had brains and stamina are remembered, as individuals, even after the names and faces of some of the old bunkhouse mates begin to fade—my little horse, Catchem, for instance. When he made the run that saved my life he did sixty miles between sun-down and sun-up, over wild country, alone, without saddle, bridle, or rider, nothing on him but his hobble rope and my note.

I had been hunting horse thieves that time in the wild Four Corners country, where New Mexico, Utah, Colorado, and Arizona come together. William C. McDonald, chief owner of the Bar W and governor of the state of New Mexico, had sent word for me to drop all other work and come at once to Santa Fe, and I knew it must be something mighty imperative. When I saw him, he told me that the north part of the state was alive with horse thieves. I wasn't known in that section, and that was one reason why the Governor picked me for the job of going after them. Catchem was the name of the horse I rode—a bright colored line-back buckskin, eight years old, half steel dust, the rest thoroughbred, a thousand pounds of fire, rubber, muscle, speed, and endurance, with lots of sense, and a good average rope horse.

The trail took me by way of Shiprock to Bluff City, the little desert town where two enormous sandstone figures, one that looks like an old man and the other like an old woman, stand guard near the road as you come in. I had been advised to see Tom Livingston there, who was said to be the only "white" white man living in the place.

"He won't talk much," my informant said, "but what he says, you can depend on."

Tom made me welcome, sat me down to a good supper, and gave me a place for Catchem. But he was sure still-tongued, and I couldn't get much information out of him. However, he went out after supper, and came back late with news about the men I was after. He had learned that they were just about to take some stolen horses down the San Juan River as far as Mexican Hat, where the plan was to deliver the bunch to men from Gable's Crossing.

"Personally," he said, "I hope you round up every last one of the gang. But livin' here, I can't afford to say that publicly."

I inquired about the country where the thieves were going, for that was where I had to go too, and it was all new terrain to me. "Is there any place ahead," I asked, "where I can buy grain for my horse?"

"Not for a hundred miles," Livingston said.

"Well," I remarked, "if Catchem ever gets loose down there, he'll go back to the last place where he was fed."

There were a number of happenings during the next few days, none of which matter for the present story, except the

fact that I collected four of the horse thieves and lodged them
in the jail at Bluff City, only to have them "escape" the same
night. When I took up their trail again, there was a gun fight,
one against several, in the course of which, while lying behind
some rocks, I was ripped down the side by a bullet—and that's
where Catchem came in. I was dizzy and losing a lot of blood,
and knew I had to have help, but was in no condition to ride.
The only thing I could do was leave it up to the horse, and trust
him to come through. I had a stub of pencil, but no paper, so
with my pocketknife I cut a piece of the white kid lining out of
the top of one boot, and wrote this message on it:

> Tom Livingston, Bluff City. Come. I need help.
> Johns Canyon.
> J. T.

I cut a slit in the kid big enough for a rope to go through,
then about sundown slid over the sandy bank of the arroyo and
landed by the side of Catchem. Pulling his head down, I
managed to work the rope hobble that he wore on his neck,
through the slit in the kid. I was pretty unsteady on my feet,
but I succeeded in unfastening the saddle straps and pulling the
saddle off, and I unbuckled the bridle and pulled it off. Catchem
then was free and wearing nothing but the hobble rope and my
message. I gave him a slap with the bridle reins and saw him go
galloping off. Then consciousness left me.

I had no idea what time it was when I came to, but I was in
fearful pain, it was dark, and I was burning up for a drink of
water. After an hour or so I dozed off again. When next I woke
up, the sun was shining in my face. I tossed and rolled, delirious
most of the time, crazy for water, but without strength
enough to crawl out of the arroyo. Everything was so still,
hour after hour after hour, that I thought I'd go mad. Finally,
however, just about dark, I heard hoofbeats and the voice of
Tom Livingston, and called out weakly to let him know where
I was. Tom had two other men with him. They poured water[5]
into my dry mouth. And Tom told me how, at daylight, he
heard a horse nickering outside his corral, and went down and
found Catchem and the message.

Photograph by New Mexico State Tourist Bureau.

THE COWBOY'S MAIN INTEREST

"There were some good horses in the country and that was what we all looked at and were interested in. . . . . A good cow horse was supper and breakfast, wife and sweetheart, pal, means of conveyance, the main tool and brains of the cow business."

A TOP ROPING HORSE

A horse well-trained for cutting a herd or standing night guard, might be of little value for roping. There were specialists in each cow-boy's string, suited by nature and training for the different kinds of riding done in cow work. This horse, "Johnnie," with Jack Thorp aboard, was a first-rate roping horse. He could go into high from the first hop, and as soon as a calf was roped, he kept the rope just taut enough to prevent the calf from rising until tied.

ABOARD A "THUNDERBOLT"

Although Jack was never a regular rodeo performer, he was a top rider and occasionally took part in the contests with other cowhands. Here he is in the saddle at a Colorado Springs rodeo in 1911, just as the horse, supposed to be a "killer," was released from the chute. Actually this animal turned out too tame to be a good house cat.

A GOOD FRIEND

Usually, when one of his horses reached the end of the trail, Jack burned the body. But when this favorite horse, "Paint," died, Jack went 'way out in the woods and dug a deep hole and buried him. "I'm not goin' to let the coyotes have him," he said. "He had more sense than a lot of men I know." It was about this horse that Jack wrote the song, "Old Paint," one verse of which appears at the top of Chapter II; and this was the horse that wouldn't let Mrs. Thorpe ride him, brushing her off against tree limbs if she tried it.

You could expect performances like that from the best cow ponies. They had brains and endurance. I don't pretend to say how well Catchem understood my situation and need, though he did have a doglike devotion to his rider; anyhow, he was a smart horse, and I was sure that he would go back, when released, to the last place where he had been fed. That's what he did; and by doing it he probably saved my life. That he would make such a distance—sixty miles—in a single night, was more than I expected.

II

The story of the cow horse has been over-romanticized, but little understood. It is one of the great chapters in the history of the West. The range cattle industry never could have existed without those small Spanish thunderbolts that turned on a dime and flashed into top speed at the flick of a spur, the progeny of Arabians brought over by the Conquistadores. A modern cowboy hauls his horse in a trailer behind his flivver till he gets to where the road ends. The old-time cowboy never saw a steering wheel. He was given a mount, usually seven horses, when he went to work for an outfit. They were his as long as he kept the job. He trained them himself, and was jealous of anybody else riding them. A ranch owner once told cowboy Pete Sommers that he had a great friend coming out from the East, and he wanted Pete's old Rusty horse for him to ride.

"Sure, cut him out"—Pete's words were like icicles on the bunkhouse roof in a long cold winter. "While you're at it, cut out the whole mount—an' make out my pay check."

A real cowhand wouldn't let anybody else ride his horses. No two men handle a horse alike, and a cow horse and his rider had to understand one another like a bean understands the pod it grows in. Some horses had natural cow sense and took right to it; others never would have any cow sense, no matter how much you trained them.

Cowboys had four main jobs for horses: roping, cutting, riding circle, and standing night guard. Almost any horse with a lot of "bottom" and endurance, but not especially good at anything else, would do for riding circle. The last man dropped might be fifteen miles from the wagon before he started hazin' cattle out of the brush and draws, and by the time he drove his gather back to the holding ground, he would have done a lot of riding. It took a good strong horse. For the other jobs, cowboys trained specialists.

A top cutting horse was a second set of brains at the round-up. If you started after a certain critter in the herd, and your horse once identified the animal you were after, you could reach over and take the bridle off, and he'd take that particular critter out of the herd by himself. He had to have lots of speed, but he never used it till he had slowly worked the animal out of the herd. In the movies you sometimes see a man supposedly cutting cattle out of the herd, running his horse hell-for-breakfast through the herd, scattering the cattle in all directions, which shows that that cowboy, or his director, knew nothing about the handling of cattle. A cutting horse didn't get to be a top animal without a lot of training, and the best cutting horses were the cowboy's pride.

A top roping horse went into high from the first hop. He watched your rope, and stopped the instant he saw you had made your catch. As you ran to make your tie of the animal's legs, he kept a strain on the rope so the animal could not get up. There were no branding chutes in the early days, and all cattle, big or little, were roped and stretched out either in corrals or on the open range. When a big steer, or a cow, or bull was roped, the roping horse kept his head to the animal and the rope tight, not only because that was what he was taught to do, but also because anything else was likely to result in his getting snarled up in the rope and thrown. The strain came just behind the horse's shoulders, and at this point he was apt to get tender and sore. Also, holding heavy cattle was hard on the front legs. Some old rope horses were just cute enough to be mighty careful not to run within roping distance of a heavy animal. I once knew two horses that grew up together and were pals, and in their prime they were top roping horses. But as they got older, while they would always make a great show of willingness to overtake a steer, they would never carry the rider quite close enough for a throw. One spring, come roundup time, these two old-timers were not to be found at all. Don't tell me they didn't know! For, within a week after the crew left for the lower end of the range and the roundup, the two old bums showed up all right at the home watering. The same thing happened the two following years, and the head man told the foreman to let them have their liberty, for they had earned it—both were more than eighteen years old.

You would never see a horse that was tops at both roping and cutting. Plenty of cowboys would brag that they owned such horses, but I never saw one, and to expect a horse to be expert at both jobs would be a little like expecting a man to be a great physician and also a great lawyer. A horse seldom became a top horse at either roping or cutting until he was around eight years old. It took that long to learn the tricks. But once he had them learned, he might keep on at the work till he was twenty. Cow horses wore out much more slowly than Eastern horses. The feet of the latter would usually be the first thing to give out, due to their being always shod, and pounding along on hard roads, and working every day except possibly Sundays and holidays. A cow horse in a seven-horse mount got a half-day of work every three days for seven months of the year—thus he had five months of absolute rest. A cutting horse working a herd would usually work only for two or three hours, then he would be pulled out and replaced.

A top night horse had to be gentle and very sure-footed in order to protect himself and his rider from falling, and he had to have a good bump of location. Chopo, another pet horse of mine, was the best night horse I ever had. Coal-black and branded O, he was one of those horses that made a good hand anywhere. If he made up his mind to catch a calf, he'd catch him; but he was not a top at it. I have even used him in a buggy team. Everything was all right with Chopo. A girl school teacher said once:

"Do you know what that little black horse of yours will do?"

"What?"

"He'll eat peppermint candy. I fed him two long sticks."

I don't think you could feed Chopo anything but what

he'd eat it. He saved my life just as surely as Catchem did—
not once, but many times. Chopo's daddy was a Morgan stud
shipped out from the East, and his mammy a sure-enough
mustang Arabian, one of the old Spanish stock that ran pretty
much all over the Southwest. He first proved himself on the
trail drive when Little Joe, the wrangler, was killed—not in the
same stampede, however.

We had just crossed the Pecos. It was one of those black
nights, so dark you could feel it. Rain began during the first
guard and increased till it was just sloshing down. Lightning,
striking here and there, seemed to rip the skies apart. In the
bright glare we could see that the cattle were on their feet.
The rain suddenly turned to hail, though it was still warm, and
some of the hailstones were half the size of hens' eggs. When a
bolt of lightning finally struck at the edge of the herd, twenty-
five hundred head of beef steers left the bed ground with a roar
like thunder.

Directions are hard to keep at night, with no stars out, but
as near as I could tell I was north of the herd when the run
started. I aimed to keep to the north and west, matching strides
with the leaders, shooting my six-gun in front of their noses in
an effort to make them turn and mill, and trusting to Chopo to
keep his feet. Every once in a while he broke through the muddy
ground, but he never fell. Had he done so, I would have been a
mincemeat cowboy in ten seconds under hundreds of hooves.
Occasionally a streak of lightnin' would show me where a steer
had fallen and those following had piled up on him.

We were wholly unable to stop the cattle. They ran for
miles without a sign of a split. Then when the split did come, it
was so dark that I didn't know it till a flash of lightning showed
I was ridin' in the lead of exactly three steers. Of course it was
no use going on. I was soaked to the skin. I had used my slicker
trying to whip the steers back and make them mill, and there
was nothing much left of it except the sleeves and collar. The
air had turned freezing cold. I knew that every hand at the
wagon would have been out to try to turn the cattle; but where
the others were, and where the wagon was, I hadn't the slightest

notion. Neither Chopo nor I had ever been in that particular section before.

Once more it was a case of trust the horse. I gave the little black his head. Hours passed, and I never heard sound or saw sign of another horse or human being. Then suddenly in the distance, I thought I saw a spark of light. Another minute, and I was sure. Chopo nickered. A horse answered. Chopo not only had made the run without once falling, but also he had brought me straight to the wagon on a night black enough to render human senses absolutely useless.

> Through rocky arroyos so dark and so deep;
> Down the sides of the mountains so slippery and steep;
> You're good judgment, sure-footed, wherever you go
> You're a safety conveyance, my little Chopo.

III

The Western cow pony was a quite different animal from the Eastern farm horse, and the story of his spread over the two continents of North and South America is as interesting in its way as the occupation of these continents by human immigrants from Europe. Horses were not indigenous here in geological time, yet wild horses have been found from Patagonia in South America to far north in Canada, and at one time it was estimated that their numbers ran into the hundreds of thousands, maybe the millions. Where did they come from?

Cortez is popularly supposed to have brought over the first horses. However, from examination of the records, it is clear that even before Cortez arrived in Mexico, several lots of stallions and mares had been landed. The very first horses, as far as anybody knows, came over in 1500, just eight years after Columbus discovered the New World. They were Arabians, and were landed on the Isthmus of Panama by Don Diego de Nicues. Six horses from this shipment went to Santo Domingo. In 1515, Don Bajados made a shipment of horses from Spain, using them as mounts for his men when fighting the Indians of Panama. In 1516, Don Antonio Velasquez brought a shipload of mares and stallions, along with other animals for breeding purposes, from Cuba to Honduras. Then in February, 1519, Cortez landed sixteen stallions and mares in San Antonio, Yucatan, astonishing the natives who thought they were giant deer. Gonzales de Sandoval, a member of the Cortez expedition, had a chestnut colored Arabian stallion which Bernal Díaz, the historian of the party, described as the most beautiful animal brought from Cuba. In October, 1524, Cortez shipped one hundred and fifty head of Spanish Arabian horses from Spain to Yucatan. One black horse, which was crippled, he left with the Itzas, who fed it fruit, fowl, and flowers, a diet that killed it. Its bones were kept as sacred relics, and an effigy carved in masonry attracted worshippers. Cortez got some more horses in 1525, some of them purchased from Don Antonio Camargo of the town of Nito, Honduras, and others brought over on a vessel from Spain.

Thus horses were introduced on these continents almost as early as European settlement began, and during the next century or so, many cargoes of horses arrived from the Old World, most of them being unloaded on the coast of Mexico. From these small bunches, brought by the early explorers and Conquistadores, the West was stocked, and eventually pretty much all of the western part of both continents. Horses in the eastern part of the United States had a different history, most of them being brought over much later from England. Few of the horses landed in Florida by Cabeza de Baca survived, at least no trace of them can be found.

The horses that came into Mexico originally were domesticated stock. But they easily went wild again when set free by accident or design, and as the habitat was a congenial one, they multiplied and spread. The immediate start of wild horses on the Isthmus of Panama was the abandonment of a considerable number of the animals by De Soto and his companions while they were in flight from Grenada to Panama, just before they reached the town of Fonseca. It must be remembered that the Arabian horses were seldom sterilized. Consequently, when animals were lost or abandoned for any cause, they naturally formed themselves into little bands, bred, increased in numbers, and under ideal conditions of feed and climate, eventually over-

ran large portions of the country. These bands usually numbered from fifteen to forty head of mares and fillies. Young
males ran with them up to a year and a half of age, when they
would be whipped out by the old stallions and forced to form
new bands of their own, often on a new range. Some of them,
gradually working north, crossed the Rio Grande and so entered
what is now the United States.

Freighters and others crossing the plains in the forties and
fifties, encountered the wild bands, and commented on the
number of pintos they saw, as well as others that seemingly were
off-colored. They were not really off-colored—just different in
color. Their Arabian ancestors ran the gamut in color: chestnut, dark sorrel, light sorrel, grey, white, buckskin, cream
color (palomino), also a few blacks and bays. By crossing and
interbreeding, there were produced grullas, apalusas, pintos, and
horses of various other paint-pot colors; yet the strain still remained pure Arabian. The mesteños that stayed on the west
side of the Rio Grande, in large measure retained their Arabian
blood, symmetry, and stamina right up to the end. It was a
different matter, however, in Texas, where homesteaders
flocked in with small bunches of horses of their own. The horses
they brought were poor stock, in the main, and in the course
of time, by crossing with wild native mares, the range of Texas
came to be overrun by thousands of inferior and nearly worthless horses.

In fact, most Easterners looking for the first time at the
Spanish thunderbolts which Westerners preferred for cow
horses, were skeptical about them. "They'll be all right when
they grow up!" they'd say. And there were many experiments
aimed at putting height and weight on the cowboy's horse. An
Indian Bureau official imported Percheron and Clydesdale stallions and bred them to little Indian ponies (blood brothers to
the cow pony) on the Navajo Reservation. The legs and bodies
of the unnatural colts which were produced were spindly, and
their feet and heads were so heavy they could hardly lift them.
I tried one for a pack horse and found it utterly worthless.

Better advised, but still not good enough, was the attempt
made in the Anchor brand, operating near White Oaks, New

Mexico. The owner was a New Yorker, who bought a ranch for his son in the hope of reforming him. He stocked it with several hundred Texas mares and a few carloads of Hambletonian stallions. The son, who was supposed to look after them, let them run practically wild, while he tried to drink up all the red-eye and play all the poker in the neighboring mining town. The horses in the brand multiplied and were pretty good animals; but cattlemen found them slow starters, too big and awkward for ranch work.

Important in the northward migration of the horse were the travels of the Spanish *padres*. A few animals were brought north by those far-traveling gentlemen as early as 1590, but it was not until 1681 that they were introduced in large numbers. Father Usebio Kino in that year strenuously undertook to convert to the Christian faith the Indian tribes living in the northern portion of the Province of Sonora. In most of their expeditions, the *padres* rode the so-called native horses of Mexico, straight descendants of the Arabians, which, according to the Fathers, stood from 56 to 58 inches at the shoulder—or as we should say today, 14 to 14½ hands, and they weighed from 750 to 800 pounds—very tiny. While he was exploring the country from Yuma to California to discover whether Lower California was an island or a peninsula, Father Kino had with him only a few Indians, but he had 130 saddle horses and mules.

Another important factor in the migration of the horse into the United States was the Plains Indian. Tribesmen living near the Missions were the first to notice the value of horses, and stole many for their own use. Later the more distant Plains Indians made long horse-stealing forays into the areas now known as western Texas, New Mexico, Sonora, and Chihuahua, until finally all Western Indians became well mounted. In after years they were generally able to out-distance the United States cavalry horses (not native Western stock) when pursued by them. In fact, if given just a short start on their little horses, and if not impeded by baggage, the Indians were practically never caught by their pursuers—thanks to the superiority of their mounts. A close observer who traveled across the plains in 1846, wrote:

The Indian horses are the most hardy animals of the kind I have ever seen. Many of the breeds higher up in the Rocky Mountains have powers of endurance nearly equal to the Mexican mule; an animal which I regard as superior to any other on the continent of America for long, toilsome, and difficult journeys.[6]

These tough little pioneer horses have largely disappeared. Why, and where? No doubt many thousands of them were victims of the "crazy weed."[7] Other thousands were killed as ruthlessly as the buffalo by ignorant stockmen, who begrudged them the grass they ate. Because the wild horses were so small compared with Eastern horses, these stockmen often cussed them out as no good, not recognizing that, despite their size, they were perfectly adapted to their environment and mode of life, and had more endurance than any other horse whatsoever that crossed their range. Another reason many ranchmen had for not liking mustangs was because, they said, after they were caught and broke, they invariably returned to the wild bunch at the first opportunity. This was perfectly true of wild horses caught when full-grown. And who would expect anything different from an animal raised for, say, four years in perfect freedom, and depending on sight and speed to stay free? Imagine such an animal roped, choked, and busted out. Under those circumstances, who wouldn't escape to freedom at the first chance? But when mustangs were taken as colts or yearlings and were given good care, I have never known one that wouldn't return as good measure to its rider as it received from him. Once, on a mustang hunt, I got as my share of the bunch two stud colts and one filly, all about nine or ten months old. These I raised, and I never owned better cow horses. The filly was kept as a pet around the ranch and was naturally gentle. After she was grown, I picked up a thoroughbred stud in El Paso—got him for a few dollars because he had been crippled on the race track. From these two I raised four colts, all of them very fast.

The endurance of the best of these Western cow ponies is illustrated by countless incidents. Thus Father Kino, at the age of fifty-one, rode from his Dolores Mission and ranch to the City of Mexico. That was a distance of fifteen hundred

miles, and the journey was made in fifty-one days with many
stops on the way for funerals and baptisms. That took a pretty
good rider and a mighty good horse, for the horse had nothing
to eat on the trip but grass. But toughness is traditional with
Arabians. It is said to have been not unusual for an Arab rider,
when crossing a desert, to canter his horse steadily for twenty-
four hours or more at a stretch, giving him not over a quart of
water and a couple of handfuls of dried beef pounded fine on a
stone.

Cases to match these were not unknown in the Southwest
in our times. I spent a winter in Chihuahua, for example, buying saddle horses, some of which, after trying them out in El
Paso, I shipped East as polo ponies. Many fine horses were to
be seen around the plazas in Mexico, looking particularly at-
tractive under their silver trappings, ridden by men in *charro*
costumes.[8] One horse in particular caught my eye one day. It
was a gray, somewhat smaller than the average, heavier, and with
tremendous muscles. A person who is constantly buying horses
can usually tell at a glance their approximate age; but this little
horse had me guessing.

I watched him as he was ridden around the plaza, and hoped
his rider would stop so I could have a better chance to look the
animal over. Presently the rider and his companion stopped.
Snapping their fingers, they summoned a couple of peons who
were lounging against the wall of a *cantina* and told them to
hold their mounts, then entered the big American bar. I knew
that the better class in Mexico are rather reticent about talking
to strangers; but I fortunately met a man I knew, who also
knew the riders, so I was introduced to them in the correct way.
Over glasses of *tequila*, the conversation drifted to horses. I
praised their mounts. The elder of the two, whose name was
Don Elfego Morrales, told me the following story about his
little gray—the horse's name was Marinero (sailor).

"Some twelve years ago," said Don Elfego, "at the time of
the peon uprising, Mexico was in a ferment over the revolution.
I was a young lieutenant in the Rurales. One day I was summoned to the *quartel* and given a letter addressed to Doctor
Felipe Samiliego, of Juarez. I was told to deliver it as soon as

possible, as it was an order for the dispatch of cavalry to Chihua-hua. The railroads had been torn up, so I had to make the journey on horseback. The date (year, month, and hour) were written across the envelope in large letters, showing the exact time when I left: 12:20 P. M. to the exact minute. I was riding Marinero. At 1:20 P. M. the following day I delivered the letter into the hands of Doctor Samiliego at Juarez—a distance of two hundred miles, which was covered in twenty-five hours.

"I know, Señor," Don Elfego continued, "you will think this improbable. But if you will kindly walk to my house, a block from here, I will show you the very envelope."

I saw the envelope and was convinced that the story was true. The fact that Don Morrales was a slim youth at the time he made the ride, weighing only a little over one hundred pounds, and that he rode a small light saddle, probably helped to make the ride possible. The evidence, at least, is in favor of his having done so, and from my knowledge of the breed of horse Marinero came from, I do not consider it an impossible ac-complishment.

After showing me the letter, Don Morrales said he would like to have me see something odd that his little horse could do. He mounted Marinero, and pulled gently on the bit. The horse began walking backwards, gradually increasing speed until he broke into a trot, which he continued around the corral. The horse's owner said his father had an old *caporál* who taught the horse this trick when he employed Yaqui Indians to dig long irrigation ditches at the hacienda. Sometimes these Indians would hide out a few bottles of mescal, and while at work, get drunk and quarrelsome, attacking the boss with picks, shovels, sticks, or whatever was handy. By having the horse trained to trot backwards, the foreman was able to keep the men covered with his pistol, and at the same time stay out of range of their missiles.

"How old," I asked, "is Marinero?"

"He will be twenty on Santa Cruz Day, the fifth of May."

"Would you care to sell him?"

"*Por Dios*, no!"

One of the crackerjack horses that I did get in Mexico was

a white one named Blanco. I had bought three hundred head or more from Don Jose Mata, who had a big ranch and about eighteen hundred people working for him. Blanco did not belong to Don Jose, but to his foreman. I asked the latter if he'd sell. He said he would.

"How much?"

"More money," he grinned, "than the gringos have."

When I pinned him down to an actual amount, he said he wanted twenty dollars. I pulled out two state of Chihuahua ten-dollar bills and offered them to him. He shook his head. He could neither read nor write, and Don Jose told me that he didn't *sabe* soft money. I then offered him an old twenty-dollar gold piece. He still shook his head. Before we could do business, I had to send the twenty-dollar gold piece to the store and have it exchanged for twenty "adobe" silver dollars. Then Don Jose, the Mexican foreman, and I, sat down on our "hunkies," and the foreman piled the 'dobe dollars up, two to the pile, and in that way counted them and was satisfied.

Blanco was almost pure Arabian, and one of the best polo ponies that ever went East. I sold him to my cousin, Frank Underhill, of Oyster Bay, for five hundred dollars, a small price for a good polo pony in those days. He was beautifully reined, and had speed and absolute bridle control. He was used at Oyster Bay, Meadow Brook, and Cedarhurst.

But these little Spanish thunderbolts weren't always good at games. I remember very well a buckskin that I bought from the chief of the Rurales, thinkin' he would be a top hand back East. He was plenty of horse all right; but he didn't like polo and wouldn't play, and nothing they tried would make him. He would just stand in the center of the field and kick!

How much performance could a cowboy get out of his mount? That differed a lot, and depended not only on the horse, but also on the rider. A forty-five-mile ride was a good ordinary hard job of work for a cowboy for one day; that's about what a man would do in a day of ridin' circle at a roundup. Eighty or ninety miles were possible on a very good horse. I once rode one hundred and ten miles to make sure of a beef contract. Kit Carson, one of the best early riders, used to lead one horse

and ride another, changing every five miles; in this way he is
said to have made some very long rides. A man who knew how
to take good care of his horse often got more out of a mediocre
pony than some riders got out of good ones, a fact which was
proved more than once in the cowboy endurance races that at
one time were a feature of the West.

IV

The spectacular side of the cowboy and his horse was ridin'
'em when they pitched. Even the gentlest horse would "go
bronc" occasionally. Take on a damp morning when you went
to saddle up, especially if the blankets were wet and cold, you'd
likely see cowboys ridin' 'em high all over the corral—even the
old trusty well-broke horses didn't like the feel of the saddle on
mornings like that, and not bein' bashful, they spoke up in the
only language they knew to tell you so. Cow hands were known
and respected largely for their skill in training and handling
their horses, including ability to stay aboard when they pitched.
A man was bound to get thrown sometimes, no matter how
good he was, if he rode the bad ones. And there was no tellin'
whether he'd come down whole, or in pieces.

We asked Red in tones solicitous
If he had made his will,
Had he any girl in Texas
Who really loved him still?

Was there any parting message
That he would like to send,
To some one in his old, old home
Who still might be his friend?

Who was his pet undertaker?
What parson should we get?
Would he have flowers on his coffin?—
I can hear old Bugger yet;

"Mosey, you four-flush punchers,
Don't weep no tears for me,
I'm a ridin' kid from Texas,
From the old 3 Bar C!"

Bronc-busting—that is, breaking the wild ones to ride—was not done just for the sake of seeing what the stars looked like close to, but was a necessary part of ranch work. A rider who was really good was likely to specialize on this, maybe traveling from one ranch to another and bustin' a bunch here, a bunch there. He was likely to get more than regular puncher wages, generally so much a head. Sometimes a big outfit would hire a second rider not quite good enough for the first riding, in order to get the wrinkles out of broncs after they had been busted by an expert. The broncs, so-called, that the public sees in rodeos are generally horses that for some reason just naturally don't want to be rode; some of them are gentle enough ordinarily, but will always pitch if their saddle straps are very tight. The worst of the bad horses were as famous in their way as race horses. Barometer, Old Steamboat, Prickly Pear, Pizen, a mare called Divine, Lop Ears, and Sky High are among the worst bucking horses the Southwest remembers. And perhaps there never was a worse one than the Bar W's Brown Fox. He knew more steps than a dancing master.

As a four-year-old, Brown Fox got in the wire and was passed up in the breaking. Next year, as a five-year-old, he was roped, blindfolded, hackamored, and saddled. He whirled and kicked the boy saddling him, so they tied up his forefeet. After the saddle was on, the bronc buster let down Fox's foot, arranged his hackamore reins, and went aboard. Brown Fox piled him at the third jump. He got on again, and again Fox piled him. Another boy who was watching, spoke up.

"Kay," he said, "you-all forgot all you ever learned about ridin'. Let a real bronc peeler strut his stuff."

The second jump got the "real" peeler. Fox kicked at him in passing, but luckily did not hit him.

They tied Brown Fox up, and half starved him, but no man was found who could stay with him over four jumps. After throwing every rider at the ranch, he was turned out till spring. When work started, a lot of driftin' Texas cowhands ("cotton pickers," we called 'em) would ride up to the Bar W wagon hunting work. Most of them were on rode-down horses and had sorry outfits, though occasionally one would prove a pretty fair hand. One of these fellows had a new saddle made by Tackleberry. He struck the foreman, Pete Johnson, for a job, and Pete asked him if he could ride, saying he was tired of hirin' men who couldn't sit in an armchair, and of havin' horses come flyin' in, with saddles but no riders, scatterin' the *remuda* at all hours. The cotton picker said he could ride anything. So Pete told him to dab his line on Brown Fox. The Texan made a pretty throw, and put on the bridle and saddle without trouble. Fox had been saddled so often that he was used to it by now, and stood still.

"If you can ride that horse six jumps," said Pete, "you have a job."

"I'm hired," said the fellow.

He crawled aboard. Old Fox went up, changed ends, and at the third jump the newcomer landed astride of the cook's pot rack. Fox, as usual, blazed both heels at him as he left. We thought the outlaw would run a little distance, then stop and come back to the *remuda*. Instead, he high-tailed it across the flats. In the first quarter of a mile he stepped on his loose reins, tore the headstall buckle off, and shed his bridle. Pete furnished the stranger with another horse and saddle to go after him so as to get his saddle back. Late that night the Texan rode in, saying he never got any closer to Fox than half a mile, and the horse had joined a bunch of *palominos*. We knew them. They were the wildest bunch in the country. A year later some men who were trapping wild horses on the Rio Salado, caught Brown Fox. The Texan's saddle was still on him and as tight as a drum, since Fox had got in better flesh. Both stirrups and leathers were gone, also the saddle blanket. When the saddle was stripped off, Fox's back was as white as snow. The heat of the saddle had scalded his back, and he had shed the brown hair, the new hair growing out white.

We never found anyone who could ride that horse. He was condemned as spoiled, and turned out. But about this time they started having rodeos, and "bad" horses were in demand. A fellow came along and bought Brown Fox for fifty dollars. Under a changed name he was carried to rodeos all over the country, and he kept throwing all the crack riders for years until his ankles gave out. One day several of us boys were in town to see a little Wild West show. Among the circus horses we recognized old Brown Fox. His ankles were twice normal size, but he could still pitch a little. Three of us chipped in thirty dollars and bought him, drove him over to the ranch and gave him his freedom.

A chestnut horse named Turk, his owner's pet, once pitched at just the right time to be the undoing of a rider who had stolen him. Turk had been kept in the corral one night to wrangle the saddle horses for the following day's work. Next morning the corral gate was found open and Turk was gone. His trail was picked up for a short distance on the clay flat, and then lost in stony ground—what there was of the trail made it perfectly clear that the horse had been ridden away from the corral—hence, stolen. Most ranchmen picked up a pretty good knowledge of tracking, and the footprints of a familiar horse and the way he was travelin', could often be read like a book. I once trailed a stolen horse for five hundred miles, apprehending the thief in Fort Worth, Texas. In the case of Turk, the owner knew that he had been ridden off, rather than just wandering off of his own accord, because the tracks went in a straight line and the horse had not once stopped to graze. A loose horse will not go straight, but zigzags more or less; also, he steps short of his front track, not quite reaching it with his hind feet. A horse with a man riding him cuts the ground deeper with his toe than a loose horse.

Turk's owner rode the range in a fifty-mile circle, but failed to find any sign by which he could track the stolen animal, and nobody who was questioned seemed to have seen him. About this time the neighboring ranchmen started a roundup, and moved their wagon to the home range of Turk's owner. At the end of the second day's drive they had several hundred head of cattle under herd, and there were seven men at the wagon who had just come in from the day's drive. Suddenly the cook hollered, and pointed to a riderless horse coming at a high lope and heading for the *remuda*, which the horse wrangler was holding about a quarter of a mile from the wagon. The stray was Turk. The wrangler caught him and led him to the wagon.

"JACK" AND "BLARNEY"

After a day hunting cattle on their ranch near La Palma, New Mexico, Jack Thorp and his wife came home down the canyon and found a friend from Santa Fe, a professional photographer named Cross, waiting for them. He wanted a picture of them just as they were; this is it. Taken about 1905. At that time, Jack was running an average of about 350 cattle at La Palma and in the Serrera Oscura country, as well as a flock of sheep and Angora goats.

The horse was carrying a handsome headstall, though the bridle lines had broken off, also a saddle heavily embossed with silver and with a name plate that bore a name familiar to all those present—Joe Crouch. This man Crouch owned a small ranch and a couple of hundred head of cattle twenty miles north, and although nothing definite had ever been proved against him, people were suspicious of him for a number of reasons.

Turk's story came out a few days later when a hand who was riding the chuck line, stopped at the wagon. Seeing the silver-mounted saddle on Turk, he examined it carefully, then burst out laughing. Asked what the joke was, he said he had seen a man thrown from that saddle only a few days before, that he had "landed in a creek, upside down, and he sure had a hard fall." The chuck-line rider said he had stopped at the Rafter B, Crouch Ranch. He went to the corral to "juice" the cow. Crouch came along, slapped this saddle on a chestnut-colored horse which was undoubtedly Turk, double-cinched him tight, stepped aboard, and brought a heavy quoit down on the horse's head. Three jumps down hill, and the rider was piled in the creek—and the horse pulled out for the tall timber.

Turk was not naturally a bucker. Like most of the horses on the range, he had always been ridden with three-quarter rig saddles—or if with a double rig, the flank cinch was left very loose or taken off altogether. Many an otherwise gentle horse, if flank-cinched, would carnival and go places with his rider. That's what Turk did with Crouch.

The incident was the end of Crouch on that range. He quit the country and left no forwardin' address.

Sometimes a pitching horse would pick his time and surprise a rider he had been layin' for for a long time. I once had a horse fall and break my left ankle while cutting a steer out of a herd on the Carrizozo flats. I had to ride more than a hundred miles to El Paso, Texas, to find a doctor; and when they let me out of the hospital, I got a job with a trail herd owned by the Nations and Moore Cattle Company. Joe Nations had several butcher shops in El Paso, and he sent me out to his butcher camp (beef camp, he called it) on the mesa where Fort Bliss is today, to get a horse. I rode out on my little pack horse.

The ranch foreman penned a bunch of saddle horses for me. Most of them seemed to be pretty well ridden down. However, there was one rangy bay that looked good to me.

"He's a good cow horse," agreed Luke, the foreman, "*if* you can ride him. He's from Nations' ranch in the Davis Mountains, and he's piled every butcher buyer who's tried to ride him. Maybe with a bum leg, you better pass him up." The horse's name, Luke said, was Seven Hellfires.

I laid my line on him. As he didn't even tighten the rope, I knew he had been handled a-plenty. I saddled him, and left him to soak a while. Nations had sent out my bedroll, and I put it on my little pack horse. Then we all moseyed over to the shack for dinner. I was sort of uneasy about the bay horse. I would not have worried over his reputation had I had two good legs under me, but I didn't favor takin' any chances of his piling me and maybe breaking my ankle again. However, I had noticed when I put the bit in his mouth that his tongue had a bad scar on it, showing that he had been ridden with a Mexican ring bit, and the chances were he was tender-mouthed. That being the case, I thought I could hold his head up so he couldn't buck. After dinner I eased into the saddle, and with Tom, another rider, left the ranch without any trouble. But I was still a little uneasy, and when a man is afraid of a horse, the horse sure knows it and sooner or later will try him out.

We made the trip to where the herd was being put up. Seven Hellfires acted a perfect gentleman all the time, and continued to do so for three months on the trail. I kept him as a night horse, and by the time we turned the herd over to the buyers in Kansas, he was as fat and slick as a seal. I felt pretty good over having tamed the horse that had thrown everybody else.

Several of us went to the general store to provision the chuck wagon for the return trip. As my old slicker leaked, I bought a new one. Like all new slickers, the oil on the outside made the arms stick together. I tied it on behind my saddle, and when the wagon was loaded, we started south toward a little creek where the grass was good and we intended to camp for the night. Several of us were riding behind the wagon, laughing and talking, when suddenly it began to rain.

"Now wasn't it lucky," I thought, "that I bought that slicker!"

I dropped the loop in my lines over the saddle horn. Since there would now be no night guard to stand, I was riding my night horse, Seven Hellfires. Turning halfway in the saddle, I reached back and untied the slicker. Freeing it from the saddle strings, I pushed my right arm through the sleeve, then my left, but halfway through, it stuck. There I sat, with both arms in the air and half behind me; and old Seven Hellfires looked back and said, "Jack, this is the chance I been waitin' for. I want you!"

Down went his head, up went his back. About the third jump, he got me over the saddle horn. By then I had both arms through the sleeves, but all I could find to grab hold of were his ears as his head came up. He pounded my bootheels into the ground so hard my legs were sore for days. Two jumps more I rode him, and then we parted company. He sure threw me, that horse did. And all those fools sat a-watchin' and laughin' at me. They knew I could ride him if I'd had a shot. I was mad all over, thinking that this horse, that had thrown 'most everybody else, had waited three months to catch me just right and strut his piece. I rode him, after that, whenever his turn came, all the way home, and he never offered to rant again.

V

Strange tales have been told of the faculty of range-bred horses for finding their way home. The instinct of horses is very strong to stay on the home range or to go back to it if they can. Some of the tales sound pretty tall, but I am inclined to think that many of them are true, or substantially so. I will tell two instances of this kind that came under my own eye.

On July 1, one year, it rained for the first time in over twelve months. Old grass was plentiful, but my range twenty miles west of the Guadalupe Mountains was parched and dry. Now, however, all the waterholes would be full and stock would

be fat. Fine! I thought. The earth roof of my house leaked
so badly that I slept under the kitchen table, which luckily was
covered with oilcoth. That spot, and the inside of my stove
oven, were the only dry places in the house. It rained for three
days and nights, and when on the morning of the Fourth the
sun appeared, you could almost hear the grass and weeds grow.
The big earth reservoir in my corral was full and running over.

I needed a saddle horse, and didn't have one caught up. One
could usually take the tracks of my gentle saddle and work
stock and trail them up, but the continuous rain had killed all
sign. With the outlying waterholes full, I knew it might be
several days before any stock would come to the home ranch,
and then only to lick salt at the troughs at the corral. So I
whistled up my hounds and shouldered my saddle gun and
started out to see what luck I would have afoot and without
any signs to guide me. I had none. I walked till almost sundown
and never found the trail of a horse or a cow. After the first
couple of miles, walking in high-heeled boots, I thought of what
Old Man Blevins once said:

"The Lord," he declared, "never intended a cowpuncher to
walk. *I can prove it by the Bible!*"

On the way home, to sort of even things up, I struck a bunch
of antelope and shot a yearling buck, which I dressed and packed
in to the ranch.

The next morning I started out afoot again, heading for my
nearest neighbor's ranch—Will Brownfield, who lived five or
six miles to the east. I thought sure he would have some horses
in his corral and I could borrow one, but as I approached his
windmill, I saw him sitting on the fence whittling.

To my question if he had a saddle horse, he answered, "Nary
one! I been perched on this rail since sun-up, waitin' for something with four legs under it to come in to water. But shucks!
there won't be nothin' now till outside waters are dried up.
Stock won't come in to drink this salty water till the rain water
is all gone."

We went in the house and cooked us a good meal, then wan-
dered out and perched on the corral fence again, praying for
almost any kind of a horse to stroll in. A cowboy without a

horse was a gone gander for sure. My gaze happened to fasten on a white chalk hill to the west, and I thought I saw a little dust arise. I called Will's attention to it.

"If it's an animal," he said glumly, "it's none of mine. All my stock run south or east of here." The puffs of white dust, however, continued to rise from the chalk-hill trail. Will was puzzled. We watched for some time, and presently were able to make out that it was a horse with something following it. "It's nobody ridin'," Will said, "dust not risin' fast enough. But I can't figure what animal it could be, coming from that direction. Whatever it is, it knows this watering, or it wouldn't be on the chalk-hill trail." The dust puffs continued coming our way, and while the animals were still much to far off for any possible identification, Will let go with an exclamation. "By hominy!" he said, "I'll tell you what's happened. Now listen to me. I'll bet you a new pair of buckskin gloves that animal we see is a four-year-old bay mare, branded E. L. Bar, with a yearling colt following her."

As I didn't see how he could possibly tell, I took the bet. But in about half an hour, sure enough, a bay mare branded E. L. Bar on the left hip, passed into the corral. She was heavy with foal, and was followed by a yearling colt. I asked Will how he had figured it out.

"Well," he said, "you know a young mare has an instinct to have her second colt at the same place where she had her first one. So as soon as I saw there was a colt following, I reckoned it must be a young mare coming home to foal where she had the last one. If it had been an old mare, maybe she wouldn't have bothered. If it was a young mare that belonged here on Crow Flat, I knew it had to be a three- or a four-year-old, and since she had a colt, the chances were she was four. And the bay color—well, that was the color of all the mares I sold."

He explained that the year before, a man named John Cavitt, who ranched on the Colorado River in western Arizona, near the town of Parker, had driven through in a buckboard and bought a hundred head of mares, some with colts by their sides, from his mother and himself. This mare we had just seen was one of them, and Will knew she had reached Arizona, because Cavitt had written to say he had made it back to his Arizona ranch with all the horses he bought. To cover the route again and make her way home, this mare must have traveled at least six hundred miles and crossed seven rivers, roughly, as far as from Cincinnati to Atlanta. In those days there were very few fences, so an animal could make such a trip.

Once on a trail drive I had a more intimate experience with the propensity of horses to go home. We were out for three months, taking a herd of beef steers from the Rio Grande in New Mexico to a ranch running the R O Y brand in southern Kansas. As there had been a severe drought in New Mexico, the stock, including the horses, were thin. Accordingly, each man had seven in his mount instead of five. The two extras in each mount were half-broncs, that is, they had been ridden a few saddles the fall before, then turned loose during the winter, and gathered again on the spring horse work. It was customary for every trail herd to carry along at least a few young horses, as trail work gentled them fast.

We crossed the Pecos River at Fort Sumner. The trail headed east to a large surface lake, then north, leaving Peach Spring Canyon to the east, then through Salt Spring pasture, and then we entered the X I T pasture, "three million acres in extent." We passed through pasture No. 7, and one other, before coming out near the railroad east of Washburn Junction. In the days of the trail herds there were no automobiles, and consequently no troughs or cattle guards, just wire gates, or occasionally one made of boards. Unless he was clever, a horse couldn't get through a wire fence. The reason for mentioning these pastures and fences will be seen presently.

In my mount my two young horses were a four-year-old and a five-year-old, both seal brown in color with stars on their foreheads and two white stockings behind. They were evidently brothers, or half-brothers. The buster who broke them out had named them French and Jew's Harp, and so I called them. The name given a horse by the first man to ride him usually stuck.

It was late July when we started, and in September up on the plains, the nights began getting cold, especially so about the time when old Torch, the morning star, poked over the rim just ahead of the sun. And up there almost every morning the horse wrangler was short two horses, French and Jew's Harp. It was very evident that these two young horses did not care for the cold early mornings and wanted to get back to the cotton-wood shelters along the Rio Grande. Of course the herd and wagon couldn't be held up to hunt for them; so the horse wrangler or trail boss would have to take the back trail of the two Harps and follow it until he found them. Usually they were still hobbled when found, but they would have traveled anywhere from two to five miles from the night's camp.

We crossed the line into Kansas to find that there had been no dought. The grass was as green as a garden and all surface lakes were full of water. In three days more we made our last camp, six miles south of the R O Y ranch. The next morning the horse wrangler was again short the two Harp horses.

"Let 'em go!" said the boss. "We'll pick 'em up on our way back." So we started the herd without them.

We were delayed at the ranch by a cranky buyer. The herd was made up of yearlings, two-year-olds, three-year-olds, and up, and to satisfy him that he was getting what he was paying for, many of the animals had to be roped, thrown, and toothed. So it was three days before we passed the old bed-ground on our return home. There all hands spread out and cut signs for the trail of the two missing horses, which was picked up some three miles south of the old camp. They were hobbling along headed due south, and the trail was easy to follow. In about five miles we picked up a broken rope hobble, and just before we stopped the wagon for noon we found the other one. So the two horses were foot-loose, and the foreman prophesied that we wouldn't catch up with them till we struck the north end of the X I T pasture fence, forty miles south.

Without the herd, the outfit was now making about thirty-five miles a day, and it was noon of the second day when we came to the big pasture fence. The wire gate was closed, our herd having been the last to go through. On top of the dust of the cattle sign was the clear trail of our two runaway horses. They had followed the fence line east. Trailing them, in less than a mile we found the fence partially down. From the tracks, it was evident that they had pawed at the wire until the staples came out of the posts and the three lower wires dropped. The horses then had evidently squatted and gone under the top wire for we found some brown hair caught in two of the barbs.

A mile further south, their trail showed again. We were following it when we camped the wagon for the night.

It took us two days to cross this pasture, and still the tracks of the Harps were headed for home. In following their trail, we could notice but few places where they had quit the trail to graze. Probably, there being a splendid stand of grama grass, they just grabbed enough to satisfy themselves and kept traveling.

A couple of days later we came to the fence and the gate heading into the next pasture. We found that the little stake on the end had come out of the two wire loops holding it to the post, and had fallen to the ground, leaving a gap through which the two horses had passed. The tracks on the north side of this gate showed that the horses had been here for several hours, and it was quite apparent that in their eagerness to get through, they had finally managed to nose the wire loop off and let the gate fall.

All along the way, from that point on, the trail of the two horses was plain. The plank gate at the end of this pasture had been left open by somebody, and the Harps' tracks showed where they had passed through. Several days later we pulled up at the ranch house among the cottonwoods along the Rio Grande and saw Williams, the ranch cook, watching for us from the gallery.

"Ain't yo' boys lost somethin'?" he grinned.

The two Harps, he said, had come in a couple of days before. French Harp's back was pretty well cut up by the wire, but the cook had greased it thoroughly and turned the two loose in the horse pasture.

That's the story of two horses that wanted to go home, and did it, though it meant an air-line walk of about six hundred miles, and openin' one gate, and takin' down part of one fence.

VI

Mustangs were not ruthlessly slaughtered in New Mexico as they were in some other states, but great roundups were held by ranchmen and *mesteñeros,* or "mustangers," as the professional wild-horse hunters were called. Some of these men were artists at their work. Among the best-known of them were "Horse" Evans, "Pony" Bob Campbell, and "Wild Horse" Gould. And there were many others, such as Bill Ike Babb and Bill Mack. Such men made a business of catching wild horses and trailing them to market; and incidentally, on a big roundup, they could usually figure on picking up around a hundred strays that the owners would pay three or four dollars apiece to have returned. Once a group of mustangers drove a bunch of wild horses clear across Texas to Louisiana, where they traded them to plantation owners raising cotton, to be used in place of mules.

A good deal of romance clings to the wild-horse herds of the Southwest, and some thrilling fiction has been written about supposedly magnificent mustang studs, untamed and unbranded, free as the wind, smart as cats. There were some beauties in the wild bunch, especially when the bands had not suffered from isolation and too much inbreeding. At the same time, wild ones as a whole were apt to be deceiving. To look at a stud snorting and raring at the head of his *manada,* you might swear he was sixteen hands high and worth five hundred dollars. But run him down, and you might find he was no more than thirteen hands, and worth at most a dollar. Many a good gentle horse was ridden down after a poor wild one. No estimate of wild-horse numbers could even approach anything like accuracy, but many years when the waterholes were full, I have seen as many as a thousand head at one watering, made up of many different *manadas.* It was a colorful and exciting spectacle, because at these times the stallions heading the *manadas* would fight for supremacy, the victors stealing the mares of the vanquished. A fight between mustang stallions was not a pretty sight. A well-directed kick on the hock might place one out of the combat, or too tight a grip on the jugular vein might mean death. In fact, death was a not uncommon result of these desperate combats. During the breeding season, early spring, the old stallions were constantly battling and whipping young males out of their *manadas*. The outcasts generally tried in retaliation to steal a few mares from their old bunch. No matter how fiercely two old stallions might be battling, if they saw some young stallion trying to steal one of their mares, they would stop till the young thief was run off, after which they would take up the fight again where they had left off.

Mustangs were wary creatures. Their eyesight was very keen. In the open country, if a *manada* happened to sight a horseman, they would head at once for the densest timber or thicket they could find; splitting up, they would come together again only after they were well out of danger. A badly-scared wild bunch would generally run toward any other bunch of animals in sight, whether antelope, wild cattle, or another bunch of mustangs, and when they had overcome their fright, the stallion would separate out his own mares, running behind the laggards and biting their rumps to make them hurry. When they were all started, he would gallop proudly into the lead.

Various methods were used to catch mustangs. Some *mesteñeros* would build a stout corral, eight feet or so high, at the edge of a mott of timber with wings extending a quarter of a mile in either direction. They would run the horses between the wings and force them into the corral. Sometimes this worked, other times it didn't.

Occasionally a horse hunter tried catching the wild ones by suspending snares or loops along brushy trails used by horses when going to or from water. Very few were caught in this way.

Three brothers, just starting as wild-horse hunters, conceived the scheme of digging a pit across a trail much traveled by horses. After a week of hard work they completed it. It was very similar to a bear pit, carefully covered with leaves and branches. The brothers then took turns watching. Presently a *manada* of about thirty head came along, with the stallion jog trotting in the lead. When he came to the side of the pit he stopped, sniffed, and led his bunch carefully around it. One exuberant colt, dashing around its mother, did fall into the pit. It took several men the best part of a day to fish him out. That one small bay colt was the net result of a week's hard work, and since the boys couldn't feed the colt, they turned him loose to join his anxious mother. The pit then had to be fenced up to prevent stray cattle from tumbling in.

One reasonably successful way of catching mustangs was to walk them down. Full moon was the time usually chosen, since the idea was to keep them going night and day, never letting them graze or rest. We would make camp as near as possible to the middle of the range used by the wild bunch—they would rarely leave it. When we first jumped the bunch we were after, they would probably break and run a mile or so, and one man would keep after them at a walk or a jog trot. When he got near them the second time, they might run for three or four miles. After reaching the limit of their range, they would double back, and as they passed camp, one of the other boys would take over the job of following them, while the first one rode in and rested, caught up a fresh horse, and got something to eat. Old mustangers would often have two men walking the *manada* at night, one in daytime. Some of these hunters used to bell a mare and turn her loose where the stallion would pick her up. Her bell was a great help in keeping track of the *manada* at night. The walking was kept up, and usually at the end of the sixth or seventh day, having had no rest and little or nothing to eat and drink, the mustangs would begin to weaken, then it was easy to throw them with a bunch of gentle stock and drive them into a corral.

Another method quite often used was to round up a *manada* of gentle mares and colts, and head the mustangs towards them. After they had run a while, the entire bunch would be checked, and if there were plenty of men on the work, all could be corraled, wild and tame alike.

After the wild ones were put on herd with the gentle bunch, however, there was still the problem of keeping them from running away at the first opportunity. In a fenceless country, that was a real problem. Often the mustangers made a surcingle of a piece of rawhide, to which they attached another piece of rawhide that they tied around one front ankle. The effect, when the horse tried to run, was much the same as if he had broken a leg, and after a couple of tumbles, the average horse thought better of running. Another scheme was to cut a piece of rawhide about six feet long and four inches wide, and fasten one end securely around the ankle of one front foot. If the mustang started to run with this on, he was bound sooner or later to step on the trailing rawhide and trip himself. Ordinarily, it's hard to throw a horse. If he has a rider, he may not care two straws if he throws *him* and breaks his neck, but he is mighty careful of his own neck.

Tall tales were told by some of the *mesteñeros*. Sometimes you had to hunt around some for the truth in what they said, but generally there was a good substantial kernel of it if you knew where to look, like "Pony" Campbell's yarn about the little "yaller" line-back mule whose mammy was a mustang, and who ran with the *manada* in which he was raised till he was five or six years old. "Pony" was a little short fellow who ran wild horses for years. He said it was largely because of the wariness of this little mule that the *manada* which the animal ran with never had been corralled. One time, on a big roundup, the band was pressed very hard. The stallion tried to keep them all together, but the little mule smartly split them up. As a result, they all got away in the brush except one mare and colt. This mare and colt at first were penned in a big winged corral with other wild ones taken on the roundup. The next morning, according to Campbell, one of the boys saw the little buckskin mule standing on the flat about a quarter of a mile away, making mule noises, and the little colt that had been caught with its mammy, nickered in reply.

"We kept the bunch in the corral for three days while workin' 'em over," "Pony" said. "On the fourth day we started to put 'em out under herd to graze. The little mule seemed to have disappeared, though at times the colt would nicker. When we turned the horses out, the mare and colt were on the nigh point of the herd. Before we got to good grass, we had to pass through a patch of post oak. Just as we entered it, we saw a small yaller flash dart into the herd and cut out that mare and colt. All three disappeared in a cloud of dust.

"And every word of that," said "Pony," "is so!"

It is a fact that wild mules did become mightily attached at times to horse colts.

Four *mesteñeros,* including "Wild Horse" Gould and Bill Ike Babb, came out from Texas one year to the mountainous region of New Mexico west of the Rio Grande, bordering the Navajo Reservation, and announced their intention of penning a bunch of twenty-one wild horses inhabiting that region and known to be extremely wary. The horses in this band were all gray, except three mares which, on account of their age, had become almost white. They were led by a steel-gray stud. Because of his unusual appearance and speed, the ranchmen had christened him Rocket. The Texans announced that they would take the bunch by walking them down. The ranchmen were very much interested, because they had tried many times to *run* the bunch down, with no success. I was a comparative youngster on the range, and watched the preparations with the closest attention.

The walk-down started, and proceeded according to schedule into the second night, when a rainstorm came up. It got so dark that the man following the mustangs lost all track of them, and even had a hard time finding his way back to camp. The range next day was too boggy for much riding; but as soon as it dried out, the *mesteñeros* tried to pick up the trail of the wild ones. This should have been easy enough to do. But they found neither track nor trace of it. On the evening of the fourth day, a cowman passing reported that he had seen the band about twenty miles to the south, on what was known as the old Salt Trail—a road long abandoned, and deeply cut by ruts and rains, that had once been used by freighters going to the salt lakes. The *mesteñeros* took up the trail early the following morning, and found the band, sure enough, grazing right alongside the Salt Trail not far from the river.

The Rio Grande, here about ten feet deep, had cut a channel near the west bank, and the old trail now ended abruptly on a bluff twenty feet above the water. Thanks to some motts of cedar, which they kept between the wild bunch and themselves, the hunters were able to get within a couple of hundred yards of their quarry before being discovered. They planned to "land" the band, that is, ride on either side of it,

knowing pretty certainly, they thought, that when the horses
came to the high bank of the river, they would have to turn and
come back, and then, the hunters believed, they could rope the
stud and maybe a few others.

As soon as the horsemen were seen, the mustangs fled
straight down the old trail towards the river, the stud at the
rear hurrying them along. As they approached the river,
Rocket, with a wild burst of speed outran his *manada*, took the
lead, and with never a pause, dove into the swimming water,
followed by every one of his mares. By the time the *mesteñeros*
arrived at the river bank, they saw the last of the mustangs
leaving the river and entering the rough hills to the east.

Ordinarily, a band would not leave its home range. But
that band did. And the fact that they did, was their salvation.
Long afterwards, in talking with Bill Ike Babb, I asked if he
ever saw those mustangs again.

"Yes," he said, "I did. Eight years later I was hunting horses
in the rough country at the head of the Pintada, and about a
hundred miles south and west of where Rocket and his band
swam the river, on a hill a mile away, I saw the old stud. On
another hill, farther on, I saw his old *manada*. He had evidently
met the fate of all the old ones, and one of the younger studs
had taken his place as leader. But when I put my bring-'em-
nears to my eyes, I saw the old fellow was watchin' my every
move. His head was erect, his tail arched. His pose seemed to
say, 'Maybe I *am* old. But jest try and catch me!' The last I
saw, he was still watchin' me as he picked his way step by step
down the trail into the depths of Portales Canyon."

Once, south of the Davis Mountains in Texas, a bunch of
us came across a family of Mexicans from Old Mexico who were
mesteñeros in a fashion all their own. We saw the dust of a
band of horses approaching us rapidly at an angle, and as they
got nearer, we observed that two riders were crowding them
along. One of the riders, to our surprise, was a girl. She was
mounted on a big white horse. As we watched, she raced alongside a mustang sorrel that on the other side was crowded against
other horses in the racing band. She reached over, grabbed the
sorrel's mane, and slipped neatly from her white horse onto the

wild one's back. Her companion, following behind, picked up the bridle reins of her white horse, and led him over to where we were.

"How come?" we asked. "How's that girl goin' to stop that horse? He's liable to run into the Gulf of Mexico with her, no?"

"No," the man said in Spanish, "she'll be back pretty soon." And sure enough, in less than half an hour she was back on her new horse.

This Mexican girl was small and wiry, maybe fourteen years old. When she jumped from her gentle horse to the mustang's back, she carried nothing but a hair rope about ten feet long. With this, she explained, she threw a little loop over the horse's head, then a couple of half hitches over his nose, making a crude *jáquimó* (halter, anglicized as hackamore). With this, after he got over his fright, she was able to check him and slowly work him where she wanted him to go. I knew that pony express riders sometimes changed horses spectacularly in this way, but they were working with gentle horses that knew just what to do. This bit of a girl was climbing onto the backs of horses that had never had a human being aboard.

We visited the camp of these people. There were six of them, all of the same family, camped in a brush *chosa* (shanty) with a little round *orno* (mud oven) to bake bread in. They had a *carreta*, drawn by three big burros, into which they dumped everything when they moved. The family consisted of the father and mother, the boy or young man we had already encountered, the girl *mesteñera* whom we had seen in action, and her two younger sisters, whom we found herding about twenty head of horses that the older girl had caught within the month, and anxiously looking forward to the time when they too could be *mesteñeras*. The captured horses were all either hobbled, side-lined, or necked two and two together, to prevent their running away. The father, we learned, when he was still light and active enough, had caught wild horses in the same way his daughter was catching them now; and at different times, while doing it, he had broken both arms and both legs. His wife had been a *mesteñera* too in her day. Their son had caught wild mustangs also, but he had quickly gotten too heavy for any horse to carry him alongside the wild ones. His sister, the present *mesteñera,* weighed about seventy pounds. Sometimes, she said, she had to race the *mesteños* two or three miles before she could attempt a leap. The gentle horses that the family owned and used for running down the wild ones, were very fine animals, each standing around sixteen hands, and weighing perhaps eleven hundred pounds. The saddle the girl used was merely a sheepskin pad, held on by a surcingle on which were fastened two brass stirrups, the whole thing weighing, I suppose, not over three pounds.

The father said that when they had caught fifty head of wild horses, they would go back to their home in the state of Chihuahua to spend the winter, selling the horses on the way or during the winter months. The ones they caught were unbranded, of course, and could be sold anywhere. They were better, he said, than most of the mustangs that were left south of the Rio Grande.

At this camp, I was much interested in the style of corral the Mexicans had built. One side was a rock bluff. The remainder was a fence built in the following fashion. Two posts were set abreast and about a foot apart, and were lashed together at the top with rawhide. Two feet further on, two more posts were set and lashed in the same way; and so on all around. Into this "cradle" of posts, cedar and oak brush had been tramped down, making a fence that was literally hog-tight, horse-high, and practically foolproof.

Here too, I was much interested the following morning to see how these Old Mexicans busted their wild horses. The boy chose a big sorrel mare out of the wild bunch, and put a blinder on her. At the same time, the little *mesteñera* and her father tied an end of each of two long horse-hair ropes around the mare's front ankles. The boy saddled up, climbed aboard, and pulled off the blinder. When the mare bucked, the girl and her father pulled on the two ropes, with the result that the mare came down on her knees. She bucked and landed on her knees six times before she decided that she had had punishment enough, and quit pitchin'. The boy told me that her knees

Photograph by New Mexico State Tourist Bureau.   BEGINNING OF THE DRIVE

"Corral gates were opened, and those wild horses came out of there a-snuffin', with only one idea in all their heads, namely, to make a break and hit the nearest trail back to ranges which many of them had known from colthood, unfenced and free."

Photograph by New Mexico State Tourist Bureau.

HIGH WATER

"The river was out of its banks making it a swimming proposition." Getting a trail herd, whether of horses or cattle, across swimming water was always attended with difficulties and sometimes with danger.

would be swollen for a few days, but no more, and that she was
probably cured of bucking for all time; but if she ever did show
any signs of wantin' to pitch, all that was necessary was to tie
a short piece of hair rope around each ankle and she'd give up
the notion in a hurry. Later I tried this method myself and
found that it worked very well, provided the horse was saddled
again while his knees were still sore.

VII

Cowboys were very various in their treatment of horses.
Some had no patience and were mean and short-tempered, and
you could depend on it that a horse of any spirit would give
that kind of rider as good as it got. In fact, you could often tell
a good deal about the kind of man a puncher was, just by noticing how the horse acted when the rider came near. Many
cowboys had respect and often affection for their horses, and
got a good deal of amusement and education out of studyin'
their ways. What I felt about one horse, and what many a well-
dispositioned cowboy felt about some horse, went into a song I
wrote but never published about a horse I owned, Old Blue.*

> And you say that horses ain't human,
> That they don't know what you say;
> Now maybe old Blue didn't speak to me
> As I turned to go away,
> When he lay out there in the pasture
> And his time had come to go.
> When he raised his head and looked at me,
> Don't tell me he didn't know!
>
> Seemed to say, "You've been a good master,
> And I've tried to play the game fair;
> I've made you a hand as a cow horse
> And we've been 'most everywhere.
> As a four-year-old I saw my first roundup:
> I was green as a country lass;
> We stood night guard together
> And never let anything pass.

---

* Jack was mistaken in saying that this song, which he called "Old Blue," had never
been published. It appeared under the title, "A Cow Pony Friend," in a copyrighted book
of songs, with music entitled *The Happy Cowboy*, and is reproduced here with the permission
of the publishers, The Paull-Pioneer Music Corp., of New York City.—N. M. C.

"Then you stabled and fed me next winter,
Taught me how to hold a steer down:
I'd set back on the rope till it almost broke,
But I'd never let one off the groun'.
Your praise was just like music—
You never a cross word spoke
When we lost the rope contest at Dixon
And I knew that, old friend, you were broke.

"And then when you got into trouble,
And we went on the dodge for a time,
And the ride that we made for the river,
And at midnight crossed the line:
Eighty miles on the sands without water,
In the heat of an August day,
Till we ran the legs off of the posse,
Crossed the border, and got away.

"When the years passed you gave me my freedom,
Wouldn't let me die in a pen,
But turned me loose on the green hills,
That I might recover again.
Good-bye, master! I'll ask a last favor:
Be as good as you've been to me
To the rest of your mount of cow horses—
When worn out and old, turn 'em free."

In many respects, horses resemble humans. Oddly enough, they seem to have about the same reaction to alcohol as human beings. I had a little pet horse that got to drinkin' water out of a bottle. One day somebody tried him on whiskey, and he got cockeyed. A saloonkeeper that I knew, had a burro which he used when he went hunting once a year, and at other times kept out back of the saloon. Beer and whiskey slops would be put out in a trough, and this little burro would drink about a gallon of it and get perfectly stupid and look at you so funny.

I had a horse named Grampa that would steal anything. If you dropped your pocketknife, he'd pick it up. He was a regular old pot-licker. At a wagon camp he would watch till he thought everyone was asleep, then he'd sneak close, taking little noiseless steps in his hobbles. Many a time I pretended to be asleep in my blankets, just to watch him. Unless stopped, he would nose the cover off the cookpot and eat the contents, whether it was beans, coffee, stew, or raw dough. Once at my Slash SW Ranch in the San Andrés Mountains, I dropped a bottle of whiskey in the wash bowl and broke it. I strained out the glass and left the bowl on the gallery while I went to the corral for something. Although I returned in a very few minutes, the whiskey was gone, and Grampa was drunker than a dime-store mirror.

Range horses had personal likes, dislikes, and prejudices just as human beings do. At one time I was cattle buyer for the San Cristobal Ranch, and was on the go pretty much all the time, trading mostly with Indians and small native ranchmen within a distance of seventy-five or a hundred miles. My only assistant was a collie pup named Bobbie Burns, who in time developed into one of the smartest cow dogs I have ever known. My horse was named Clay, a genuine old line-back buckskin that in the past had had the reputation of being a bucking fool, but with me was as gentle as one could wish.

On long trips, Bobbie Burns would get tired, and I would let him ride in the *morral*, or nosebag, which hung on the horn of the saddle. There he would sit with his paws hanging over the sides, looking at the jack rabbits and other scenery. When he got too big for that, he would have to take it mostly afoot. During this time, Clay became very much attached to the dog, and whenever I saw that Bobbie was getting too tired, I would stop, reach over, and pull him up by his collar, laying him across in front of me on the saddle. Clay never objected. In fact, dog and horse got so accustomed to this act, that when I called Bobbie, he would run and jump as high as he could, landing against the horse's shoulder, and I would grab him and scramble him into the saddle. When full grown, he could make it onto the horse's back without assistance. The dog and horse were thrown together in this way for about two years, with no other companions to speak of, and that no doubt accounts for the great fondness that grew up between them. When Clay was turned into a small pasture occasionally for a day's rest, the two would remain together, Clay sometimes whinnying to call the dog to him. Often Bobbie would jump on his back and sit there while the horse continued to graze, both seemingly perfectly happy.

Another horse that knew what he liked was Old Speck, a red roan with a switch tail, no beauty, but all horse. I brought him as a three-year-old from Devil's River, Texas. He was naturally gentle and never had to be broken, and adapted himself to any place I wanted to use him, saddle or buggy. He was six years old when I was married, and since he seemed like such a good horse, I gave him to my wife, with a new side saddle, as a wedding present. Sometime later a fine shorthorn bull of mine strayed to Canyon Blanco, some thirty miles away, and I suggested to my wife that she go along and help me drive him home. We made the trip out by road, and had no trouble. We spent some time watching a celebration of a native *matachine* dance, after which we started back toward the ranch with the bull. The country in that section is heavily timbered, mostly with cedar and piñon and a few small pines on the ridges. As soon as we climbed out of the canyon we were among the trees. My wife was riding Speck at the right of the bull. Presently she called to me, and I saw that she was having trouble. Old Speck was trying to brush her off the saddle under a piñon tree. I got them straightened out, but we had not gone far before Speck tried to repeat the performance. This idea, in fact, became so fixed in his mind that it resolved itself into a game. Every inviting looking limb he saw, he would head for. Finally he became so insistent that she and I had to change horses. Why Speck didn't want my wife to ride him was a mystery to me, for she weighed only about half as much as I did. Whenever she tried to ride him after that, he went through the same stunt.

I thought perhaps he merely objected to a woman rider. But that was not the case. A young schoolteacher who was staying for the winter at the ranch, could ride Speck, and with her aboard he behaved himself perfectly. The only explanation I ever hit on that seemed to make sense was that my wife was a brunette and the schoolteacher a blonde, and old Speck was a gentleman!

If horses could talk, they might be able to tell us just how smart they are, as some humans do! However, some of the things they did seemed to speak about as loud as words. For instance, the incident told me by Don Jacobo Yrisarri about a white stud, called El Salvador, in the famous Turkey Track brand. The old Monte de Encino Ranch in the Estancia Valley, Turkey Track headquarters, was both a cattle and a horse ranch; but it was known especially for its horses, and the range that they covered was a big one. On a final roundup, one band in the brand was found watering at Tularosa Creek, about a hundred and twenty-five miles to the south, while many others were gathered along the Pecos River from the Texas line north to Anton Chico, and still others on the Rio Grande. This white stud, El Salvador, was one of the wildest on the range, seldom coming to the ranch for water, and then only at night. As a result of eating loco weed, many of the mares in his band had died. Finally only eight were left.

It was the time of year, Don Jacobo said, when surface waterholes on the range were drying up. Many horses, consequently, began coming to the ranch for water. Looking out one morning, the Don saw the white stud standing outside the corral gate all alone. This was so unusual that he called his *caporál* and they looked the stud over carefully for fresh scars, thinking that he might have been whipped and his harem stolen by a rival. This, however, did not appear to be the case. But what, then, could be wrong? El Salvador had never before been seen without his *manada*, and almost never was he seen at the watering in the daytime. His curiosity aroused, Don Jacobo told the *caporál* to saddle up, take another *vaquero,* and follow the stud as soon as he finished watering. This was done. Presently El Salvador set off at a high trot with the two *vaqueros* trailing him. In about ten miles the stud led them to a long slough which, when drying up, was known to be very boggy. There they found all eight of the stud's band bogged down to their backs in the mud, and completely helpless. Putting two ropes on each horse, the *vaqueros* succeeded in pulling them out.

Don Jacobo insisted that the stud, seeing his mares' danger, purposely put in an appearance at the ranch in order to call attention to his need for help. Seeing that horses do not talk, I can only take the Don's word for it!

The worst scare I ever had was given me by a pet horse named Fiddle. I was riding alone, trying to catch up with the chuck wagon, the *remuda,* and the rest of the outfit, which had got half a day's start of me out of Deming. We were bound for Palomas Lake, south of the border in Old Mexico. Forty miles below Deming, after covering some of the lonesomest country I know of, with only a couple of windmills in sight along the trail to indicate human beings, and the bleak Tres Hermanos Mountains over to the east, I reached the Boca Grande (not Rio Grande) which roughly marks the line between Old and New Mexico. The Boca Grande is only a little river, but it is always running, and there are several little falls in it, not high, but just big enough to make the water noisy. That's where the river gets its name: *boca grande,* big voice. I was unarmed on this trip, except for my six-shooter. I carried a slicker, more for style than anything else, as it seldom rains in that country. Since I knew I would have to lay out, I had had some sand-wiches put up for myself, and a *morral* full of grain for my horse.

The night before I started, word had reached Deming that *bandidos* had killed and robbed a couple of freighters at the crossing of the Boca Grande, and left the bodies lying in the road. I reached the stream about sunset, and before arrivin' could make out the freighters' wagons ahead. When I got up close I saw how the loads had been ransacked, boxes broken open, and their contents scattered. The bodies of the two men were still sprawled on the ground beside their wagons. From the horse sign, I figured that there had been four or five of the bandits. I didn't know but they might still be in the vicinity.

About half a mile to the west of the wagons was a mesquite thicket. Picking up a couple of cans of tomatoes which had been overlooked in the looting of the boxes, I moseyed over to the thicket, removed Fiddle's saddle and bridle, and with only a rope around his neck, led him the short distance to the Boca Grande to water him. Fiddle was one of those horses that just naturally broke out gentle. He never had a mean idea, wouldn't pitch, wouldn't even run, and just trotted off gentle under his first saddle. With a half hitch around his nose, you could jump on him bareback and ride him anywhere.

Back in camp, I hung the *morral* with the corn on Fiddle's head, ate my sandwiches, and rolled me a cigarette. Not wishing to attract attention, I decided not to make a fire, and kept my eye open for any riders. As soon as Fiddle had finished what I thought was about half of the corn, I took the *morral* away from him, meaning to save the rest for his breakfast. I hid it from him by placing it under my saddle, which had been turned upside down to serve as my pillow. I had two saddle blankets with me, and spreading my leather chaps on the ground, I put one blanket over them, and used the other blanket and the slicker for cover.

The sun had been down close to an hour when I noticed Fiddle looking over toward the east. He didn't nicker, just stood and watched. At last I made out what he saw—two riders, skylighted away to the east. They didn't worry me much, for they weren't headed my way, but I suppose they did sort of color my thoughts.

I pulled off my boots and rolled into bed with my six-shooter in my hand under the covers and between my legs. I was soon dreaming of *bandidos* and such, and the next thing I knew, something struck me sharply and suddenly in the face. One jump, and I was out of bed and on my feet, with my gun jammed against the outlaw's belly. But it was only my little horse, Fiddle.

The rascal had hobbled into camp, nosed out the *morral* of corn from under the saddle, grabbed it by the bottom with his teeth, and spilled the corn in my face. He had figured it must be time for breakfast!

I have owned hundreds of horses, but the smartest, without much doubt, was a steel-dust called Little Sam. The first time I saw him, he was following his mammy, who was being led behind a covered wagon coming from Texas. She was a quarter-mile mare, and very fast. Sam himself was no race horse, but he had plenty of speed and was stout on a rope. He died at Moriarty, New Mexico, when he was twenty-one years old, after he had been pretty well all over the country with me.

He knew all I knew, and a little bit more. I'd say, "Sam do you like brown bread?" (or white) and he wouldn't move. But if I said, "Do you like hot biscuits?" he'd nod like a starving cowboy. If I said, "Do you like boys?" he'd shake his head sideways. But if I said, "Do you like girls?" he'd nod. I taught him with a pin, and afterwards he connected the words.

As he grew up, you would usually find Sam in that part of the horse pasture nearest the house, waiting for his corn. He'd play around with the milk calves as they came up at night, nip them with his teeth, and carry on for all the world like a mischievous kid. For a while he took up with a bay horse I had, and when they were both loose in the pasture, they were always together.

I had taken the job of milking the cow of mornings, and I always rode Little Sam when on this chore. I'd leave the calf in the corral and drive the milk cow up the canyon to water, then bring her back past the corral and throw her outside the horse pasture to graze during the day, and at night I penned her and turned the calf loose. That way we managed to save some milk for ourselves. Sam understood all this like a book.

One morning I delegated the milking chore to a boy unfamiliar with the routine. He saddled Sam's mate, and supposing that I drove cow and calf to water together, he opened the corral gate, and the calf, not used to this freedom, kicked up his heels and lit out up the canyon. Sam knew this was wrong. He dashed after the calf, headed it back, put it in the corral unaided, and stood crosswise in the gate till I came and closed it. That ornery little horse screwed his head sideways and looked at us and almost winked, as much as to say, like a kid who thinks he has done something pretty cute, "Didn't I do right!"

BAREFOOT HORSES

(The biggest bunch of horses ever to leave New Mexico in a single cloud of dust, to the best of my belief, was trailed out by Bar W cowboys. Although I did not make that drive myself, I have written the story of it as if I were along; as I might have been, since I was a Bar W hand and knew all the boys who went. Those who made the drive were Allen Hightower, "Tie" Randolph Reynolds, Charlie Zellner, Bart Roberts, a boy horse wrangler, and an Irish cook.)

I

WE WERE squattin' on our hunkers one day on the rough board floor of the old Bar W Ranch house, doing nothing but scratch and listen to bits of news from the *Las Vegas Optic* which Allen considered fit for us to hear. The ranch house was a big adobe building, with I don't know how many rooms, and walls two to three feet thick. No Indian could shoot through those walls, and they kept the building warm in winter and cool in summer. There was a fireplace in every room, big logs to support the ceilings, and crude furniture—a table and chairs, mainly used for card playin', a couple of cots, and in the room where we were, ten or fifteen old buffalo guns, out of use for years, and stacked up like an Indian wigwam. The enclosure behind the building was protected by a wall ten feet high, where a few saddle horses could be kept, and often were, in Indian times. Just below the house was a spring with big cottonwoods around it. William C. (Bill) McDonald, one of the owners and the big boss, had a very nice new house down below about half a mile, where he lived with his family. The old ranch house was strictly for men, and there wasn't a woman on the place, not even the cook, *especially* not the cook! Although Indian

troubles were infrequent in '89, still, the country hadn't grown
up by any means. Carrizozo today is a modern looking town
a couple of miles away, but in those days there was no Carrizozo
at all. Just a lot of wide-open scenery, good grama-grass
range, cows, and ozone. Except for a few cottonwoods, like
those at the spring, trees were practically absent.

"Boys," said Allen, "listen to this!" He read out that Con-
gressman Springer was pushing strong on other Congressmen at
Washington, D. C., to get public lands opened for settlement in
Oklahoma. The opening, as we knew, had been agitated for
a long time. Now the paper said it looked like it was going
through. If it did, the idea was to make a public run for it,
from four sides to the middle. The first person on a piece of
land and claiming it, was supposed to have it. "Gee whishity
damn," said Allen, "let's us go!"

"And be a fool plowman?" says I.

"No"—witheringly—"sell horses."

Now we already knew, from different riders passing through,
that horses were in good demand around the Indian Territory;
and it seemed certain that if those Oklahoma lands were opened
up, there would be a chance to sell a lot of broomtails. And
Allen Hightower was this kind of a *hombre*: a born promoter
and horse trader. Tall, slim, brown-eyed and brown-haired, he
could start out on a "first Monday" (Texas slang for horse-
trading day) with nothing but one old horseshoe, and back he'd
come at sundown with a good horse and saddle under him, and
complete legal right to both. Yes, he was just a born trader.

But we had no time to more than kind of roll Allen's idea
over in our minds, when he said, "Shut up, boys; here comes
Mac."

"Nobody," said Randolph reasonably, "is doin' any talkin'
but you."

"Maybe so; and you all keep on lettin' me do it."

Bill McDonald entered the room quick and full of business.
He was generally accounted one of the best all-around men that
ever hit New Mexico. Physically he was rather slight, about
five-feet-ten, with a drooping mustache and almost bald. He
was well educated, and had come to White Oaks, New Mexico,

the mining town, originally as a surveyor, and there he started in and built himself up. The cattle company running the Bar W brand was built mostly on English money, and there was a rule that no man could manage the outfit unless he owned at least twenty-five thousand dollars' worth of stock. Now, when the previous manager got wild and hocked his stock to George Ulrich, the banker, McDonald bought it for ten cents on the dollar and stepped into his shoes. He didn't know a cow from Holy Bible, but he was a good business man, and the Bar W as he ran it was a good place to work, and the owners made money too. McDonald was so well liked and widely known that he was induced to run for governor when New Mexico was admitted as a state, and although he was a Republican and it was a Democratic year, the state goin' for Woodrow Wilson by four thousand votes, Mac was elected.[10]

"Mac," said Allen, busting with his big idea, "what will you take for the Anchor brand of horses?"

McDonald was cautious. "Who wants to buy them?"

"We do." With a sweep of his hand, Allen indicated the rest of us. "We'll pay a dollar a head for all grown stock."

"Now, now," said Mac, beginning to walk up and down the room in his excitable way, and shaking a skinny finger at Allen and us, "you know that's no price for those horses. A dollar a head? Why, there ain't a scrub colt in the bunch but is worth more than that."

"Had any bids?" asked Allen. He knew the answer was no; and McDonald knew that he knew it.

"What would you boys do with them? Where do you expect to sell them?"

"Oklahoma!"

I had better explain about the Anchor brand, which was an orphan. In the year 1884, a wealthy Easterner came to New Mexico hoping, among other things, to find a location for his son, who wanted to start a horse ranch, at least, he guessed he would like that as well as any other job that was work. This boy was reputedly as wild as a jackass with a tin can tied to his tail, and the old man thought that starting him in the ranch business would help to tame him. The father already owned an interest in mines at the then booming camp of White Oaks, and he decided to locate his son in that vicinity. The range itself was open; so he bought a ranch site with a good watering a few miles from White Oaks, and turned it over to the boy, who registered an anchor as his brand. The old man stocked the place with four hundred head of old Mexico mares, and a carload of standard breed trotting stallions from the East. These Hambletonian stallions ("Hamlins," we called them) were all right in their place, but they never were meant to cross with Mexican mares and raise cow horses, which have to show top speed from the jump. A trained cow horse, when you loosened up on the bridle, was on a dead run—he had to catch up with the calf or steer before it got started, not walk awhile, trot a piece, and finally decide to break into a run. However, the country east of the Anchor Ranch made ideal horse range, with nothing to interfere except a few varmints that lived in the Jakes Hills. These were a succession of little lava hills, none of them as much as a hundred feet high, and the varmints would occasionally kill a colt, but not often enough to amount to anything. So the stock of Anchor horses, without receiving much attention, multiplied and scattered all the way from the head of Three Rivers to Salt Creek on the west side of the White Sands. They ran wild, few of the younger horses ever being branded.

The boy who owned them learned that a wild mining camp on the boom furnished plenty of excitement, and although the amusements were somewhat cruder than those on New York's Great White Way, the liquor was just as potent, and the game called poker was played by the same rules, except for calling certain cards "wild." Becoming fascinated with the life, he sat in a poker game, and, if history is correct, practically stayed in it for several years. Then, having lost all available cash, he wrote his dad a farewell letter, and shot himself dead. After the boy's death, the father in New York apparently forgot all about the existence of the Anchor brand. George Ulrich, the banker, and Jeff Grumbells took charge of the horses, and ran them for about two years, but they stuck at paying the taxes, so the county assessor wrote and reminded the old man that he owed a certain considerable sum of money. Thereupon, he asked his neighbor, Bill McDonald, to dispose of his New Mexico interests to the best advantage. McDonald himself bought the Anchor watering and other ranch holdings, and he had the say-so about the stock in the Anchor brand.

That was the situation when Allen, out of a clear sky, broached the idea of us four boys buying the Anchor horses for a dollar a head. McDonald was inclined to hold out for a bigger price. But Allen pointed out some plain facts. "You got to figure," he said, "that we have to pay wages, put up the outfit, buy grub and horse feed, and gather the horses—an' they sure are snaky. If your outfit made the gather, they'd cost you four dollars a head by the time you put 'em in the railroad corrals at Roswell or San Antonio. And your outfit wouldn't get there with over half the herd. The price we offer you is clear gain."

The horse-swapping talk continued until late. But as Mc-Donald had been unable to get even a bid from anybody else, he finally ended up by telling us we could have the horses at our price, all last year's animals and small colts to be thrown in free.

Financing the deal was no worry at all to us. I suppose the four of us didn't have a hundred dollars all throwed together, in the kind o' money the dealer wants to see when you sit in a game of stud. But in those days, if you worked for an outfit, your credit was good. I personally never knew of anybody trying to beat another out of anything on a stock deal. I once bought eight hundred head of cattle on credit without a scratch on paper, and paid every cent of the purchase price when due. Moreover, the seller spoke to the bank, and my drafts were honored up to forty-five thousand dollars. It was a lot different then from now, when you can't borrow a nickel unless you get the Lord and all His Disciples to go on your note.

II

On February 1, the four of us quit working for the Bar W outfit. We each owned two private horses, and we put them on grain to give them strength, which they would need. We borrowed a wagon and a four-mule team from McDonald to haul grain and supplies from the railroad, and Charlie Zellner was sent to Rio Bonito to rustle a wagon and a couple of sets of harness for the roundup and the drive, while Reynolds and I, with a pack outfit, went off to locate the work mules belonging to the Anchor brand, which would be tallied in as stock horses at the completion of the work. Those mules were sure hard to find. We spent several days combing Willow, Jakes Spring, and other waterings, but only succeeded in finding three of them— two wheelers, and one lead mule. However we picked up nine head of Anchor saddle horses while we were at it. With these, and the supplies brought by McDonald's wagon and loaded into our own wagon from the Rio Bonito, we headed for Milagra Springs, where there were good corrals for animals, and a small board shack that we could use to camp in if we wanted.

Rain threatened the first night, and we unrolled our bedding inside the shack where we had some visitors who smelled our food and came to claim their cut of it. Tie Randolph, bunking nearest the door, received preliminary notice of their arrival.

"Whoops," he yelled, "hydrophoby skunks!" Every head disappeared under a tarpaulin.

Cowboys might not mind lightning, flood, stampede, or schoolma'ams, but they gave a little black and white polecat all the leeway he ever asked for, not only because of the un- pleasant consequences of any argument, but also because of the prevailing opinion that his bite was worse than a mad dog's. I couldn't say from personal experience, but I knew a cowhand who swore up and down that he had witnessed two deaths caused by the bites of these animals. This shack where we slept, inci- dentally, was the same one where Jim Red, after spending Christmas week in town in pursuit of poker, liquor, and the new biscuit-shooter at the hotel, started to spend the night while on his muddled way home to the ranch where he worked. Accord- ing to facts which are well vouched for, he had just settled down on his saddle blankets, when he saw what looked like two small lamps in the far corner. He feared nothing in the world, prac- tically, except being mad bit by a skunk. First he threw a small stone at the animal, then his hat, his quirt, and his bridle, and finally, when the animal wouldn't move, he got up and shot all the cartridges out of his six-shooter at it. Still it wouldn't go, and Jim Red, getting mad, began chasing it, but it always kept just out of his reach. Jim, being shaky in the legs by then, finally lay down on his blankets and said prayerfully half-aloud that it was damn cold.

"Yes," said the animal, which Jim now saw was a giant cat, "it is."

Jim made a sudden jump for his saddle and blankets, and said it was going to be a damn sight colder where *he* was going, and he went out and saddled up and put the spurs and quirt to old Rooster, his horse, and headed in a bee-line for the home ranch. After seven or eight miles at a pretty hot pace, he pulled up, considering it safe to do so, and said to Rooster, "We've had a pretty stiff run."

"Yes," answered the cat, which Jim now saw was hanging to his stirrup, "we have."

For the next week, they say, the boys around the home ranch were busy burying cats which Jim Red began shooting just as soon as he got some reloads for his six-gun.

The roundup of Anchor horses was the customary job in such cases. The first few days were taken up with shoeing all our saddle horses, because the east side of the Anchor range was mountainous and rocky, and in the lava hills a barefoot horse with a man aboard would not last long. We also went over the Anchor horse-pasture fence and stapled it up. In many places due to neglect, the wire had come off the posts and lay on the ground. This fence surrounded five or more sections of land, maybe thirty-five hundred acres, and every day's catch of Anchor horses was thrown inside it, since we were too short-handed to hold them under day herd.

At the end of the first week, some five hundred head of stock horses had been turned into the pasture. Not all of these were in the Anchor brand, but we rounded up and held all stray saddle horses that did not belong on the Carrizozo flats, since it was customary for the owners of long-strayed horses to pay a little something for their recovery. We next combed Salt Creek, the old S L Y Ranch, Mound Springs, and one other unnamed watering hole, picking up almost a hundred and fifty more horses, and some fifty burros that we needed to neck the old Lavina mares to. A burro out West is the same animal as a donkey in the East, but he grows smaller because he has slimmer pastures to graze in. What he lacks in size, however, he makes up by knowing his own mind. He is the stubbornest thing there is, outside of a Baptist minister, and just about the most wonderful little animal in the world. Neck a burro to a full-grown mare right up close, so that they can't bite each other or run, and that little burro will take the biggest mare to just one place, namely, where the burro is going.

We next worked Tularosa, Nogal Creek, and Three Rivers, where we found seven Anchor saddle horses, the fourth work mule which Reynolds and I hadn't been able to locate, and about two hundred head of stock horses. After this came Duck Lake, Indian Tanks, and Red Lake, these three waterings contributing over a hundred and fifty head.

The Anchor horses were practically as wild as if none of their ancestors had ever heard of a bridle. We picked them up in scattered little bands, like *manadas* of *mesteños,* each band composed of a stud and several mares and colts; and the studs were jealous of their family prerogatives, just like the wild ones. Even when all the horses were thrown into a single road herd, each one kept his little band separate. Every morning when they got off the bed ground, we would see the studs commence looking and whistling to get their own bunches together. And if we ever tried to keep two stallions and their bunches overnight in the same corral, by morning we were liable to find a crippled or dead stud.

After working the vicinity of Red Lake, we figured that the range was pretty well cleaned up of Anchor stock, and news that we received made us anxious to be on our way. Things had been happening in Washington, D. C. The Senators turned down Mr. Springer's Oklahoma bill, but the Congressmen, who were for it, tacked it as a rider onto the appropriations bill, which *had* to pass, otherwise, a lot of government porkers would have found no swill in their trough. This rider directed the President to open certain lands in Oklahoma to settlement. The Senators, it seemed, did not like it, but they had to swallow it, and President Cleveland signed the bill just a few hours before his term was up. The new President, Benjamin Harrison, announced the grand opening day was to be April 22, and he invited everybody who wanted a slice of government land, to be ready and waiting for the run on that day at the crack o' noon. Allen read us all this out of the newspapers he got hold of.

"We'll be there!" said Tie Randolph.

"If we make it!" said Charlie Zellner, who was six-feet-two, slim as a bed slat, and a born pessimist, which was perhaps due to the fact that he always owned a race horse or two.

Allen, of course, was high salty,[11] though we were all equal partners in the deal. At the Bar W we picked up the Irish cook, who had come over from the railroad on a freighting wagon, also a boy from the Sacramento Mountains to work as horse wrangler, and we were then all set and ready to go. However, we laid over one more day, because McDonald told us that if we would wait, he would get his outfit together and help us on the first day's drive. That would see us past Lincoln and out of the timber and rough country, and from then on, the idea was that we could easily handle the herd ourselves. During the layover we corralled the bunch in the Bar W corral, necked up the worst of the old mares with burros, and counted out into the big east corral. The tally was one thousand and thirty head. One thousand barefoot horses, and six hundred miles to go! Zellner had some reason for doubting if we'd ever get them there.

"You can pull out tomorrow at daylight." Allen told the cook that last night. "Follow the *remuda*," he said, "the wrangler knows the trail. Have grub ready on the Salado flat— that will be about halfway on the day's drive."

By the dawn's early light, the drive began.

III

Corral gates were opened, and those wild horses came out of there a-snuffin, with only one idea in all their heads, namely, to make a break and hit the nearest trail back to ranges which many of them had known from colthood, unfenced and free. A cowboy could sympathize with how they felt, without aiding them to accomplish their plan. Riders were so thick and close together that they kept the wild bunch laned and headed east, in spite of all they could do. Every once in a while some stud with his bunch would try to make a break for the rough country and freedom; most of them had ranged to the south, and that was the direction they headed for mainly. But a whole string of McDonald's riders on that side kept them strung out, and the wild ones were always hazed back. Pete Johnson, the Bar W foreman, rode ahead leading a gentle bell mare. After the herd became road broke, we knew they would get used to hearing that bell and follow it, and miss it if it wasn't there; and even that first day, the bell mare helped to keep the bunch in some order. However, we were willing for the broomtails to run their fool heads off at first if they wanted to, for we knew that afterwards they would be easier to handle. They were fat and rollicky, and in consequence harder to handle than if they had been thin. After the first ten miles, a lot of the run was out of them. They slowed down considerable, but we made the Salado flat by early noon. The *remuda* and chuck wagon had arrived well ahead of us, and all hands helped loose-herd till the Irish *cocinero* hollered, "Come en git it!"

The big corral at the foot of Picacho Hill was where we aimed to get to the first day. This was a thirty-five-mile drive— a fast clip for so big a herd. We figured that a speedy drive not only would take the horses off their home range, but also would be a big help towards getting them road-broke. So after the stop for grub, we roped fresh horses out of the *remuda* and started for Picacho, arriving at sundown. Even the wild studs were tired by that time, and had practically quit fighting; and the mares were willing to take it easy. It was so early in the spring when we started, that the mares had not yet foaled, except one. Her colt, little and cream-colored, was the only animal under a yearling in the herd. He was no more than six weeks old, but he kept right alongside his mammy and ran like an antelope, and that was what we called him—Antelope.

An amusing incident occurred while we were corralling the horses the first night. There was a big black stud in the herd that we had christened Brigham Young, an account of the big harem of mares he had acquired. He had no less than thirty-six of them, all black, except two that were seal brown. Brigham was as mean as they come, and Tie Randolph had remarked more than once that if he ever got a good chance, he was going to pick up his paws and turn him a cat, meaning, rope him by the forefeet while he was running, and make him turn a somersault, an enlightening experience for any horse that considered himself extra smart. Randolph got his chance, after a fashion, at the Picacho corral. Brigham Young whirled suddenly and started out of the herd, headed for freedom. Randolph was the nearest rider. He had no chance to try for the stud's feet, but he did dab his rope over the big black's head as he ran past.

Now the stud was stout, but the rope was strong. But Randolph, unluckily, was riding a horse named Simon, which was cold-jawed. A cold-jawed horse is one that has been abused around the mouth; maybe at some time he had been pulled up hard and the nerves killed by a Mexican ring-bit, which is one of the cruelest things you can put in a horse's mouth. Anyhow, a cold-jawed horse has no feeling for the bit, and he does not respond to a mere touch, as a cow horse should. So when Tie roped the Brigham stud, Simon did not swing around quickly, as he should have done parallel to the line of travel of the stud when the rope went taut, and was caught sideways.

Knowing what would happen, Tie stepped out of the saddle a second before the pull came, Simon was jerked flat on his side; but the experience of trying to drag another horse by means of a rope knotted around his own neck, was probably a brand new one for Brigham, and not very pleasant, apparently, for it slowed him to a standstill and knocked all idea of running out of him. After that, he went into the corral as meek as a day-old colt. Such an experience, or a hard fall, would generally knock ideas out of the rantiest wild horse's head. I have seen mares roped so hard that they fell and when they hit the ground went "Umph!"—and never once, when they got up, did they try to run again.

Brigham was an interesting case for a horse psychologist. He was a hot-blooded Hambletonian trotting horse, hand-raised behind a fence in Kentucky bluegrass pasture, and at four years of age was as gentle as they make them. Then he was brought West, burned with the Anchor brand, and turned loose on the open range where fences were as scarce as hiccups in a prayer meeting. In the next six years he forgot all he knew about being gentle, and moreover learned all the tricks of the range-wise wild mares. With never a bit in his mouth nor a saddle on his back, he became as wild as a hare and as slick at looking out for himself as any range-raised stud. That he could fight with the best and better than most was proved by the size of his *manada*, mostly stolen through victorious battles with other stallions. If folks ever try to tell you that a horse once gentled is always gentle, don't believe them!

Tie Randolph, who roped Brigham on this occasion, was a heavy-set puncher, black-haired, of medium height, and at the time was considered New Mexico's top roper. This is how he got his curious nickname of "Tie." He was once guiding a party of college men on a hunt, and overheard one of them use the phrase, *sic semper tyrannis*. Randolph did not have much book education, but he was blessed with a wonderful memory, and he tucked away every strange word he heard until such time as he could learn its meaning and make use of it. Some months later, while with the Bar W wagon, he was roping calves for branding, and upon making an especially fancy catch, he hollered out:

"Sic distemper tierandolph!"

The boys never forgot it. He was "Tie" from then on.

Gypsies that steal the horses they sell, had hardly anything on us, with our herd of wild ones bought at a dollar a head. We could sell any animal in our bunch for almost nothing, and still make a profit. So as we drove along from day to day, we sold or traded as opportunity offered, refusing no reasonable offer, be it cash or kind. One day two or three of us rode in to the wagon from a side trip to a near-by ranch, and saw Tie Randolph and the cook squatted on their hunkers and admiring a Jersey milk cow and her calf which were grazing near the chuck wagon—a strange sight on the Western range, where a cow was a critter born to produce steaks, and milk by the law of nature was known to come out of tin cans and probably, as some cowboy once said, was produced by eagles, since the cans all said "Eagle Brand."

"Where did them come from?" asked Zellner, nodding at the Jersey and her calf.

"Traded."

"You ain't goin' homesteadin'?" Tie refused to give this insulting remark any notice.

"Well," chirped in Allen, "you and the cook done traded for this critter, Tie, an' it's up to you an' him to do the milkin' of her."

"Not me!" says Tie in great alarm. "I'm no churn-twister. I haven't milked a cow since I ran away from home."

"I never knew you ran away from home," said Zellner.

Things have changed some since, but in those days you could hardly get a cowboy to do anything but ride a horse. Once I saw sixteen men sitting around the ranch house with nothing at all to do (and doing it loyally), when the boss, in a sour temper, walked in and told them to go get a mowing machine and cut hay. One after another, the whole sixteen quit rather than do such a low, menial task. Next day, when he got in a good humor again, the boss hired them all back. As for milking, a cowboy would almost rather walk two miles and die of thirst. I remember a time once when I was riding north from Langtry, Texas. The trail dipped into a valley, called Johnsons Run, which joined Devils River not far from the Prosser Ranch. When I got into the valley, I saw a ranch house, and as I got nearer, noticed a woman of middle age crossing the gallery with a grip in her hand, full of business and headed for a buckboard and team which stood in front of the house.

"Hello, young feller," she said, spying me, "which way?"

"I'm jest lookin' for a comfortable place to settle down for life," I replied.

"How about right here?" That was an invitation, and I had heard that the old lady fed the cowboys awful good apple pies.

"Might I use that armchair I see on the gallery?" I inquired. "I feel like meditatin'."

"Goodness!" she said. "If you're that bad, you better take

some Black Draft; there's a bottle of it on the kitchen shelf."
She stepped into the buckboard and gathered up the lines.

"By the way, lady," I said, "how long will you be gone?"

"Not later than tomorrow night. I just got word my daughter is downright sick in Ozona, and I must go." She got out her whip and was ready to split the wind. "Don't forget to milk the cow!" she said, and was off—was it "cow" she said, or "cows"?

I made myself at home, and that armchair was one of the comfortable kind. A little before sundown I saw a lone cow approaching, and a calf bawled behind the house. As the cow passed, I noticed that her bag was as large as a pillow. "How in the world can I ever milk her?" I wondered. It would take a day, at least. Presently from behind a little raise appeared another cow, then another, and another, till in all there were six large-bagged cows, and six calves bawling lustily from the corral. I went to the milk house and got a bucket and proceeded to the corral, where the faithful cows with their tongues between the cedar posts were licking their calves' noses. The sight reminded me of Lord Lincoln, the Englishman, who had been working on a ranch on the big mesa to "get experience," and in writing a letter home, told his relatives that the ranch had ten thousand cows. He received a reply in which his own brother called him to account for having acquired the American habit of yarning.

"Look!" said the brother, mindful that hardly anybody in England ever kept more than ten or a dozen cows, and those only for the milk they gave, "Where in the world would they get the milkmaids to milk that prodigious number?"

Well, I got one of the cows inside, and began to milk. Sometimes the stream hit the bucket, sometimes the ground. My left hand seemed to be out of commission, because I couldn't get any milk at all on the port side. An hour must have passed, but I was making progress, for there was at least half an inch of milk in the pail. Pausing to rest, I noticed how fat the cows were, and how thin the calves. "Poor things!" I thought, "That woman is starving you." This worried me, and I wondered what the S. P. C. A. would say. The more I thought about it, the more it seemed that a good deed a day was called for; so I opened the gate and let the cows and calves get together. The cows' bags receded, and the calves' tummies swelled, and everybody was happy.

While we were admiring the Jersey cow, Zellner, who had been brooding over the matter, remarked idly, "Tie, how did you come to run away from home?"

"Well, it was this-a-way, Charlie," Randolph soberly replied, reaching for the makin's, and rolling one. "When I was about ten, Dad bought a new corn planter, painted red, easy to look at, but hard to push. I was a hard worker, and pushed that planter so fast I burned out the bearin's. And Lord! How Dad did whip me. So that night I saddled my pony and quit home."

Two days' drive saw our barefoot herd penned in the Roswell stockyard. It was here that I called at the post office and received a pair of new boots which I had ordered through the mail from a Kansas bootmaker several weeks before. Like most cowhands, I was proud of my small feet, and in consequence, when taking my measure, I undersized them some, so they were a little bit tight, in spite of costing forty dollars cash. The first night I hardly did get them off at all, but finally, by forcing the heel between two spokes of the chuck wagon wheel, and having Allen put both arms around my waist and pull, the boot instead of my leg came off. After the first night I used a human bootjack. This, as all cowhands know, meant that one of the other boys backed up to you, while you stuck a foot between his legs. He would grab the boot heel with both hands, and pull. With your other foot on the boy's rump, you would push him for all you were worth, and off the boot would come, though sometimes the helper went face first in the dust. Cowboys' shop-made boots were nearly always a little tight at first, but in time they would loosen up and fit the foot like a glove.

In Roswell we sold a hundred or so of our horses, which put some cash in our pockets, and from that point we grazed the herd north up along the Pecos River towards Fort Sumner, Billy the Kid's old stamping ground. We kept selling for cash if we could, or trading for gentle stock, and generally reckoned that two picked broncs out of the wild herd, or two mares with colts by their side, were worth the price of one gentled saddle horse. If a buyer insisted, we would halter-break a wild one for him.

Halter-breaking meant training a horse to know what a rope around his neck meant, so he could be led, and was often done in the following fashion in New Mexico. We would take a good-sized timber log, not too big, but not too small either, and tie one end of a rope around it good and tight. Then we would rope our bronc, throw him on his side, and blindfold him; this was the only way to get the halter around his neck. Then we'd tie the free end of the log rope through the halter ring, snap off the blindfold, and let nature take her course. The bronc would get up scared and snorting, and start to run, and that's where the log came in. It had to be heavy enough to check him, but not heavy enough to break his neck. Tie a wild bronc to a solid hitching post or a tree with no give to it, and he would break his fool neck trying to pull free. The right-sized log, however, he would drag a little ways. But it would be more than he cared to keep on handling, and it would choke him some too, so he was soon taught the scriptural meaning of a halter. After one experience of it he knew the feel, and usually was willing to be led.

The first night out of Roswell, camp was made in a large grove of cottonwood trees, where we were visited by several Mexican *vaqueros* and small ranchers. One of them traded us a good pair of mules for ten head of mares and a stud. He seemed to think he was getting a fine bargain, and maybe he was.

Next night it rained, and we stayed with another Mexican. He had a large pole enclosure where we corralled the horses, making it unnecessary to stand night guard, a job which was never much fun after a day's work, and twice as little fun when it rained. It was a real pleasure to sit in front of a home-cooked meal and a fire, and have a roof over our heads for once when we rolled up for the night, and hear the rain a-sloshin' down. However, it was not so much fun next morning when we put wet blankets on wet-backed saddle horses and every last one of 'em "went bronc," furnishing plenty of excitement for the *ranchero* and his family, who watched from windows and doorways.

The third night after leaving Roswell, we drove the herd into the government's old adobe corral at Fort Sumner, and the few people still living there sat on the walls and passed remarks, mostly favorable, about our horses. During the evening a few head were sold, and we made an early morning start next day for Puerto de Luna, a little Mexican town some miles to the north; here we spent a night without seeing a single gringo besides ourselves. It was part of our plan to stop at towns whenever we could, so as to sell as many horses as possible. Two nights later, without any special happenings, we corralled at Tucumcari, on the old stage route from Missouri to Santa Fe, and here, after selling or trading about forty horses, we had the craziest stampede that almost ever happened.

We had left the corrals, and were on our way out of town, with the herd strung out along the main street, one man on the point, another with the drags, and two on the swing. The *remuda* was ahead, but the chuck wagon was late and hadn't caught up. We were almost out of town when somebody let out a yell, "Runaway a-comin'!"

Down a crossroad. headed our way, raced a scared and dangerous team dragging an overturned wagon. Tie Randolph, who was working the swing on that side, made the best preparations he could to stop them. He jerked down his rope and built a big blocker, and when they came by, he made his throw and caught both runaway horses in the loop. Tie's rope horse, Old Lug, was no cold-jaw, like Simon, and he played his part perfectly. He squatted, and when the team came to the end of the rope, the pull almost brought them to a halt. It did stop them sharply enough to turn the wagon right side up. But Tie's luck was running kind of muddy that day, and the strain was too much for his rope; it broke off at the *honda,* where it was already worn thin. The freed team again took up their crazy race, and cut the herd in two.

Sooner than a flea could hop, pandemonium was loose. Every horse in Tucumcari, wild or tame, seemed to think it was the day for all good horses to get together and run. The original runaways, instead of continuing in one direction, circled behind the trail herd. Our horses immediately whirled in their tracks and at full speed raced back through the main street of town. As it was Saturday, a lot of saddle horses were tied to the hitch rails, or stood waiting with their lines hanging down. They all joined the racing herd. Two horses hitched to a white-topped hack standing outside the hotel, thought what fun, and away they went, hack and all. A man named Brass, a fat saloon-keeper, had just driven up to his place of business in his expensive new buggy. One look up the street showed him what was coming. He jumped to safety inside his saloon door, and watched his fancy outfit being swallowed up in the tide of horses. A bunch of cowboys who were already half-lit and raring for excitement, rushed out of another saloon and with their six-shooters punched the air full of holes, and this did not tend to slow up the racing horses to any extent. All the school children in town who had their ponies saddled up, immediately took after the fast disappearing herd.

For three miles south of town the road was as straight as an arrow, then it turned at a sharp angle to the left. We started with our horses on the run, heading for that turn, with the intention of checking the runaways at that point. I rode alongside Zellner, who between cussing spells almost cried.

"Now we've lost 'em," he mumbled, riding hell-for-leather. "All our hard work thrown away. We'll never gather the half of 'em. Allen, why did I ever let you talk me into this fool deal!"

Four miles of hard riding brought us to the lead horses, and we stopped them, but what we stopped· was only a small part of the herd. In the excitement, several bunches had split off, and where they might have got to was anybody's guess. It took us three days of hard work from sunup to dark, combing the flats with a lot of volunteers, mostly boys, before we got them together again and made another start for the next town, Nara Visa. Before we left, Allen made a dicker with the owner of the runaway team that had caused all the trouble. He traded him ten mares and colts for the pair. The chuck wagon mules were turned into the herd, and the new horses were hitched in their harness.

"Now," said old dough-wrangler Pat, climbin' aboard the

driver's seat with a gleam in his Irish eye, "lean in the collars, ye divils. Lean! I'll be right behind ye!"

Old *cocinero* made those two pay a-plenty for the riot they had caused!

After this stampede, the colts began coming in big numbers. The night following the run, the herd was bedded out, and the last guard, reaching the wagon at daylight, reported the arrival of several colts. Antelope soon had any amount of company his own age, or near it. This meant shorter drives, and choosing trails where plenty of water could be found. But the grass was fine, and there had been recent rains, and water in many places still lay in surface lakes. There's an old belief among stockmen that colts, even if they grow up into white horses, are never white when born, but always come a cream color, slate, or blueish. In fact, many a man raised on the range has never seen a white new-born colt. But one morning on the bed ground we found one, a horse colt, and pure snow white.

Grazing slowly along, it was the evening of the third day when we reached Nara Visa, just a little settlement, but one where the people seemed to need horses, and liked ours. One rancher bought a hundred head of mares and three studs. After that trade, Allen figured where we stood to date on our deals. We still had about five hundred head of horses left, besides enough cash to pay McDonald and everybody else we owed money to, and practically eight hundred dollars in cash. Even counting all the time we had put in, this looked better than working for wages; and besides, we were headed for Oklahoma and ringside seats at the big excitement. Even Zellner began to see signs of a silver lining. Nara Visa is close to the state line of Texas, and it was here that the stock inspector checked us out.

Now we came to a branch of the Canadian River which, owing to heavy rains in the north, was out of its banks, making it a swimming proposition. We waited several days before we figured it was safe to cross; and then when we did, Zellner had a little hard luck. His horse stepped in a hole under water, stumbled, and fell, and threw Zellner into the muddy water. As he could not swim, with the instinct of self preservation he grabbed the nearest thing within reach, which happened to be the tail of a swimming horse.

"Oh, Lord, Lord, Lord," he kept saying over and over. "Save me, save me, save me!"

"What were you so worried about?" we asked him afterwards. "You were gettin' a free ride, weren't you?"

"I was afraid the horse's tail would pull out," he said.

"You ought to know that a swimming horse can pull as much with his tail, as when hitched to a wagon."

"Yeah, but I was thinkin' what if my boots shrunk."

Beyond here the grass was belly high, and in spite of fairly recent rains, as dry as tinder.

"Just think how easy that stuff would burn!" Allen remarked.

He might have been a prophet. It was hardly as long as four bits lasts in a game of stud before we saw dense smoke ahead. A high wind was driving the flames of a grass fire in waves right toward us. The wild Anchor horses had their heads up, looking. There is no better animal for spotting danger than a horse, because of exceptionally keen eyesight. Many a time when hunting wild horses I have come to the brow of a hill and through field glasses located a bunch miles away, but already on the move. With naked eyes they had seen me topping the rise sooner than I could get the glasses on them. You would usually find antelope and wild cattle grazing close to wild horses for safety's sake. The horses would spot danger and telegraph the alarm before the other animals had any inkling of it. I remember once seeing a bunch of frightened mustangs on the gallop; right behind them came a herd of antelope, and behind the antelope came a bunch of wild cattle. All were running from some danger that the horses had seen first.

Wild life of all kinds now began coming towards us, and away from the fire. They were more afraid of it than of us. First two racing coyotes appeared and dove into a hole close to the herd. Then out of the smoke came a big bunch of antelope, evidently from the size a number of bunches banded together. They headed for the restless horses and scattered among them.

Although the horses were excited, the fire was still a good ways off. Allen was riding one point. He checked the leaders till the herd bunched up. Then we started back-firing. The only sure way to fight fire on the prairies was with fire. Settlers used to plow double furrows a hundred feet or so apart in a circle around their houses and fire the grass between, making a ring of protection that no ordinary prairie fire could cross. The method we used was as follows. We put baling wire around a couple of rolled-up gunnysacks soaked in coal oil, and set fire to them. Dragging a burning sack apiece at the end of a rope, two of us set off in opposite directions, each one riding for half a mile or so behind the herd. The burning sacks set fire to the heavy grass, with the result that we were caught between two fires, but the wind was carrying one fire toward us, the other away. Soon, a good big space was burned over behind us, and in ten minutes or so it was cool enough so we moved the horses and chuck wagon back on it. The fire ahead, reaching our burned-over ground, had nothing further to feed on, and died out.

The danger of any prairie fire depended to quite an extent on the speed of the wind. Sometimes a grass fire was gone in a minute—it just seemed to fly past, *whoosh!* not stopping at all. I have seen such fires curve over a place where the grass was high, like a big wave. Grass fires were usually started by a camp-fire or a lighted cigarette, sometimes by Indians, and sometimes by lightning. Occasionally they would burn for forty or fifty miles before they struck any obstruction sufficient to stop them: maybe an arroyo or a succession of roads. If the wind were high enough, a fire might jump right over a good-sized creek.

The rest of that day we traveled over the burned area, and having no grass, the horses made good time. In fact, we made fast time all the way from here. We crossed No Man's Land, which is now the handle end of the Oklahoma pan, but then was a tail belonging to no dog. It was part of no state and no territory, had no government, and no form of justice other than a rope or a six-shooter. Some wicked things happened there. because it was a gathering place for some pretty bad *hombres*. But several thousand people had moved in, mostly cattle ranch-ers, and most of them respectable, and Beaver City, through which we passed, was already a good-sized settlement; but property was held by squatter's rights only, and a man couldn't even get married legally. Considerable dust was being raised for law and order, however, and a provisional legislature was calling the region the Territory of Cimarron, but the United States Government never did recognize it, and violence, bloodshed, and theft were daily happenings.

As soon as we moved across this strip into Kansas, we were in country showing signs of civilization, and the closer we got to Caldwell, Kansas, the more we began to hear about the Oklahoma excitement. In fact, from Caldwell east to Arkansas City, Kansas, there was almost a continuous camp of home-seekers, thousands of them in wagons, tents, and buggies, their campfires flaring at night, all waiting for noon of April 22. Or not waiting. Some chose to take a chance and slip across the line at night to select good farms or town lots ahead of the crowd. "Sooners," these cheaters were called. They were supposed to be caught by soldiers and put off, and many were, but in the excitement, others counted on picking likely spots, and did so, hiding out in the tall grass, and when those making the run came along, they'd pop up with their claims all staked out, and say they had just arrived.

Speed was the big thing among the people who were going to make the run, and there was need for a lot of horses. We soon got rid of all that we still had at good prices. When we divided the pot, we weren't wealthy, but we had poker money.

IV

So with our barefoot horses we had escaped safe from fire, flood, stampede, and a Jersey milking cow, and here we were at the Oklahoma opening a week ahead of time. That opening was something to come and see. This first run, in '89, was maybe not quite as big as the opening of the Cherokee Outlet four years later, but it was the original and first of its kind and nothing like it had been seen or thought of before. I have read accounts people have tried to write, but as they generally say themselves, they don't do justice to it. Nobody could, in writing. You had to see it to believe it. Just figure: all those wagons, buggies, and saddle horses, thousands of them, with people from every part of the country, and their belongings. Many of them had cattle, hens, sheep, and other livestock, ready to settle down and go to housekeeping. There were gamblers, preachers, storekeepers, office clerks, lawyers, doctors, and as one feller said, some farmers. An old maid lady was camped next to us, and she came over to pay a call and get acquainted, and like as not put her line on a husband.

"My name is Miss Mary Campbell," she announced. "I'm a schoolteacher." Singling out Allen as high salty of our outfit, she said sharply. "Have you had any education?"—just like a gospel preacher askin' if he had been saved. One thing that cowboys generally managed to do was to attend to their own private business, and they liked for others to do the same.

"Lady," Allen replied, fingering his hat brim, "I had just enough learning so I learned not to talk about it."

Poker, blackjack, and craps flourished among the waiting crowds all day and often late into the night. Occasionally we would hear the crack of a gun. Kansas was dry on the liquor question, as it still is more or less, but that did not stop the bootleggers. The most up-and-coming member of this profession that we saw was an old fellow who rode up and down on a white mule that he called Preacher—so we called the rider Parson. On each side of his saddle hung cantinas holding gallon jugs full of homemade corn whiskey.

"Guarantee her to scorch the hide off a rhinoceros!" Parson said.

"Her" sure did!

We four New Mexico cowboys and wild-horse nurses never had any idea of claiming government land in Oklahoma for ourselves, but since we were on hand, we decided to make the run just for the fun of it. Along towards noon of the twenty-second, everybody began to move up and toe the mark. There were soldiers in front to keep anybody from starting too soon, and nobody was letting his near neighbor get more 'n a flea's breadth the head start. You can imagine a little what it was like if you have ever been to a horse race and have seen the horses lined up at the barrier and snuffin' to go, only here, instead of maybe six or eight horses, the starters were numbered by the thousands. It's anybody's guess, but I'd say probably a hundred thousand people were massed on all four sides of the land to be opened, and I've heard tell there were more. Where we were, the line extended solidly for as far as we could see in both directions. There were fifteen passenger trains, too, with steam up and people crowded inside and out, hanging on cowcatchers or wherever they could grab a handhold. I never heard of another race, horse or any kind, to beat it.

The line got dead quiet in the last few minutes. You hardly dared to think for fear people would say you were too noisy. Then at last, 'way down the line, faintly, we heard a bugle call. Quick as scat it was taken up and rolled down the line to us, and on past, and far beyond, different buglers sounding it from east to west. In a second, hell busted loose a-yelling, and the rush was on.

As I say, it's impossible to describe it so it seems real. In the morning, the town site of Guthrie was waving prairie, and by night fifteen thousand people were more or less settled down and living there. Oklahoma City had ten thousand or more, and Kingfisher and Norman likewise. Every town lot and desirable quarter section had from one to several claimants, some of them being ex-claimants on account of a bullet causing them to quit breathing. It wasn't always the first person who came to a claim who held it in the end. Sometimes it was the one who could run the biggest bluff or draw a gun the quickest. "Sooners" who sneaked in and lived to keep what they claimed (some didn't) got some of the choicest spots. All the first habitations were tents or stick houses, but presently portable houses were brought in, and the place took on a settled look.

The four of us had been running side by side for some distance from the starting line, when we came to a nice looking field where a man was plowing with a team of oxen. He had several acres plowed. Now, we had started at the crack of noon and hadn't stopped, and we had good horses under us.

"Mister," said Allen, reining in to speak to the man with the oxen, "when did you enter?"

"One minute past twelve."

"Done all this plowing since then?"

"Certainly have!" He slapped the reins on the backs of the oxen. "Sure had to hustle, though. Giddap, bullies!"

Tie Randolph brushed back his hat brim and shook his brown head. "Gee wickles!" he said, his brown eyes very astonished, "All the born liars don't live in New Mexico, do they!"

FIVE-HUNDRED-MILE HORSE RACE

Oh, music springs under the galloping hoofs,
  Out on the plains;
Where mile after mile drops behind with a smile,
And tomorrow seems always to tempt and beguile—
  Out on the plains.

I

THERE was always a horse race brewing or in prospect when cowhands got together. The usual kind, which was for a short distance, such as a half mile or less, could be gotten up almost anywhere, in a few minutes, impromptu, with no jockey club rules to worry about. The boys would go to a level place, step off the distance, strip their ponies to save weight, and ride. Whoever had money bet on the outcome. Lacking money, almost anything else of value would do for what our English highness, Lord Lincoln, usually called a wager. I remember a race I saw in the little town of Pecos when I was coming back from my first song hunt. The "race track" was the main street of the town, and the "grandstands" were the sidewalks, which were lined with dozens of cowboys from different outfits. The two horses contending for honors were cow horses owned locally, and several thousand dollars, not to mention saddles, silver-mounted bridles, hair ropes, spurs, and what-have-you, changed hands in a few minutes on the outcome. I personally bet all my cash capital except five dollars, naturally on the wrong horse.

One completely impromptu race was run the day the Englishman, McQueen, announced he was going to have a horse sale, old-country style. McQueen raised trotting horses which were fast enough, but of no earthly use as cow horses; however, in announcing the sale, he promised free "breakfasts" for all— meaning high-noon breakfast, or course, but cowboys from ranches near and far began showing up soon after sunup. They found McQueen and his flunkies dressed in English riding clothes, carrying little rattan sticks in their hands, and there was plenty of champagne and other alcoholic dynamite on hand for the flunkies to pour. I have known cowpunchers to get loaded when they had to fill their own glasses, but when there were flunkies to do the filling, kid o' mine! Some of them told McQueen that they had decided to initiate him into the Cowpunchers' Union, and did so in the stables, the main part of the ceremony being that he had to take eleven drinks, one after another, swaller for swaller, with each of the brothers present, a feat which didn't tend to sober him. He was then introduced to the game of fuzzy-guzzy,* which was new and fascinating to him, and at which he lost all his ready cash, then his silver flask, and finally his watch, and after that a horse race was proposed, which to a cowhand was like a gold-mounted invita- tion to set the boss's good-looking daughter. McQueen agreed to run a big fat mare he owned with a colt by her side, against a smoky horse owned by a cowboy named Tobe, the distance half a mile, terms horse for horse, colt thrown in.

Now, there was a little exercise track in front of the house, and all of McQueen's horses knew that track like a book from much use of it, but it was no race track to them, just a place to jog and have fun. The route for the race was laid out with the track as part of it, and when the handkerchief was dropped, McQueen's fat mare shot far ahead of Tobe's horse until she came to the track, but there she dropped back into a jog and couldn't be whipped or cussed into going faster. Tobe reached the finish line all alone, McQueen's horse ending up at the tables where the drinks were laid out.

"I say, old chaps," said McQueen, "I hardly call that a fair test, don't yer know." And he insisted on running the race again.

* Played with a small top with four sides on which are marked the letters A, N, W, and L —meaning all, nothing, win, lose.

The result was the same, not only the second time, but each of half a dozen times. In fact, they might be running the same race yet if McQueen hadn't got so drunk he couldn't ride any more, and finally admitted, to the tune of "God Save McQueen," that he was beat.

There were all sorts of crazy horse races run in the West, one of the craziest being one that was proposed and won by Calamity Jane herself. She was sitting in front of a saloon beside her horse, Jim, when a stranger rode up and invited her to trade horses. He was willing, he said, to prove that his horse could outrun hers under any conditions, for money, marbles, or whiskey. She said the idea of a race sort of appealed to her and inquired if she might name the distance and conditions. The stranger said he was willing, and each of them put one hundred dollars in the hands of a stake holder, winner to take all. Calamity Jane then had a notary write down the terms of the race, and it was signed and witnessed by two passing gamblers. The terms she dictated were as follows: "We'll start twenty feet back of the platform where the horses are now standing, jump the horses up on the platform, ride into the saloon, take a drink, ride out through the back door, enter the next saloon by the back door, have a drink there, and out the front, enter the next saloon, and so on all the way down the street until all eleven saloons and dance halls on that side of the street are visited in turn. First horse at the bar of the last saloon gets the money." Her horse had been trained to do this stunt and had done it for years, and when he got to a bar, he could even take a bottle in his teeth, up-end it, and drink just like a man—and with about the same physical consequences. Calamity Jane won the race by three saloons and four drinks.

There was a different class of horse race entirely, the outcome of which depended very little on flashy speed or tricks, and very much on the stamina of the horse and the horsemanship of the rider. Cowboys' endurance races are a thing of the past now, but in their day, sponsored by different people and especially Buffalo Bill, they had a peculiar place in the West and were a picturesque part of the life. I got the detailed story of one such race, which was run in the early eighties, from Jack

Best, who was one of the contestants. He rode in this race, he told me, the year he went north with a trail herd from southern New Mexico, which was about the time when my brother and I had a ranch south of Stanton, Nebraska, on Maple Creek. The conditions of the race were as follows: it was to start at Deadwood, South Dakota, and finish at Omaha, Nebraska. No horse entered would be over fifteen hands. He must be a qualified cow horse, and carry a rider and saddle, six-gun and chaps, all to weigh not less than one hundred and ninety pounds. The nearest distance from Deadwood to Omaha was approximately five hundred and thirty miles, but the riders could choose their routes to suit themselves. Each rider was allowed a helper to drive his buckboard or hack, which went along to carry chuck, horse feed, and bedding. Creeks and rivers had to be forded as they were come to. Starting time was a Saturday morning at six o'clock, in Deadwood, and the contestants had to check in at the fair grounds at Omaha not later than midnight the following Saturday in order to qualify. The condition of the horse on arrival was supposed to count 60 per cent, the time of arrival 40 per cent. There were four purses. The first prize was one thousand dollars in cash, and Buffalo Bill in person was to hand the money to the winner.

Following is the account of the ride Jack Best made in that race, in my words but as if he were telling it, as in fact he did tell it to me.

II

A bucking horse reared high, and pitched through the crowd that had gathered to see the first stage of the big race, which was just about to start. Suddenly the bucker fell. Somebody piled on his head to prevent his scrambling to his feet and trampling the rider, who was pinned underneath. When they worked the horse off, it was found that the rider, Hank Singleton, had a broken leg. That was a hard line of luck for Hank, who was one of the ten entrants in the race. What had happened was that he had left the corral riding the young horse which bucked, and leading Once Again, the horse he meant to ride in the race.

The noise of the crowd frightened the young horse, and whirling, he got the rope of the led horse under his tail, clamped down on it, became more frightened, started pitching, then lost his footing and fell.

Hank, with a broken leg, was out of the race before it began. But his sister was following on another horse, intending to lead the young saddle horse back to the corral; however, as soon as she saw that her brother was being cared for, she went to the judges and asked for a chance to take his place. They gave her permission to do so. When we started, therefore, there were nine men riders, and one girl.

I don't remember the names of all the horses that lined up at the start, but the four that went the whole way and finished were a black named Coaly, a bay named Ranger, a sorrel named Hornet, and my own little horse, Johnnie Dun. Of all ten horses in the race, Johnnie Dun was the smallest in height, standing just fourteen-two hands. He had a dark line down his back, a black mane and tail, was glass-eyed, wore a naught-size shoe, and was branded Diamond A. He had a fast walk, a good running fox trot, an easy lope, and like all of his color and kind, a lot of bottom. For a month before the race, Dunnie had been getting his exercise daily to make him hard and fit. Starting at ten miles a day, with three feeds of oats and good mountain hay, I had increased the training distance daily, and the week before the start of the event he was going thirty miles every day, and was as hard as rocks.

A good deal of fun was poked at Johnnie Dun when we lined up to start, because he was so small; the other horses were all around fifteen hands. Now my own idea was that some of them were too fat, and others too long coupled, to stand a long, hard grind. However, the gamblers thought otherwise. They were makin' books and layin' all kinds of odds, and at Deadwood, Ranger and Hornet seemed to be the general favorites. Once Again, ridden now by Singleton's sister, was also carrying a lot of money to win. But Johnnie Dun was the joke horse of the race, as far as the gamblers went, and nobody was willing to make a bet on such a long shot except one old cowhand who, a year or so previously, had ridden Dunnie up the trail from New

Mexico, and had a feeling of affection for him. More because of that than any real belief that he could win, this feller placed a twenty-five-dollar bet that I would finish in the money, that is, that I'd be one of the first four. The gamblers gave him odds of four to one that number eight, which was Dunnie's number that I wore on a card on my back, wouldn't show.

Amid a lot of shouting and excitement, we received our final instructions, and got away. Three of the ten starters went off in a high lope, cutting a great swath, throwing dust and gravel as they sped down the flat. Five galloped, trotted, or fox-trotted. Dunnie was fishing at the bit and wanted to make as showy a start as anybody. But I figured that a five-hundred-mile race wasn't going to be won in the first mile, and I held him down to a flat-foot walk. The Singleton girl, whose number was nine, did the same thing with her mount, Once Again; in fact, she rode at my side, taking it easy, and we chatted and got acquainted. Her father, she said, was driving her hack; he had a pair of spotted ponies hitched to it. I told her that my brother Bill was driving our outfit, and he had a pair of long-legged mules that could walk around five miles an hour and not worry. Bill, I might as well remark here, carried a keg of water, plenty of food, a few bales of hay, and two sacks of oats; also a bucket and sponge, a bottle of rubbing alcohol, and a blanket for Dunnie in case the nights were cold or rainy. The girl asked what I thought of her horse. I had to tell her the truth, which was that I was afraid he was too soft and fat. "But if you hold him down the first few days," I said, "you might have a chance. Don't expect me to pull you out of any bogs, though!" Helping a girl was one thing, but that thousand-dollar purse at the end of the long grind was another.

"Cowboy," she said, understanding perfectly well what I was thinking, "this is a hoss race!"

At eleven o'clock, five hours after the start, she and I were still riding along together, and my original opinion about her horse was unchanged. My hack had stopped, and when I came up to it, Bill was cooking up a meal. "Good luck!" I said, and pulled off the road. The girl went on to overtake her own outfit.

I unsaddled Dunnie, fed him, had a good dinner myself, and

rested. The five-hour ride hadn't been more than a good morning's exercise for either of us, but I once read about a party of
men who were left afoot in a desert, with very little food, at
a place where they were at least fifty miles from water. If they
had lost their heads thinking about it, they might have tried
to get to that moisture quick and died of exhaustion. But their
leader had a watch, and he made a rule that the party should
walk fifteen minutes, then rest ten, walk fifteen and rest ten,
and keep it up; and by not ever lettin' any of the party tire
themselves out, he got them through to water safely. My idea
in this race was something like that for Dunnie. By one o'clock
I was saddled and on my way again. We had covered almost
twenty-five miles, and had left the town of Calcite some distance behind.

The tracks of the hacks showed that all of the riders, like
ourselves, were making a beeline for the town of Interior. However, I didn't catch up with any of them that first afternoon;
they seemed to smell the Omaha "moisture," and were making
for it as fast and hard as they could go. My brother, with our
hack, passed me with his mules at a trot, and handed me a couple
of doughnuts he had brought from Deadwood. "I'll camp about
six," he said. "That should bring us five miles or so beyond Box
Elder Creek, and I'll have supper ready when you come." He
whipped up and drove on. I held Dunnie to his slow and steady
pace. About an hour after getting out of the hills, I came to Box
Elder Creek, and here both Dunnie and I had a good drink. He
stood in the water for a few minutes, cooling off his legs and
feet. Refreshed by this short rest, we rode on several miles
more and reached the camp which Bill had made in a mott of
timber.

On the wheel of the buckboard, Bill had rigged up what he
called a buggy-o-meter, by means of which he could figure out
more or less correctly the miles we traveled. It was based on
the number of revolutions of the wheel, times its circumference.
After consulting this contraption and doing the necessary mul-
tiplying, Bill announced that we had covered something more
than forty-eight miles so far. I was well satisfied with that.
After watering Dunnie, I threw him some hay, stripped off the

saddle, threw a sheet over him, then ate my own supper. I must say that Bill, without being a regular *cocinero,* could toss up some mighty fine grub over a campfire, and it sure tasted good to a feller who half the time was hungrier than a red-headed woodpecker.

After we ate, Bill and I went into a huddle. As I said, I had a general idea of how I meant to run the race, and of how I thought a man and a horse might win it. You probably gathered that my plan did not depend very much on speed in any given short distance, but I knew, from long experience with cow ponies, that a horse that was given specially good care, many times would travel a long distance faster and in better shape than a naturally better horse that was ridden harder and faster for short distances, but wasn't given equal care. My main thought, accordingly, was to keep Dunnie going, not fast or hard, but steadily, for just as much of the time as was possible without wearing him down, letting him rest frequently. That first evening, therefore, knowing that the moon would soon be up, I decided to put a few more miles behind me as soon as Dunnie finished his supper. By nine o'clock I felt good and rested, and Dunnie looked as fit as when we started, so I saddled him and pulled out. Within five miles, Bill caught up and passed me. Soon I saw a rig camped beside the road. Behind the buckboard and the spotted ponies was the Singleton girl's fat horse, Once Again. The girl and her father were apparently fast asleep, so I kept right on, and in another six miles or so, came to the camp Bill had made. He said that some other outfit was camped immediately ahead, but whose it was he didn't know. He also said that according to the buggy-o-meter we had put fifty-nine miles behind us, just about half the distance to our first goal, the town of Interior.

I offered Dunnie water, but he didn't want any. I sponged off his back, legs, and shoulders with alcohol, rubbed him dry, and threw a sheet and blanket over him, then broke out some good hay for him, fed him grain, and finally turned into my own hot-roll for a good night's sleep.

Bill called me at four. I smelled the coffee and bacon he had ready and waiting, and he told me that he had already given

Dunnie a good rubbing with a flannel cloth to take out any stiffness that the first day's trip might have caused. Now as part of my equipment I was carrying two double Navajo saddle blankets. One had been used the day before, and was sweaty and liable to cause chafing. I gave that one to Bill and asked him to wash it out at the first creek he came to. The other one, which was clean, I put under the saddle. On a long ride, no horse is better than his back, and I meant to keep Dunnie's back in good shape if it was in my power to do so.

In the course of the first two miles or so that morning, I came to a camp and saw the horse, Ranger, which carried number one in the race. His rider and helper were just eating breakfast as I went by at an easy trot. About a mile further on I passed number ten, and close by, numbers two and six. I was fox-trotting along easily when the sorrel horse named Hornet (number three in the race) came out of the brush, and his rider and I rode along together for a while. This feller was long and skinny, and when he was standing on the ground he looked like a rattlesnake on stilts. Some distance on we passed number seven, then in a little while number four, who was just saddling up. Most of those horses had gone a lot faster while they were going, the day before, than Dunnie. Yet here we were, right along with them. Hornet's rider remarked that the weather was sure cool. Yes, I agreed, it sure was. He remarked that I was traveling pretty slow, wasn't I? Yes, I said, I reckon I was. He said he guessed he would try to make better time. I told him not to let me stop him. So he struck out at a high lope, and as I watched horse and rider disappear, I thought of a saying of my old Swiss grandmother:

A long race,
A slow pace.

Dunnie and I weren't going to be hurried. We continued to keep our slow and easy gait, and one after another, all the horses in the race, except Once Again, with the Singleton girl aboard, caught up and passed us.

Bill and I camped for grub and rest at eleven o'clock, and it ·was close to noon before Once Again finally put in an appearance, following close behind the girl's rig, and carrying his head low. I knew by the look of him that he wasn't going to get much farther. Father and daughter pulled up close to us.

"Light an' take a load off your saddle," I said.

Bill invited them to eat dinner with us. The girl seemed discouraged as she looked after her horse, but declared she would keep going till that night anyhow. Then if Once Again didn't perk up, she said, she would drop out. I rode off from that camp at about one o'clock. But before I went, the Singleton girl had a talk with Bill and me that showed her heart was in the right place.

"Jack," she said, "from what you've told me, you live a long ways from here, an' don't know a whole lot about people in these parts."

I told her I was practically born poppin' longhorns out o' the tornial along the Rio Grande.

"Well," she said, "all the horses in this race are local horses, except Coaly and your Johnny Dun. Coaly is supposed to have been sent here by a ring of gamblers, to win the race. He's a clean thoroughbred, and his rider has a reputation for winning, no matter how. Ranger and Hornet are carryin' most of the Deadwood gamblers' money, but the big money has been bet in Lincoln and Omaha on this big black horse, Coaly.

"If you don't think Coaly is fast," she went on, "you don't know the feel of cactus when you're settin' in the middle of it. If those other riders ever find that you fellers have any sort of a look-in to win, they won't stop at much. At least, that's my notion. They'll try to dope or cripple your horse, if they can, or they'll put you out some other way. Keep your eyes peeled. Remember that there's probably a hundred thousand dollars at stake."

Her own horse, she admitted, was in no condition to compete. "I'll probably drop out; but I wish you boys luck. That's why I'm warnin' you to be on the lookout. Take care of yourself, and your horse."

Bill and I felt grateful, and said so.

"That's all right," she replied. "I may hop the train and see you in Omaha. *Adios.*"

I climbed aboard Dunnie and rode off, and never saw her again.

III

The next few days were a steady grind of riding, resting, eating, riding, resting, eating, with a few highlights and incidents along the way. Nearly every night we made our last camp ahead of the others, or got an earlier start next day, and nearly every morning the others passed me, one by one, until Dunnie and I were again at the tail of the procession. On Monday morning, for example, I left camp at five o'clock, and in the next two hours passed seven of the outfits camped along the road. I was just thinking that another horse must be ahead or dropped out, when suddenly I passed Coaly's camp as the rider and his helper were having breakfast.

"Come and have coffee," they called.

I shook my head and thanked them, saying I had eaten, and kept right on. Shortly after crossing Pass Creek, the brown horse, number seven, galloped by under a full head of steam. His rider waved. "I'll order supper for you in Omaha!" he shouted.

I felt like saying, "Brother, you'll never get to Omaha on *that horse!*"—but I didn't. And as a matter of fact, neither did he—get to Omaha, I mean.

They all passed me, horses and rigs both. As Bill went by, he called, "I'm goin' to stop at nine today, Jack, an' we'll have some coffee and rest a while." That was our regular routine— ride, rest, ride. And whenever we were making one of those rests, even a short one, I would sponge Dunnie's head, wash out his nostrils, take off the saddle, give him an alcohol rub, and let him munch some hay. In half an hour we would be going again, refreshed like a prize fighter after the rest between rounds. I gave the horse every attention I could think of that would keep him fit, and anybody with eyes could see that under that kind of treatment he was standing up well; but I was thinking a lot, and very seriously, about that thoroughbred, Coaly, and about what the Singleton girl had said about the money that was down on him, and about those other horses, Ranger and Hornet, both of which were built bigger and stronger than Dunnie. I figured that the load of money on these three would not have been wagered unless it was supposed that one of them was almost sure to win. However, neither Bill nor I ever had any notion of quitting. We were raised with horses, and we felt that if any of the other riders thought they could run any rani-cum-boogerie on us, they were welcome to try. It was real competition that we were up against. Dad, who had been a horseman all his life, used to say, when he matched one of his horses in a race, "I may not win myself, but I'll sure make the other feller think he has been to a hoss race."

We passed Norris on Black Pine Creek in the middle of Monday morning, and got to White River at about eleven o'clock. All the other riders were bunched up there, afraid of the water, but Bill never even stopped; he drove right in, hollering to me to keep on the lower side of the team. Twice we struck swimming water, but it didn't cause us any trouble, in fact, Dunnie seemed to enjoy the swim and the look and feel of the clear water. We went into camp on the far side, and soon all the other riders came across. I laid up here till one-thirty, and when I pulled out, some of the other riders trailed along with me. Soon, however, my speed proved too slow for their liking, and they galloped on ahead. Bill and I camped at six on the other side of Mission, about a hundred and seventy-five miles from Deadwood, laid up till eleven, then rode for another hour, camping at midnight at Rock Creek, where we found seven other outfits camped. This was the only night when so many of us were together. The missing outfits, I discovered, were numbers seven and nine, one being the Singleton girl on Once Again, and the other the rider who had promised when he passed me, to order supper for me in Omaha. There was one other casualty. Number ten, who was camped next to us, said his horse had been sick half the night with colic, and he would have to drop out and turn back. The left only seven of us.

Next day Bill and I had a piece of luck, the only important bit of luck that came our way from first to last in all the five hundred miles of the race. I left at five o'clock, just as most of the others were lighting their campfires; and eight o'clock saw me crossing the Keyapaha River. Bill caught up and passed me there. Nine miles further on he was waiting for me; none of the other riders had caught up yet.

"We're campin' here till they pass," he said.

He had news.

One by one the riders went by us, and when the last one was out of sight, we went too—but by a different road. The news Bill had picked up was that for many miles the straight road ahead was a quagmire. He and I turned to the left, paralleling the muddy stretch on higher ground. Our way was a few miles farther, but the going was fine, and when we hit the Niobrara that evening at the town of Riverview, and got Nebraska instead of Dakota under our feet, we learned that we were ahead of everybody. And by eleven that night when we set out again and put ten more miles behind us, none of the other riders had yet appeared. In fact, it was not till nine o'clock next morning that I saw any of them. At that time Hornet and Ranger caught up with me. The two horses were coated with dried mud up to their knees, and looked drawn and tired, and the riders told me they had pulled through twenty miles of heavy bog mud the day before, and that all the hacks but one got stuck. They said there was another horse right behind, but they didn't know which one it was, and two more of the riders had dropped out.

Tired though Hornet and Ranger were after that hard mud, their riders could not long bear to crawl along at the slow and steady pace which I made Dunnie take. They galloped on ahead. But when I reached Bill's camp at eleven o'clock, there they were, waiting for their own hack (they were both using the same one now), and smelling Bill's coffee with hungry looks. They ate with us, and before we were through, their hack came along.

Following my usual routine, I pulled out again at one-thirty, walking Dunnie for an hour, then fox-trotting him for another hour. We camped again at six. About nine, three riders and two hacks passed—the horses were Ranger, Coaly, and Hornet. They all camped near us, but Bill and I pulled out again at eleven, and as I was passing, Hornet's rider told me that another horse had now dropped out and there were only four of us left in the race. Covering another ten miles in the dark before turning in for the long sleep, we found we were about three hundred and ten miles on our journey, and we had Thursday, Friday, and Saturday yet to go. Those next two hundred miles, we knew, would furnish the real test. Coaly already looked awful; Ranger and Hornet seemed to be dead tired. Dunnie, thanks to the care I constantly gave him, looked fine. But he probably wasn't as much of a horse, I knew, as the others were. The race, I told myself, was still far from over.

The others overtook me the next day at about nine o'clock, as usual, and I let them go ahead.

"Don't hurry," Bill said, grinning like a mountain cat over a fresh-killed deer, "we've got 'em licked."

But no rooster ever ought to crow till his chickens are hatched. It was eleven o'clock when I next caught up with Bill; and I didn't find him at the side of the road with a fire built, and coffee on to boil, and beans in the pan, and biscuits comin' up.

> Bacon in the pan,
> Coffee in the pot;
> Get up an' get it—
> Get it while it's hot.

No, his hack was standing in the middle of the road, tip-tilted like a stovepipe hat on a drunk's head. He had hit a boulder and knocked every spoke out of the right hind wheel.

"So we've got 'em licked, have we!" says I, lighting to inspect the damage. Without Bill and the hack to take care of all the little chores and leave me free to care for Dunnie, I knew I wouldn't stand any chance at all of taking the race. "*Now* what are we goin' to do?"

"*We* aren't goin' to do a thing," said Bill, who was peeled down to his undershirt and sweatin' with an ax. "You fork your horse an' hit the road. I'll have this fixed an' beat you in to O'Neill yet."

I never thought he could do it, but he sure did. He cut a long pole and tied it on top of the front axle and under the rear one, with the end of the pole dragging along behind. The hack sagged

a little on the pole corner, but it stayed up, and when Bill waved
his whip and spoke kind words to those long-legged mules of
his, riding on three wheels and a bob-sled, he split the breeze
about as fast as on four wheels. When I got to O'Neill I found
him strutting around like a turkey gobbler in a hen pen, admiring the hack, which now had four good wheels and looked the
same as ever. Bill had rustled an old wheel from somebody's
buggy shop, and though it had taken our last cent of cash
money to buy it, once more we had hopes of shaking the hand
of Buffalo Bill and sharing the promised purse. O'Neill was
called three hundred and forty miles from Deadwood.

I left there at one o'clock, riding along the Elkhorn River.
Bill passed me, but none of the other riders or hacks came in
sight. At six-thirty I rode into the camp Bill had made, and
smelled something that made my stomach get right up and wave
its hat. As a special celebration, Bill had borrowed a chicken and
fried it for our supper. I took good care of my half of the fowl,
as well as Dunnie, giving the little horse an alcohol rub and
bandaging his legs with wet cloths. We went on again after
eleven for about an hour and a half, the buggy-o-meter tallying
three hundred and eighty miles when we stopped for the night.
One hundred and fifty miles still to go, and two days to make it
in!

Next day none of the riders appeared until Bill and I were
nooning. Then all three came by together, trailing behind their
two hacks, and when they saw us, they camped a little beyond.
Their horses, with heads hanging, looked gaunt and tired. Presently the three riders strolled over to where we were.

"Keep your eyeballs oiled," said Bill, when he saw them
coming. But a cowhand foaled in Texas and busted out in New
Mexico didn't need that warning.

It was easy to see that the three had some serious business on
their minds. I hunkered down near Dunnie, just in case their
intentions had any reference to him. But as it turned out, they
were mostly interested in mathematics and long division. They
started edging into the subject by pointing out what all of us
knew by heart, namely, that there were four prizes offered for

this race—$1,000, $500, $300, and $200—making a grand total of $2,000.

"Cut the deck deeper, fellers," said Bill, "Jack and I don't *sabe*."

"Only four of us," Hornet's rider pointed out, "are left, and it's still anybody's race." He then went on to say that $2,000 could be cut four ways, making four even piles of $500 each. "Why not make a pool of it," he said, "we can let the horses take it easier. We'll cut cards to see who comes in first, but whatever the cards say, we'll split the money four ways even. That's the way she lays with us. How about you two?"

A certain kind of smell always means a skunk. This Hornet feller had been friendly enough to me, even if he was so skinny that a man would need an extra batch of luck to hit him with a handful of gravel, but his talk wasn't the kind I liked to trouble my ears with. I'm no professor with a deck of cards, but I have met people who can make them act real educated. It passed through my mind that tens of thousands of dollars had been bet on each of the other three horses left in the race, and only twenty-five dollars on Dunnie; and it seemed as plain as plowed ground that if we did cut cards with those three, there was one rider present who would not cut the high card, and the name of his horse was Johnny Dun. I shook my head, and Bill, backing me up, said "No!"

"It's still a hoss race, fur's I'm concerned," I said.

"Reckon I know how you feel," said Hornet's rider smoothly. "That prize money is warm in your pocket already, ain't it? But," rising to his feet, "you know there's never any certainty in a hoss race—*is* there?"

That was the end of the parley. "We'll have to watch those *hombres* like hawks," said Bill when we were alone again. "If I ever heard a plain warnin', that's it."

"An' we're only two against five."

"They may not try to pull anything; and again, they may. We won't camp near them again. And nobody hangs around our camp any time, day or night. Whenever you use the water bucket, Jack, put it away in a gunnysack an' tie the end good— don't give 'em any possible chance to dope Dunnie."

Now it was that same afternoon as I was passing through the town of Neleigh, that a crowd cheered me. One fellow came running out and thrust a bottle of whiskey into my hand. "Go it, old Diamond-A!" he yelled, adding that he used to work for that outfit down in Deming, New Mexico. About five miles farther on I caught up with Bill and offered him a jolt of the rye, and I sure didn't have to twist his arm to make him take it. We ate supper, and I hit the hay, Bill keeping one eye wide open. At nine-thirty he called me. We went eight miles farther, passing Warnersville before we made our last night camp. About midnight the hacks of our rivals pulled up and passed, and presently the three riders trailed along too. We saw them apparently make camp at a little distance, but we did not call attention to ourselves in any way. I think Bill slept with one eye open all night, expecting somebody to creep up out of the dark and try something on Dunnie. I turned in and told him to call me at four.

Well, we were expecting a surprise from those other riders, but not the surprise we got.

Dunnie and I at this point had only seventy miles to go to the fair grounds at Omaha, and we had until twelve o'clock midnight to do it—just twenty-four hours. Easy? After the grind we had been through? Don't you think it!

IV

I was up and ready to go at four-thirty next morning. It was still only half light, and I saw no signs of activity in the camp of the other riders. Since it was the last big day, I tied a bright new silk handkerchief around my neck, and pulled out aboard Dunnie all dressed up for the home stretch. The little horse still looked good. Nothing had happened to us so far; maybe nothing would. As Hornet's rider had said, the prize money was already hot in my pocket. And then I passed the camp of the other riders.

It wasn't a camp any more. In fact, it was as quiet as a hoss-thief after a hanging — not because the other riders weren't awake yet, but because they had gone. In the dark of the night they had stolen a march on us. At what time they had left, neither Bill nor I had any idea. But gone they were, and by now they might be ten, twenty, or even twenty-five miles ahead. Bill saw the possibilities at a glance; and with his mules at a keen trot left me behind.

"Keep your eyes open," he hollered. "I might leave a message for you at the station in Nickerson."

I figured my chances as I rode. If those riders had traveled all night, as seemed likely, even if their horses couldn't strike a lope and hold it, I realized that maybe just by walking they could make it to the fair grounds ahead of me. I had a powerful itch to make Dunnie lay out his legs and run. Though he was tired, I knew he still had a lot up his sleeve. But I decided against changing my style of riding, even if I was to lose the race for it. I walked the little horse for an hour, then fox-trotted him for an hour, then walked him, and kept it up, like the party in the desert walking fifteen minutes and resting ten.

Two farmers came out of a cross lane. "Here comes another cowboy from the Black Hills," they yelled, wavin' their hats. "Go it, sonny!"

A little later I met a team and a buggy coming towards me, and I hailed the driver. "Seen anything of three men on horseback," I asked, "an' a couple o' hacks?"

Yes, he said with a grin, he had seen 'em.

"How far ahead?"

"About ten miles."

"How are they makin' it?"

"A slow walk, an' about played out."

"*Bueno!*" I went on feeling a little better.

I caught up with Bill about thirty miles from the last night's camp. It was then ten-thirty in the morning. He had met a fellow who told him that the other riders were now only about four miles ahead and going very slowly. It was hard to sit down for two hours and a half in the face of those facts, and just do nothing but rest, knowing that every minute carried them yards closer to the winning line and the big prize; but that's what we did, for I knew what the rest would do for Dunnie. He had lost some flesh during the long grind, but he

still didn't look drawn or gaunt. When I left that camping
place, at one o'clock, I had forty-odd miles to go, and eleven
hours to make it in.

Bill and I passed through Nickerson together at about four.
He then went on ahead, and when I caught up with him at six,
he had a good supper cooked. He had passed the other outfits, he
said, and they had passed him in turn while he was fixing supper.
He said they looked about all in, and were urging their dead-
tired horses for all they were worth.

This was our last camp. I fed Dunnie once more, and gave
him a final rubdown with the last few drops of alcohol. But we
were up and off at seven. Bill hit a six-mile gait and I stayed
alongside till we came to the last hack. Right ahead of it we
saw the other one. It was then nine-thirty, with thirteen miles
to go. At ten we overtook the three riders and a dozen or so
off Buffalo Bill's cowboys who had come out to escort us in.

"Let's pull around 'em!" said Bill.

We did so. The cowboys from the show gave a rousing cheer
as Dunnie and I tore out on the last stretch. "Tore" isn't just
the word. We were making two miles to the other's one, but
neither Bill nor I knew how much reserve power those other
horses might have. They might not be nearly as tired as they
looked. We had been assured that the big black was a thoroughbred, and though he certainly seemed to be dead on his feet, I
knew you never could tell just how much last-minute power
a really good horse might have. There was no question as to
Dunnie's being in the best condition of any of the horses, but if
I let this Coaly horse get too close, could he in a last-quarter
drive beat me? Blood, I knew, will tell. In consequence, I decided to go at a saddle gait and put just as much distance as
possible between us.

Three of the cowboys from the show rode along with Bill
and me. At eleven-fifteen they sent word to the fair grounds
that we would soon be in, as we had only three more miles to go.
Just about then, Bill yelled at me:

"Here they come, Jack. Look out!"

I took a quick look over my shoulder. We were now inside
the city limits. Although it was late, the town was lighted up

and was almost as bright as day. The sidewalks were lined with people, and the crowds got denser, the yells louder, the nearer we came to the finish line. In my quick look back I saw the thoroughbred, Coaly, come pounding up from behind. He passed me and took the lead.

"Don't race him!" Bill yelled excitedly. "Push him at a good gallop, but keep just behind. He'll come back to you in a mile."

And pretty soon one of the cowboys said, "There's only a mile more to go, buddy."

Away we hammered. People shouted, and waved hats and handkerchiefs. Dunnie, being the smaller horse, got more 'n his share of the cheering—"Come on, you little buckskin!" But Coaly, though he looked to be gutted, was a wonder and got plenty of the yells too—"Come on, you black!" Once when the big horse stumbled, I thought sure he would fall. But with a thoroughbred's great grit, he recovered himself and kept on. Hornet and Ranger were left blocks behind. Bill threw the leather into his galloping mules and kept pace with me.

Inch by inch, Dunnie edged up on the big black. Now we were abreast of him. I could see that he was really dead on his feet. But he was trained to be a race horse, and a race horse he was to the last, even when he was running on nothing but breeding and nerve. A great horse—greater than Johnnie Dun—but not as well taken care of during the long week of that race. I gave Dunnie the spurs in earnest for almost the first time in five hundred miles, and with a spurt of speed that the black simply couldn't match, we shot ahead and through the fairground gate, breaking the string that was stretched between the posts, two good lengths in the lead. That was all. Just two lengths in a five-hundred-mile race.

A wild, screaming mob pulled me out of the saddle and carried me to the judges' stand, right up to say "Howdy!" to Buffalo Bill himself—and to this day I don't know what he said to me, but the check he handed me said one thousand dollars!

ON THE DODGE

Last week I found a stake-pin I had lost,
Jest an iron one—'bout a dollar it had cost—
On it was tied a rope,
En it almost got my goat,
When I found the other end tied to a horse!

I'm as innocent as any man can be,
But I'm afraid the Judge will not agree,
As there isn't any use
In dishin' up a poor excuse,
I might as well jest saddle up and flee!

I

BILL MUGGRIDGE and I were heading north from El Paso with a four-horse team and a wagon loaded with valuable supplies, and approached the Hueco Tanks about dusk, meaning to camp there for the night. The Tanks are a formation of big lava boulders, with natural reservoirs of fresh water, located near the Texas-New Mexico line. Bill, who was my partner in a ranch proposition, was an English remittance man of the kind you've read about. The night before, in El Paso, we had gone to see a minstrel show. A black-face comedian pulled one joke that was a corker; I nearly fell off the seat laughing at it. But poor old Bill sat as solemn as soap, never cracking a smile, because the point failed to percolate his skull. He had slept on it all night, ridden all day, and now, just as we were making for our camping place, he suddenly saw the point and burst out laughing.

"By God! old chap," he exclaimed, "wasn't that a bully wheeze that nigger got off."

Bill might be slow on the uptake with an American min-strel joke, but not otherwise. Suddenly I felt a sharp dig of his elbow. He said nothing, and kept right on laughing, but I fol-lowed the direction of his eyes, and in the shadows of the lava boulders saw a man, half-crouched, dragging a rifle.

We carried a Winchester in a holster tied to the wagon bow on my side, but you had to get off the wagon to get it out. I braced myself, sprang to the ground, whirled, and jerked out the gun, all in practically one motion. "Whoops!" I said, throwing down on the skulking figure, "what do you want?"

The man moved out of the shadows in a hurry, waving peaceably. "No harm," he said, "nothing, nothing. I was goin' to cook supper. Jest thought," nervously, "I'd see who was a-comin'."

"Where's your horse?" I asked. I didn't see one staked out, and had noticed no tracks. The stranger admitted that he had come there afoot. This was odd enough in the West, where to travel afoot from the front gallery to the horse corral was quite a *pasear,* but having satisfied ourselves that the stranger was alone and had no designs on us or our property, we asked him to take a load off his feet and share our chuck.

That was the evening of John Collier's first day on the dodge. Bill and I asked him no pertinent personal questions. Too much curiosity about other folks was considered bad form and not too healthy on the range. But we knew perfectly well that our guest had been up to some devilment, even though the nature of it might be no concern of ours. Mentioning the name he was going by, the feller said he was on the lookout for a job, and as Bill and I were drilling a stock-water well and needed help, we hired him. Some time later when I was in El Paso again, the sheriff gave me a letter-perfect description of John Collier, our hired hand.

"I don't know what name he's usin'," the sheriff said, "but I wouldn't much wonder if he headed your way."

"What's he wanted for?" I asked.

"Killin' Diamond Dick—" a Canadian gambler of unpleas-ant reputation. "The cuss probably needed killin'," the sheriff added. "Still, we need the man that done it. Don't reckon you seen him?"

"Sheriff," I said, "do you know I got just the worst kind of memory for faces!"

He knew what I meant; and I knew that he knew.

Going on the dodge was one of the peculiar institutions of the old West. It corresponded with what is known in certain circles today as "taking it on the lam." There were other rangeland phrases for it, such as hiding out, riding the lone trails, hunting the high places, laying out with the dry cattle—this last referring to cattle that range a long way and come infrequently to water. The country was big, and the spirit was one of live and let live. A man who got into trouble in one place might easily light out and make good somewhere else, if he changed his name and more or less walked in the paths of righteousness henceforth. It was an unwritten rule not to bother a man on the dodge or be too inquisitive about him; but he better behave himself in his new surroundings and not be caught riding horses with the wrong brands or selling the wrong man's beef!

The majority of men on the dodge in the West were not what would be called bad men, judging by those I knew. A good many were like Collier—victims of circumstances, or of quick temper, carelessness, daredeviltry, and thoughtlessness. I never knew exactly what happened between Collier and the gambler he killed. Probably it was hasty words over a game of cards and purely an accident that the gambler collected the bullet in a vital spot instead of Collier. The latter was a great windy, nothing special as a gunman, and he couldn't on any account tell the truth. Bill Muggridge and I put him to work on the well we were drilling, and one day while we were hoisting a slush bucket, he got his right thumb caught in the sprocket chain, smashing it so badly that it had to be amputated. Collier bawled like a baby at the pain. Many years later I dropped into a saloon in Santa Fe and heard him telling a bunch of open-mouthed townies how that thumb had been shot off in a gun battle. Happening to look up and see me listening with considerable interest to the details of his story, of which he was the outstanding hero, he seemed to forget all the last part of it.

The way Collier made his getaway after killing the gambler was rather interesting. He had no horse, and set out afoot from the little town of Isleta, near El Paso, hoping to put as much distance behind him as possible. Now, if he had walked at the side of the road, or straight across the desert, where the going would have been easiest, a man on horseback could have tracked him at a lope, and he soon would have been caught. But Collier was smart enough to walk in the deep sand of the wheel tracks; the loose sand that he displaced dropped right back in, and his tracks were gone as soon as they were made, like other footsteps in the sands of time. He walked through thirty-five miles of that loose sand, in the daytime heat of Texas and southern New Mexico, to get to the Hueco Tanks where we found him.

In fifty-odd years as a cowboy and cattleman, and occasionally as a special officer, I knew a lot of men on the dodge. I hired them, worked cattle with them, camped and ate, drank, sang, and swapped stories with them, and at times trailed and caught them for horse stealing or worse. Some were plenty hard, but as I say, only a small percentage were downright villainous. By accident, or in a passion, a man committed offenses that you or I, in the same fix, might have committed. In a country so lonely, the law was often a long ways off. I have ranched in a spot fifty-five miles from the nearest town, and eighty-five miles from the county seat. I know if I'd got in a tight out there, I would have protected myself. Wait for the sheriff? No, sir!

II

Men on the dodge were as varied in character as the whole band of pioneers who fought for and built the West. Some were brave, others were cowards; some you could trust with your last poker chip, others would steal a stakepin; some were modest, honest, quiet, others could on no account tell the truth or shut their mouths and stop the drip. The trouble with many who had to go on the dodge was simply that they got off on the wrong foot.

In Socorro, New Mexico, not long ago, they buried a man
whom everybody called Jack. He was a short, square, heavy-set
little fellow, who always wore a mustache, a hard-riding man
whose tough body and spirit served him well to the end of his
long life. He was past eighty when, just a year or so before he
died, he went with a party of us ten miles up a draw to gather
horses. I was on the south side of the creek, where the land
lay flat, and hardly any side arroyos came in, hence, I had easy
riding. Jack was on the north side, near the hills, and every few
minutes he had to cross a dry wash. Old as he was, I noticed
that at every arroyo he gave his horse the whip and took it the
quick but hard way, never once hesitating or trying to spare
himself.

Not over half a dozen people in New Mexico knew that
Jack's surname was assumed. I think even his wife did not
know that actually he was Joe Jackson, the one member of the
famous Sam Bass gang who escaped with his life when those
daring train robbers were ambushed at Round Rock, Texas.

> Sam met his fate at Round Rock, July the twenty-first;
> They pierced poor Sam with rifle balls and emptied out his purse.
> Poor Sam he is a corpse and six foot under clay,
> And Jackson in the bushes trying to get away.*

Jackson did get away, and he came to New Mexico, where,
in isolated cow camps under another name, he lived his life out,
giving up the ways he had followed as an outlaw, running a few
cattle, and I figure, like thousands of others, living his life the
way he wanted to and not requiring anybody's pity. A few
influential New Mexicans who knew his story, tried, without
betraying him, to win him a pardon from the Governor of Texas.

---

* There was another wife who also didn't know that "Jack" was Jackson. I
remember very well the time when my Jack met him; they had once been friends,
but had not seen one another for years. Jackson was a rather secretive-appearing,
hard-visaged old fellow, many years older than when they had known one another,
but Jack recognized him at once. "Hello, old-timer!" he said, holding out his hand.
Jackson gave him a sharp look, then reached out and took Jack's hand, and said,
"What are *you* doin' around here?" That was all. No recollections or reminiscences.
I saw Jackson occasionally after that, at our house or elsewhere, but Jack never said
much about him, and nothing about his past. But one day the news came that
Jackson was dead—and then Jack let me in on the secret. "Why didn't you tell me
sooner?" I said. Jack just laughed. "What good would it have done?" he said. It
was the code of men like Jack, that the less talk there was about the private affairs
of others, the better for all.—ANNETTE THORP.

The attempt failed, apparently because it was feared that to admit that Jackson had been alive under an assumed name for fifty years or so, would be a reflection on the great reputation of the Texas Rangers. Jack's secret has gone undisclosed, I believe, until this very moment.

Now, how did a man like that "go bad" at the outset? The story he told me and others was that once he and a younger brother, as boys, had gone fishing in a creek near their home. The brother tried his luck upstream, and pretty soon Jack heard him yelling as if the Apaches had him and were takin' his hair. Dropping his rod, he ran to see what was up, and found a man twice his own size holding his brother and beating him over the head with a stick, presumably as a punishment for trespassing. Never stopping to think twice, Jack hurled a rock which caught the man squarely over the left eye. The frightened boys fled, leaving him on the ground with blood streaming from a wicked gash. They didn't know whether he was alive or dead; in fact, Jack never did know if the man died or not, for as soon as they got home, he saddled his pony and lit out. In a hundred miles or so he got a job wrangling horses for a trail herd just starting north. The boss of that herd was Sam Bass. Jackson's big sin was protecting his brother, running away, and accidentally meeting a man who later turned train robber. Maybe he was just a poor picker of stars to be born under.

Strange too was the case of "Will Finn," as he was called to the day he died. In his early twenties, Finn took a job as horse wrangler for the Block cow outfit in Eddy County, New Mexico. One day, along with a bunch of Block peelers, he visited the saloon in the little settlement of Seven Rivers, and during the ensuing celebration there was some shooting at the heels of strangers to see how fancy they could dance; and somehow there was an "accident." When the smoke cleared, a man lay dead on the floor. None of those present knew, or would admit knowing whose gun had done the killing, but they knew the sheriff would have to be told a good story. So they agreed to load the blame on the drink-befuddled young horse wrangler, who was completely unknown in the neighborhood, and help him get away. Finn came to with a new name and no recollection of the shooting, which under the circumstances was not strange. From what he was told, he was satisfied in his own mind that he was guilty. He escaped to the Navajo country, where he worked for a famous Indian trader who later was killed in a fight with a Navajo. Finn then married the trader's widow and lived the rest of his life believing himself responsible for the crime that had caused him to change his name. Even yet, I suppose, comparatively few people know the truth. The fact is that Finn had nothing to do with the shooting. Another man did it—a man about whom there would be considerable eye-lifting if the facts ever came out. But *he* never went on the dodge. The hair grows long on some human critters, just like on cows, and you've got to look sharp to read the brands correctly.

"Silent" Moore was another odd one on the dodge. For many years he lived as lonesome as a lobo in one of the numerous canyons of the Guadalupes, visiting nobody, welcoming no guests. People thought he was cracked, but he wasn't. He was just law-shy.

One day religion came to the cow country in the warbag of one of the best converters from Texas, who held revival meetings in a stake-and-sawboard synagogue, on the banks of the Pecos River. Cowboys from all over came to

> hear the pastor tell
> Salvation's touching story,
> And how the new road misses hell
> And leads you straight to glory.

More than one of them stacked heavy burdens of cowboy sin on the altar and swore they were through. Some who were said to have escaped hanging in Texas only because they got up earlier and rode faster horses than the sheriff, joined hands and shouted hallelujah, and promised to give up "drinkin', cussin', card-playin'," and all similar wickedness forever from that day forth. To the astonishment of all who knew him, Silent Moore showed up and sat through every one of the services. At the last meeting, when the preacher extended the usual invitation to sinners to confess and be saved, Silent was one of the first to come forward. He was dipped, bathed, and had all his sins washed away, and told publicly how, years before, he had killed a man, his wife's lover, he said; and not a day had passed, he declared, that he had not relived the whole scene in his imagination. Moore, he admitted, was not his real name, but he did not say what his real name was, nor did he ever tell where or when the crime was committed. He had been on the dodge for ten years, and he said he sure felt a lot better for telling about his crime and joining the heaven-bound herd, branded with a "C" instead of a "D."

Silent Moore left those parts right after the final meeting, in the company of the preacher and his organist, and a couple of years later word drifted back to our range that Brother Moore had forsaken his solitude completely and was now a preacher of the gospel himself. But he still went by the name of Moore, and he was still on the dodge.

III

A large percentage of the crimes in the old West were committed against property, or against persons when trying to gain illegal control of property. As a general thing, these crimes were not very subtle, and followed a more or less common pattern of violence. Once in a while, to be sure, some cowhand or cattleman gone bad would think up a twist that would do a city con man credit. There was the case of the smooth horses, for example. A ranchman in South Texas went broke in the cow game, and had nothing but twelve head of good horses left when he closed out. By selling these horses in the usual way, he figured that he would have little more than eating money, so he thought up something different. Throwing in with a feller named McLaughlin, he turned over eleven of the twelve horses to him, keeping just one big blue roan for himself. McLaughlin then pulled out with the eleven horses, selling one here and another there whenever he got the chance. The real owner, following on his trail a week or so later, claimed that the horses had been stolen from him, proved his ownership of the brand by showing a certificate of registration, and the unlucky buyers had to let the salt go in the gravy and give him back the horses McLaughlin had sold. The partners in crime met every now and then to divide the proceeds, and to place the recovered horses in McLaughlin's hands so he could sell them again. Starting way down near San Saba, Texas, those slick *hombres* worked north, selling the same horses a dozen times and never taking less than forty dollars for any horse and sometimes getting as much as seventy. In a couple of months they cleaned up several thousand dollars. However, they were caught up with and landed in the penitentiary.

The most valuable property in the range country, counting totals, was cows. They walked around on four legs without bodyguards in wide open spaces, and it was commonplace knowledge that many respected citizens considered it all right that they themselves had stolen a start in cattle, their possessions as first consisting of nothing but a running iron, a rope, and an easy conscience, but they didn't approve the same methods in others after they had their own piles. Of course anyone could brand a maverick without reproach, but if he was caught making one brand into something different, it was quite often a propitious idea for him to go on the dodge, provided he could make it away ahead of the posse. From filching cows to filching other kinds of property was often a short step for the man willing to take it, and the commoner kinds of nefarious activity were train and stage holdups. Gold was the great objective, and for various reasons connected with the nature of the country, it is probable that there is more lost buried treasure in New Mexico today than in any other state. Valuables were often buried by the men who stole them, or by others to keep them from being stolen, and in both cases it happened time and again that the man who did the burying never came back to get the stuff, or if he did come, failed to find it.

Stories of men on the dodge seem to go naturally with stories of buried treasure. I have no direct evidence that my friend Singleton, the famous outlaw, who was on the dodge all the time I knew him, discovered such a treasure, but I am satisfied in my own mind that he may very well have done so. He was in the right place for it—and there were some very odd circumstances.

My acquaintance with Singleton began when I was driving a mount of saddle horses from Black River to Crow Flat, by a trail which skirted a point of the Guadalupe Mountains. There is a bluff there which runs up two thousand feet or more, and if you get the sun on it at the right angle, you see an enormous cross. At a peculiarly lonely spot along the trail, my eye lighted on a charred piece of fat pine. There was nothing especially odd about that since any passing cowboy might have built a fire, or travelers of any kind might have made a camp there. But what did strike me as odd was the fact that there was no sign of a fire having been built; that lone piece of charred pine was just lying out there all by itself, as lonely as a teetotaler in Uncle Johnny Root's saloon.

Now, cattlemen were great sign-noticers. On the range, preservation of property and good health might depend on noticing signs, and figuring out what they meant. One of the little but important things, for example, was the fact that cowboys' horses were shod with shoes that had heels; town horses were not. The wrong kind of hooftrack in the wrong place might send a cowman traveling out of his way for a half a day to see just what strange rider was in those parts, and what he might be up to. If the sign was not washed out by rain in the meantime, or obscured in some other way, as by a band of sheep being driven over it, it was often possible to follow it for long distances, no matter how much trouble the fugitive took to avoid being seen.

I had occasion once to trail a man who had stolen a horse. He had also just escaped from the penitentiary, so he had a double reason for going on the dodge and hiding his trail. For the first twenty-five miles he followed a rough and rocky route through the hills, and it was slow trailing and hard to be sure of him. But after he hit the clay flats, he left plain reading all the way, the tracks being those of a fully shod horse. This rider carefully avoided all ranches, watering only at windmills or reservoirs far from houses, cutting across country and giving traveled roads a wide berth. Never once in a ride of hundreds of miles did he sleep in a house, though many times I found the remains of small campfires and of rabbits he had shot, cooked, and eaten; and several times he had entered line camps while the punchers were away, and apparently taken what grub he needed.

Any cowhand who was familiar with a certain horse, would be apt to recognize that horse's tracks as soon as they caught his eye. "Joe was sure cuttin' the wind across here on old Buzzard," or, "Wonder what the boss was doin' out this way on old Spade?"

So it was not odd that I threw my horses off the trail to graze, and rode quietly back to the place where the charred pine lay. I dismounted and made an inspection of the neighborhood, and soon discovered the mouth of a cave. There are many dry caves in the Guadalupes, some of them offering hiding places that might escape a careful search for years. In sandy clay at the entrance to this cave I saw a shod horse track, and marks of a cowboy's high-heeled boot. Apparently somebody had a hangout here. Who, and why? It might pay to learn the answer.

Knowing that sound travels readily through rock, I rested one ear against the cliff wall and listened as hard as I could, and was pretty sure I heard a voice or voices deep in the cave. It sounded like just one man talking to himself, as a feller gets to doing if he is out by himself a long time alone; but I knew it might be two or a gang. I began edging along the rocky passage, being careful to make no noise, and drawing my gun, not so much because I expected to use it against humans as because of the possibility of mountain lions, which I believed might lay up in such caves during the day. It was pitch dark in the passage, but I judged I had gone fifty feet or so when I reached a turn. Peering around the corner, I saw a small fire, and one man. After observing him a moment, I called out, "Hello, fellow!"

Somebody handy with a gun and extra nervous, might have put a bullet crease in my eyebrow in reply. However, what I did get was a crisp order to move back out—"Out to daylight! I'll follow."

Since I was a trespasser, I considered it polite to do as I was told, and the stranger soon appeared. He was a young man, not over twenty-four, tall and slim, the type of a rider, and very handsome. His voice was low and quiet, and he carried a saddle

PEARL HART
This Canadian-born female "gunman" of the old West ended a rather drab career of outlawry when she was caught with her partner, Joe Boot, while hiding-out after an unprofitable stage hold-up.

"CALAMITY JANE"

One of the most famous of the women outlaws and tough characters of the old West was the woman known as "Calamity Jane." Her real name was Martha Canary. One of her impromptu horse races was won by three saloons and four drinks!

gun with which he kept me covered; and he asked if there was anything in particular I wanted.

"Not a thing," I told him, "curiosity got the best of me."

"Queer curiosity, feller, leadin' you straight to my cave."

I explained about the half-burned piece of fat pine. He considered this for a moment, and I noticed the beginning of a smile. "Yeah," he said, the point of his gun droppin' a little, "that pine was so fat it like to smoked me out o' the cave; I tossed it out."[12] He seemed to hesitate between doubt of me, and a wish to be friendly. "You're my first visitor," he said. "I been livin' here two years and more, an' might like to stay considerable longer."

"I haven't any notice in my pocket sayin' you got to move," I said.

I told him my name, and he said the one he used was Singleton. It was near noon when I found him, so I caught up my pack horse and got out my frying pan, coffee pot, cold biscuits, and slab of bacon. While I was doing this, Singleton disappeared. Soon he came back with a hunk of fresh beef.

"Ranch friend gave it to me," was all he said.

I was naturally asking no questions, but I was pretty sure that the "friend" who gave it was not aware of being so generous.

I got to know Singleton well in the next few months. He used to ride over and spend considerable time at my ranch, which was twenty miles to the west, and every two or three months, when I rode in to the little town of Florence on the Black River (the town has since disappeared), Singleton would have me inquire for mail for him. The name I gave at the post office, of course, was not Singleton.

Of all the men on the dodge I knew, Singleton was perhaps the most likeable. I knew he was a thief. In the cave he used for a home, he always had a quarter of beef hung up, yet he didn't own a cow—to have plenty of grub was the main thing for a fellow riding the high places. He had a frying pan, a lard bucket for coffee, and a Dutch oven. I don't know who he "borrowed" these from. But if he was a thief, he was an affable one. In my song hunt he gave me one, "Westward Ho!" that I used in the book:

I love not Colorado
Where the faro table grows,
And down the desperado
The rippling Bourbon flows.

By his own admission, Singleton was a killer. When I knew
him better, he told me that he had been raised in the mountains
of either West Virginia or the Bluegrass State. For several generations his family had been feuding, he said—an old Kentucky
custom. His three older brothers were killed. When he came of
age, the family code required him to avenge them, which he did,
then in the dead of night rode away. Eventually he found
sanctuary in his cave at the point of the Guadalupes; then between suns, he disappeared and left no message, either for me or
for anyone else.

Why? He hinted once that some of his enemies had learned
where he was. But there were some odd things about Singleton.
He had no visible means of support, yet he wore fourteen-dollar
cowboy pants, and expensive boots, and he had a one-hundred-
and-fifty-dollar saddle and bridle—and he never brought that
outfit from the East. Also, he rode a magnificent thoroughbred.
Did he, while prowling alone in the mountains, come across a
cached gold hoard? Was that the source of the funds which he
never seemed to lack?

I don't know, but it could have been. At almost the point
where his cave was located, there once was established a garrison
of soldiers to protect the trail against bandits and highwaymen,
who were so numerous and bold thereabouts that even the
military ambulance carrying the government payroll was held
up, the scout killed, and all the money stolen. Probably more
stagecoaches were held up in that vicinity than in any area of
similar size in the United States. This route was used for many
years by the Butterfield Stages, which carried shipments of gold
from the diggings in California, and a favorite place for holding
them up was between the point of the Guadalupes and Red Bluff
on the Pecos River to the east. Wagon tires from stage coaches
burned in bandit attacks are still kept as curiosities at different
little ranches along the Black River. The situation got so bad
at last that the route was changed, the stages going further

north, by way of Santa Fe and Las Vegas. Now, the bandits naturally had to have hiding places for their plunder, and the caves of the Guadalupes were made to order for that purpose. A considerable part of it undoubtedly is still there, the bandits for various reasons never finding it possible to come back and claim it. Singleton in his prowls might very well have come across a hoard big enough to set him up for life.[13]

This is pure supposition, but it is not far fetched when you consider the unsettled conditions on the frontier. Law and order arrived late. Banks were few and far between. Once at White Oaks in the Jicarilla Mountains, an Indian trader called my attention to the hearthstone of a ruined and partly burned building.

"My partner and I," he said, "recovered fifteen thousand dollars in gold dust from under there."

It belonged to them, to be sure. There had been some trouble with the Indians, and the traders had to get out in a hurry. In the course of trade, they had taken in considerable unminted gold, a good deal of the metal being found in that area, though in pretty scattered spots. Knowing it wouldn't be safe to take it with them in their flight, they buried it. Indians set fire to the building, but failed to find the cache. In due time the owners came back and got it.

Incidents of that kind were repeated many times, either by law-abiding citizens or by men on the dodge. In the regular course of ranch business, money had to be kept on hand, sometimes in large quantities. The owner of the famous Maxwell land grant is reputed to have kept as much as a hundred thousand dollars loose in the bottom drawer of his dresser.

One buried treasure believed to have been dug up by a man who had no legal right to it, belonged originally to Antonio Garcia, a rich sheepman living near Albuquerque, who first buried his money at the time Texas Confederate troops raided New Mexico in 1862. With his son and daughter and a burro-load of treasure, Garcia went in the dead of night to a house he owned on Candelarias Road, where the money, presumably about $150,000, was buried under the fireplace and a big flag-stone placed on it. The daughter and son went away to college for two or three years. Garcia died. His widow moved the gold back and buried it in her own house in a room with an earth floor. Later a Mexican came and lived rent-free on the premises as a pensioner. After a while, though having no known source of income, he became very prosperous. It is said that the Garcias never recovered any substantial part of the buried fortune themselves.

Those who buried their gold, even if they came back for it and it was still there, could not always find it. This was most often true, perhaps, of men on the dodge, who had to dispose of their stolen loot in a hurry and in their excitement failed to take accurate bearings so as to be able to come back to the exact spot. I know of one buried hoard which was hunted for vainly, month in and month out, by one of the men who stole and helped to bury it. He was an outlaw associated with "Bronco Bill," alias William Walters, whose real name was Walter Brown, and who was the son of the sheriff after whom Brown County, Texas, was named. Bronco Bill's gang held up and robbed a Santa Fe train between the towns of Shawnee and Grants, New Mexico, getting away with a sum variously estimated at from ten to forty thousand dollars, about half of it in gold coin. Sheriff Vigil took their trail, and with the help of Indian trailers, caught up with them while they were sound asleep. It would have been easy for him to disarm and tie them up, but he had had no previous experience with outlaws, and he considered it his duty to wait till they woke up and then politely read them the warrant for their arrest. Unfortunately for him, they woke up shooting, and he was killed instantly with a bullet through the forehead. His Indian trailers were driven off, but not, however, before they drove off the bandits' horses.

Afoot, and with a twenty-mile walk ahead of them, Bronco Bill and his partners were forced to cache most of their loot, keeping out only enough to buy a good horse and saddle apiece. The spot they chose for burying the money was alongside the Rio Puerco. The river banks here range anywhere from ten to twenty feet high, and the river itself is almost wide enough to carry the main flow of a Mississippi flood, but at most seasons there isn't enough water in its wide and sandy bed to cover a hungry lizard. Somewhere in those thirsty banks, Bronco Bill and his partners buried their loot, choosing a crevice which in their hurry seemed to them distinctive and easy to find. The members of the gang were captured and sent to the penitentiary at Santa Fe, most of them with life sentences, before any of them could come back to dig up the money. The youngest member of the gang was let off easy by the judge, and got out inside of five years. He is still alive. I became acquainted with him and won his confidence, and he told me that for months and months he had hunted for that cache. He believed at first that he could walk straight to it; but he soon found that there were a hundred thousand crevices along the Rio Puerco, all exactly alike, and long ago he gave up hope of ever finding the right one. He believes the money is still there, perhaps hidden by a cave-in, and he thinks some day someone who never even heard of its existence may walk by after another cave-in and stumble on it.

Sometimes the thieves did come back and get their buried loot. One day not many years ago, a line rider on a Sándoval County cattle ranch noticed signs showing that an automobile had stopped by the fence. Apparently several men had walked across the field to an old abandoned shack that stood there. Suspecting that a beef might have been killed, the rider thought it worth his while to investigate. Closer study of the tracks showed him that instead of several men making the trip, one man had made the same trip several times. Inside the shack he found a freshly-dug hole in the dirt floor, and beside the hole an old Indian olla, empty now, which had evidently been buried for some time at that spot. What had it contained? The rider put two and two together to his own satisfaction. Wells, Fargo agents had been held up and fifty thousand dollars in gold taken a few miles from this spot several years before. The bandits had been captured near by, but none of the gold was recovered. Now he remembered that the newspapers had reported, about a month before, that one of the bandits was being released.

"Just think," he said disgustedly, "that I had been in that old shack a million times, with a patched pocket, an' nothing in it, an' I never guessed what I was standin' on!"

IV

Some of those who rode the lone trails, of course, were really vicious. They made a business of crime and shot to kill, not in a sudden heat of passion and excitement, but cold-bloodedly, for profit, or to save their hides. It was hard to think very charitably of them; though if a feller could see deep enough, he might find reasons. One sizable fortune that presumably is still buried somewhere in Grant County, New Mexico, is connected with that vicious type of men, the Greer gang. Whoever finds the gold the Greers buried after robbing the Chino Copper Company pay car, their most successful haul, can probably keep it.

The Greers' list of crimes was a long one. Late one evening, just before a southbound Santa Fe train pulled out of Carrizozo, in Lincoln County, New Mexico, a youngish man who looked as if he were just a cowpuncher dressed up like the king of spades, stepped on the rear platform of the Pullman. His hair was black and curly, he was powerfully built, and he was all of six feet tall. He walked through the car, and took a seat near the front. The train passed through Three Rivers and Tularosa, and nothing unusual happened; but a couple of miles north of Alamogordo, the stranger rose from his seat, drew his six-shooter, faced the passengers, calmly told them it was a holdup, and advised them to dig deep for their valuables and deposit them in his hat as he passed down the aisle.

"My partner on the back platform has you covered," he said, "and anybody who fails to do as I say, will be almighty sorry."

The bandit collected pocketbooks, silver, rings, and a few good watches, the whole loot being worth about two thousand dollars. In the outskirts of Alamogordo he dropped off the moving train and disappeared in the darkness. There was no back-platform partner, of course, and the exploit was characteristic of the cool daring of John Greer, elder of the two Greer brothers. The younger brother, Ted, and John Gates (alias Frazer), the third member of the gang, were waiting in Alamogordo, and it is supposed that the three of them had intended to hold up the mail and express car, for ordinarily they were not interested in little stickups like this. They were engaged in train robbing as a business, presumably with the idea of collecting enough so they could retire, go back East, and be somebody. But on this occasion the mail and express car robbery for some reason did not come off.

After this affair, the three men rode towards the west, and split up. Gates was surprised sometime later at Deming, and was held in jail there for the officers from Tucson, Arizona, where he was wanted for burglary. John and Ted Greer heard of his arrest and boldly rode into Deming. Finding a deputy alone at the jail, except for the prisoner, they threw down on him, and ordered Gates turned loose. In fear of his life, the deputy said he couldn't do it, because he didn't have the keys.

"Where are they?"

"Dwight has 'em"—Dwight Stevens, the newly-elected sheriff of Luna County.

John went to find Stevens, leaving Ted in charge of the deputy. Deming was just a tiny cow town then, drowsing in the sun except when cowboys rode in for drinks and excitement, its one principal street, bordered by shacks and saloons, starting at the Harvey House on the railroad and straggling lazily down towards Mexico. The sheriff was sleeping peacefully, with his chair tipped against a saloon wall, when John Greer found him. A gun in the stomach brought him up grunting, and he was invited to walk to his own jail. There, under threat, the keys were forthcoming. Gates was freed, and the sheriff and his deputy were locked in cells, but not before a little incident occurred which was to cast its shadow on subsequent events.

"Well, well!" said the released man, eyeing the sheriff's gaudy gun, "that's just what I need, I always did crave a pearl-handled six-shooter." He transferred the weapon to his own pocket. The three outlaws then mounted and rode out of town.

A posse was quickly organized and took their trail. Pushed hard, the outlaws rode into a corral belonging to the V-Cross-T, probably to get fresh horses, and here the posse caught up and surrounded them. It was a trap from which there was only one way out. The bandits threw the gate open and raced through in a cloud of dust, guns in hand, lead flying. They killed Tom

Hall, a famous trailer, and Al Smithers, an ex-Arizona ranger; and members of the posse in turn killed John Greer. Gates and Ted Greer got away. The posse pursued them to rough country north and west of Cooks Peak, and in Arabe Canyon pressed them so hard that they had to quit their horses and take to the brush afoot. Young Greer climbed a strategic cliff with his saddle gun, and made the vicinity so hot for the pursuers that they withdrew. However, they took the bandits' horses.

That gives you a rough picture of the kind of men who earlier had robbed the Chino pay car. That holdup itself was not spectacular. The automobile in which the payroll was carried had to take the highway from Deming to Santa Rita. The Greer gang stopped it on a lonely stretch east of Hurley and took all the money, reputedly about thirty thousand dollars. The occupants were not harmed, and the car was sent on its way.

The swag, it was learned later, was buried close by, and it is almost certainly there today, though the canvas sacks that held it undoubtedly must have rotted after all these years. The reason for this belief is partly the story told by Gates. After John Greer was killed, and Gates and Ted had abandoned their horses, and the posse had taken them, those two found themselves in a desperate situation. They split up, thinking that singly they would stand a better chance of escaping detection. They traveled at night and laid up during the day, Ted heading east for the Sacramento Mountains, Gates turning south towards Texas. Nothing further was heard of either of them for some time. But one day a man walked into an El Paso pawnshop and asked how much cash he could get on his pearl-handled six-shooter. After the murderous episode outside of Deming, word had gone out to watch for such a gun. The pawnbroker kept the customer waiting on some pretext, and sent for the sheriff. The latter arrived, arrested the fellow, and held him on suspicion. The gun was later found to be the one that was taken off of Dwight Stevens, the Deming sheriff; and the man who had tried to pawn it was identified by eyewitnesses as one of the bandits who had taken part in the bloody battle at the V-Cross-T corral. It was Gates, of course. He was taken to Socorro, tried, convicted, and hung. But before execution he made an illuminating statement.

Go back for a moment to the Chino holdup. Some months after that affair, signs of an old camp were discovered about half a mile south and half a mile east of where the payroll car was stopped. There were remains of a campfire here, burnt matches, an empty whiskey bottle, and a letter addressed to Ted Greer, doubtless lost from his hip pocket when he mounted his horse. In his pre-execution statement, Gates admitted participation in the Chino affair, and gave details indicating that the camp was theirs. He said he had had a pint of whiskey wrapped in his slicker, and after the holdup, he and his partners had ridden on for several miles, dismounted, buried the money, built a fire over the spot to conceal evidences of digging, made coffee, and roasted a goat's leg they had gotten from a herder. They finished the whiskey, and Gates remembered leaving the empty bottle. This all tallied.

Many have dug for the buried money at that spot or near it. Those who have followed the matter closely, however, are pretty certain that it has never been found. Ted Greer was never heard of again, and seems to have flown right off into space. Probably he went back East. The gang is believed to have had swag cached in three or four places, and there is no evidence that any of it has been recovered.

There were curious contradictions in the characters of some of the really bad men who went on the dodge, for example, "Bad Man" Moore, in no way related to the Silent Moore who was branded with religion on the Pecos. I suppose not one man in a thousand would have had the nerve to do the thing Bad Man once did in an honest cause. Yet, though he had great managerial ability, he proved time and again that he was far from an honest or, upon occasion, a kindly man.

Moore was born in eastern California, where he was known as one of the finest *vaqueros* and ropers of that state. Handsome, a great worker, a natural leader, Moore had one distinctive physical feature, a cast in his left eye, which made it hard for him, when on the dodge, to hide himself successfully. He usually kept that eye half closed, and always wore his hat on the left side of his head with the brim pulled down; but even so, you couldn't miss seeing the cast. Among the character traits that did him no good were a high temper, bull-headedness, and a complete lack of scruples about the property rights of others.

Moore's first killing was done in hot blood when he was twenty-five years old. The victim was his brother-in-law, a very popular young man, and Moore rode off ahead of a posse that had every intention of tieing his neck to a cottonwood limb, but he succeeded in outdistancing these riders after reaching the neighborhood of Elko, Nevada, at the foot of the Bull Run Mountains.

I knew Moore, but my authority for the following incident is Charlie Siringo, the famous cowboy detective, who at one time worked for Moore in Texas, and met him under various circumstances in the later stages of his dark career. It seems that the day after Moore out-rode the posse, he saw a lone horseman approaching. He apparently thought it might be somebody after him, or somebody who would carry news of seeing him. He was still badly scared, and anything right then was a booger. Without waiting for a parley of any sort, he threw down on the stranger and killed him, leaving the body in the lonely spot where it fell. That's the story Siringo told.

Moore kept on riding till he reached Cheyenne, Wyoming. Few questions were asked of men when they were hired in the cow country, save whether they could ride a horse and handle a rope. Moore could do both of these things with the best of them, so he had no difficulty in being taken on as a cowhand with the Swan Land and Cattle Company, an outfit which at that time claimed to run over a hundred thousand head of cattle, and because he was a worker and a leader, he was soon made a range foreman and later district manager. But for his vicious temper and lack of scruples, he might have gone a long way in the legitimate cattle business. But one day in a rage he killed a Negro hand, and had to leave Wyoming whipping his horse and on the dodge again.

Moore next turned up at the Bates & Beals LX Ranch in the Panhandle of Texas, riding a tired horse and looking for a job. Again few questions were asked. He was taken on as a hand,

and as a result of his ability, here too he presently became foreman and later manager. And now he began making financial
hay. He secretly started a ranch of his own at Coldwater
Springs in No Man's Land, now a part of Oklahoma. There
were always a certain number of "wanted" men on the average
cowspread payroll, and there were more than the usual number
working for Moore. One day a curious incident occurred. A
party of six or eight men appeared on the range, well armed,
outfitted with a chuck wagon, hack, and saddle horses. They
told nobody their business, but late one evening they pulled up
close to the LX wagon and camped. Next morning over half
of Moore's cowhands were missing. The rumor had got about
that the strangers were Texas Rangers in disguise, and those
cowhands figured that the next state would be healthier for
them! Actually the strangers were surveyors laying out a new
mail route.

With cowhands of this type working for him, Moore found
it easy to persuade several of them, while drawing LX money,
to help him steal LX cattle and throw them over on the Coldwater Springs ranch. During the five years that he worked for
the LX outfit, Moore continued doing just this without being
caught, and he succeeded in feathering his own nest very nicely.
Men who knew him at that time without knowing his past,
believed him to be a master cowman (he was), and personally a
chap who would do to ride the river with (that was open to
serious debate). Toward strangers he always assumed an attitude of dignified reserve; to his own men he was completely
loyal. And he was unquestionably fearless. He finally sold his
secret ranch in No Man's Land for about seventy-five thousand
dollars, and quit his job with the LX, locating a new ranch for
himself in the American Valley, in the extreme northwestern
part of New Mexico.

Here, although he was now well fixed for money, Moore
got into another murdering fit and had to go on the dodge again.
Adjoining his ranch was one owned by two partners, on which
was a fine spring of water. In that thirsty region, such a spring
controlled a big stretch of open range, and Moore was bound
and determined to buy the partners out in order to get the

watering. They refused to sell. At last, in a cold fury, Moore
rode over and killed both of them. That did him just no good
at all, for he had to hit the high places again. Under the name
of Johnny Ward, he drifted south to the little town of Alma,
New Mexico, and went to work for the WS outfit, which was
owned by Englishmen, but was actively operated by as daring
a bunch of train robbers, under the leadership of Butch Cassidy,
as ever got together in one crew in the old West. Their operations extended from Alma in New Mexico to the hole-in-the-
wall country in Wyoming. Moore stayed here for several
months, but he moved on suddenly when detectives (Charlie
Siringo was one of them) arrived at Alma. These detectives
were actually trying to trace some paper money stolen in a train
robbery, an affair with which Moore had no connection; but
Moore didn't know that. He thought they might be after him,
and like his own LX hands when the supposed Texas Rangers
camped near by, he lit out. That was one of the things that
made it tough for a man on the dodge; he never knew when
somebody who had known him in the old days might turn up
as an officer, or for purposes of revenge. I knew a few hated and
hunted men in the West who would never sit down except with
their backs to the wall and their eyes on the door.

After this, Moore was always on the slick and downhill trail.
He made his way north and west, crossed into Canada, and the
next authentic news of him came from Juneau, Alaska, where
Siringo, on still another man hunt, found that he had opened a
saloon and was doing fairly well. Eventually he was killed in a
drunken brawl, ending a stormy and rather pointless career.
He was a man of fine parts, and great managerial ability, but
unscrupulous, and deadly when his temper was ruffled. Yet
there was at least one occasion when he proved the manhood
that makes even the worst of us contradictory in character—
"Show me a perfect man and I'll show you Christ." The incident occurred before Moore's last two killings, while he was
in the American Valley.

Word came that a man just across the state line in Arizona
had killed a rancher. The family of the murdered man appealed
for a posse to go after the murderer. Moore got a few men

together and took the trail. The man they were after was trailed to a log house, and there it was found that he had barricaded himself for a hard defense. Moore called for him to come out and surrender. A shot, which barely missed Moore's ear, was the only answer from the inside of the house. Moore repeated the invitation. Again the reply was a shot that missed its mark by a fraction of an inch.

"All right," yelled Moore, "if you won't come out, I'll come in!"

Facing what looked like certain death, he picked up a large rock, hurled it and broke down the door, grabbed the murderer, and hauled him out. Moore was five times a killer himself, yet he risked life and everything for the sake of bringing another killer to justice. Neither he nor anybody else knew in advance that with the second shot the barricaded man had used up his last cartridge. Moore had courage.

The fact is, I guess, that it would take a finer instrument than human beings know how to build, to drive the cowboy herd on the scales and weigh and judge them for all the things they did that the law would say was wrong. Grant Wheeler, for one, was a tramp cowpuncher who drifted into New Mexico, and later into Arizona, working at different times for the Diamond A and the three C's, and no different, so to speak, from any other bragging cowhand who boasted around the campfire that his roping or cutting horse was the best in the land, bar none, who got tight on hard liquor when he rode to town, did the tough jobs he was set to do on the range, and considered himself as a free and self-respecting citizen, head-high with anybody. But fighting cattle for thirty dollars a month was not exactly Grant's idea of a quick and speedy road to wealth. He saw others riding silver-mounted outfits, and they no better cowhands or Christians than he was. How did they get them? He decided, without very much debating over ethics and the fine points of morals, to try a short cut. His partner in his adventures was Joe George, another cowhand, who was raised in the Sacramento Mountains of New Mexico.

Their first important exploit was the holdup of a Southern

Pacific train five miles west of Wilcox, Arizona. Now it takes five men to hold up a train successfully, according to the train robbers' official book of rules, and calls for careful organization, expert technique, and what they call "fin-essy." Joe George and Grant Wheeler, however, figured that the fewer the hands, the larger the profits per hand, so they went it alone, and botched the job. The express messenger escaped with most of the valuables while they were taking care of the fireman and engineer. Not knowing this, they blew off the safe door, holding their giant powder down with the bags of Mexican silver dollars which they found in the express car. Of course they found the safe empty. The only people who profited by that robbery were Mexican track workers, who were busy up and down the right-of-way for weeks, gathering in the scattered pesos.

A quirt and a pair of spurs were found at the point where the boys had tied their horses, and this led to the identification of Joe and Grant as the robbers. Having to go on the dodge, they escaped into the Chiricahua Mountains, but they did not give up lightly their get-rich-quick dreams.

At Steins Pass, in New Mexico, they held up a train a few weeks later. Whether by design or accident, it was the very same train as before, and the same engine crew, and Grant Wheeler, sticking his gun into the engineer's familiar ribs, said cheerily, "Well, old-timer, here we are again!" Once more, however, the robbery was a failure, due this time to the blunder in the bandits' excitement, of cutting off only the mail car and leaving all the valuables behind in the express car. Thoroughly disgusted, they did not mess around with the contents of the mail car, but exploded their giant powder in the woods and rode off still as poor as preachers, but now on the dodge for sure.

About three weeks after this holdup, an officer who was detailed to catch the two, got a clue which led him to Durango, Colorado. It was a warm trail. He pursued it to a ranch near Farmington, New Mexico; thence to Hidden Springs, a favorite resort of cattle thieves; thence to Cortez, Colorado, not far from the Blue Mountains of Utah; and finally to the little town of Mancos on the river of that name, which the officer reached after dark. And here, as far as "bad man" Grant Wheeler was concerned, the trail came to an end. The officer had a discreet talk with the liveryman, who happened to know that Wheeler at that very moment was camped in a pasture a quarter of a mile from town. Two local deputy sheriffs were enlisted to help. One of them rode into the pasture where Wheeler was camped on the pretense of hunting a stray horse. He saw Wheeler on top of the haystack where he had slept, and passed the time of day with him. Wheeler said he was coming into town directly, and had to catch up his own horses and if he found the stray, he said he would bring it in. Meanwhile, the officer who was after Wheeler had been keeping a peeled eye on him from a hotel window. Presently he saw Wheeler put a packsaddle on one of his horses, and a riding saddle on the other, and head, not towards town, but down into a gulch where he disappeared. Thinking it was a get away, he mounted his own horse, summoned the deputies, and rode off in pursuit. They no sooner reached the gulch than, to their surprise, Wheeler came up the bank in plain sight. He had not been leaving the neighborhood but was cooking his breakfast.

"Throw 'em up!" the officer said.

"I've done nothing," Wheeler crisply replied, refusing to comply. One of the deputies fired a shot of warning, and Wheeler ducked back into the gulch.

It looked as if a battle would be necessary in order to capture him. But before any further preparations could be made, a shot —just one—was heard in the gulch, and what it meant, none of them knew. One of the deputies raced his horse past the mouth of the gulch at top speed, and glimpsed Wheeler lying with his head almost in the fire which he had built to cook his breakfast. They approached with caution and found him dead from a bullet fired from his own gun by his own hand. Yes, I guess he preferred to end it that way. He had tried a tough game and failed. He had no notion of sitting behind bars after riding the range free and handsome, as he had done. At the coroner's inquest it came out that Wheeler had said to a cowboy friend only the day before, "The officers are after me. I don't want to kill anybody. But they won't take me alive."

Get six jolly cowboys to carry my coffin;
Get six pretty maidens to bear up my pall;
Put bunches of roses all over my coffin,
Put roses to deaden the clods as they fall.

Then swing your rope slowly and rattle your spurs lowly,
And give a wild whoop as you bear me along;
And in the grave throw me, and roll the sod over me.
For I'm a young cowboy, and I know I've done wrong.

It was learned later that Joe George had parted from Grant Wheeler at the Blue River. Joe headed either for Socorro or the Sacramento Mountains where he had friends and relatives. After crossing the Blue, however, he might as well have ridden off into space, and climbed the sky on wings. He has never again been heard of by any officer inquiring into the train robberies, and if he's still alive and anybody remembers, he's still on the dodge.

V

Women sometimes hunted the high places too, not as often as men, to be sure, but there were a few who rode the dangerous trails, and lived and died, gun in hand sometimes, with a price on their heads.

There's a touch of human pathos
A glamour of the West,
Round the names of women outlaws
Who have now gone to their rest—

Bronco Sue, Belle Starr, and Shudders,
Pike Kate, and Altar Doane,
Calamity Jane, Sister Cummings,
And the Rose of Cimmaron.

Some of these women killed, some stole, some tried holdups, and others shared in any or all of the crimes of men. Some were birds of gay plumage and some were barroom toughs. A few, like Pearl Hart, who was born in Lindsay, Ontario, in 1872, and who among other exploits outside of the law, tried holding up a stage, were romantically infatuated with the "wild and wooly" West. Pearl first saw it vividly depicted at some of the

W. C. ("BAD MAN") MOORE

A first-rate cattleman and manager, and once manager of the big Bates & Beals LX Ranch in Texas, "Bad Man" Moore nevertheless was a killer and a cow-thief, and had to go on the dodge to escape consequences. He is supposed to have been killed in a saloon brawl in Alaska.

PAT F. GARRETT

In his capacity as sheriff of Lincoln County, Garrett shot and killed Billy the Kid in the dead of night in Pete Maxwell's bedroom in old Fort Sumner. Garrett's book, *The Authentic Life of Billy the Kid*, which was "ghost-written" for him by a newspaperman named Upson, was admittedly made in many places "out of whole cloth."

concessions on the Midway at the World's Columbian Exposition, and it was there that she got a big hat and a pair of boots which, contrasting with her small figure, made her noticeable anywhere. She lived a pretty shabby life, but colorful, to her, with different men and in different jobs after she quit her first husband, who was a worthless small-town sport. Pearl was known in such places as Trinidad, Colorado, where she was a biscuit-shooter in a restaurant when that city was at its roaringest; in Phoenix, Arizona, where she found her worthless husband for a second time, and lived with him long enough to become the mother of two children; in Mammoth, Arizona, where she was a cook and waitress; and in Cane Spring Canyon, where she hid out and was caught with Joe Boot, her partner in the ill-starred stage holdup.

A number of women who went on the dodge came from highly respected families. Many were Southerners who, during the turmoil of the Civil War period, became estranged to former ways of living, through their families' sudden loss of fortune. Like most Southern girls of that day, they were excellent horsewomen, and took quite naturally to the adventurous life of the range and the hills. Some of these women outlaws I knew. From old records and letters written by the characters themselves to relatives, lovers, and friends, I traced the lives of more than twenty of them. The evidence is overwhelming that they were more sinned against than sinning, victims of circumstance that they refused to bow down to without a struggle, and often unable to gain their ends within the law.

Altar Doane, for example, as a girl of fifteen, left Independence, Missouri, with her father, mother, and brother Jed in a covered wagon drawn by four mules. The family was lured West by reports of rich gold strikes. Altar's father was a strict-living, high-tempered, vindictive man, who, when aroused, was dangerous. Her mother was a meek little woman in failing health, who found the hardships of the journey too much for her, and died before they reached their destination. Altar strongly resembled her father in looks and disposition, and after her mother's death, and even before it, camp duties and responsibilities fell on her young shoulders. Nine months after leaving

Missouri, the Doanes pulled into a little gold camp then known as the Essaus Diggings, where they found a few placer miners at work. They made camp and panned the sands here for a while without any special luck, then moved somewhat farther upstream, where at a likely-looking place they built some sluice boxes, and every night added a little gold to the slowly-accumulating hoard in the buckskin bag that was their bank. One morning they struck a pocket under some boulders from which they gathered nuggets worth around five hundred dollars. Somehow the news of this strike, small though it was, became known—probably it leaked out through the boy, Jed, when he went to the store for supplies. The next day, when suppertime came, and her father and brother did not return, Altar went in search of them. She found them sprawled out in the sand, shot through the head, both dead, and the claim jumped.

Altar made her preparations methodically. First she disposed of her mules and outfit, receiving in exchange some cash, a saddle, and a fine thoroughbred horse, very fast, which made her probably the best mounted horsewoman in the state. Then she took her leave, publicly. How far she rode is not known. But apparently she circled around, and came back. The day after she left, the two claim jumpers were found dead, each shot through the head, and lying almost exactly where she had found her father and brother. Altar Doane had become a killer, and though a miner's court might have acquitted her, she chose to go on the dodge.

One other little incident in her career shows her cool nerve. She turned up one day in Montana mounted on her thoroughbred, near where the town of Kalispell now stands. She was sitting on her horse watching a race between two locally-owned horses, neither of which seemed very fast to her. She made a remark to that effect to her neighbor, a hard-looking customer whose name was Marsh, and who, as it turned out, owned a half interest in the horse that won the race. Marsh asked if she would like to run her horse against the winner for some real money. After some talk, she agreed, confident that she could win by five jumps and a hoggin' string. The terms of the race were as follows: distance, four hundred and forty yards; price, a dollar a yard put up by each entrant; time, the next afternoon at four o'clock; weight, each horse to carry one hundred and thirty-five pounds. A stakeholder was agreed on, and the money was put up. Not until that night did Altar learn that the stakeholder owned the other half interest in the horse which her horse was to run against, and that the race was almost certain to be rigged against her somehow.

At the hour agreed on, the two horses with their riders appeared, Marsh's son riding the second horse, and Altar riding for herself. Everybody except the starter went to the far end of the straightaway track to see the finish. The two horses scored a long while, Altar's opponent making several bad breaks. The starter called Altar to bring her horse back to the score each time; and then once, when she was headed the wrong way, he dropped his flag, sending the other horse away to a flying start. Altar whirled and followed, but the other horse by then had a lead of ten lengths. The girl closed the gap, lapping the other horse at the finish, but lost. Naturally, she was mad.

It was dark when she rode back to her hotel. Once more she made her plans methodically. She tied her horse to a post back of the building, then went in and ate her supper. Marsh and another man came in and ate while she was there. Later, Altar went out to the office and sat down. When Marsh went up to his room, she followed, knocked at his door, went in, stuck a gun in his face, and told him to fork over the roll that he and the crooked starter had robbed her of. Marsh took a look at the gun, which she held perfectly steady, and decided it was sweeter to go on living than to enter into any immediate argument. He counted out eight hundred and eighty dollars (her bet and his), and handed the roll over.

"Now, Mister," said Altar, tucking the money in her pocket, "you can have your choice. I'm willin' to kill you here and now. But if you'd rather, you can take a ten-minutes' walk with me, not once makin' a break or openin' your mouth, and if you act nice, I'll spare you your hide." Marsh naturally chose the second alternative. "Remember," she promised, "if you make one false move or say a word to anybody. I'll drop you."

He marched to the lobby with her, as peaceful as a lamb. Altar paid her bill, and Marsh stayed right with her like her little boy, until she reached her horse. Then she mounted and dashed off in the darkness, and left him. She crossed the line into Canada, and the last trace we have of her was in the Rustercruse country, where she is said to have married a member of the Canadian Mounted Police.

Belle Starr, another famous woman outlaw, dealt in stolen horses and had a gang working for her. She was not my idea of complete depravity.* "Battle Axe" also dealt in stolen horses. She got her odd nickname from the fact that she was never known to be without a plug of Battle Axe chewing tobacco. She was born and raised west of the line of Arkansas, in "the Strip" (or as some called it, No Man's Land) where even the lilies of the field were born rough and grew spines as they aged. She had a strain of Indian blood in her veins, but was not a full-blooded Indian. Sometimes she worked with a gang, but mostly she carried on alone. Once she stole a bunch of good horses at Bloomburg, Arkansas, and in twenty-four hours turned up with them near Sulphur Bluff, Texas, a distance of almost a hundred miles, and she had no help. The owner of the horses and a deputy sheriff trailed her on this occasion, and the second day, at sunrise, rode up to the post corral where the horses were penned. Battle Axe was camped on the opposite side of the corral, about two hundred feet away. She wore a man's hat, chaps, and brush jacket, and undoubtedly her pursuers thought she was a man. They opened fire with their pistols, but Battle Axe dropped to the ground unhurt, and with her saddle gun killed them both. She then drove the horses north and east to Hart's Bluff, where she sold them.

She partnered for a while with the Broken Bow gang, which headquartered near Broken Bow, Indian Territory, the gang consisting of Jack Spain, Tom Cree, and a few others. This gang was surprised in camp while on a raid near the head of Clover Creek, and Battle Axe's left shoulder stopped a bullet fired by one of the officers. However, she managed to get away, and hid out in the brush. It was her practice never to sleep

* See Chapter I, page 35.

close to camp, so her saddle and outfit were overlooked by the officers, and she got away from the scene on an old pack horse that was too poor to interest the officers. Late in the afternoon, weak and sick from her wound, she had no alternative when she reached a lonely cabin but to ride right up and hail it. Strangely enough (strange, because women in those parts were scarce, and a "Montgomery Ward wife" was the only chance some cowhands had at matrimony), a woman came to the door. When she saw that her visitor was a woman and wounded, she made her get down and come in. Battle Axe made up a story, saying she had been riding along and heard some shooting, and a stray bullet struck her. There was no doctor within a hundred miles, but Mrs. James, the ranch wife, bathed and bandaged the wound and put her to bed, and Battle Axe lay there for a month before she was able to ride again.

Now, the James woman had a little girl named Ethel May, who was a cripple. The child's leg had been broken by a horse's falling with her, and some quack who tried to set it did such a poor job that the little girl could hardly walk. Battle Axe and Ethel May James became great friends. When Battle Axe was getting ready to pull out, she asked Mrs. James how much she owed her for all the trouble and care. Mrs. James wouldn't take a cent. Battle Axe thanked her and climbed aboard her old pack horse, which had fattened up considerably in the meantime. Not long after she had gone, Mrs. James, making up the bed, found an envelope under the pillow addressed to Ethel May, and inside it this badly scrawled message:

"To pay for having your off hind leg fixed up right."

The enclosure was three hundred dollars in bills.

A turning point in Battle Axe's career occurred at Hot Springs, Arkansas, when she was about twenty-seven years old. She was dressed in woman's clothes, and was not at all bad looking—in fact, quite a lady, medium tall, five feet, six and a half, with an olive skin, black eyes, and a figure that indicated plenty of outdoor activity and good health. She was never in any sense a carouser or wastrel. Although she had never had an opportunity for much education, she could read, she wrote a fairly good hand, and she knew how to save her money. In

Hot Springs, on this Saturday afternoon, she went to the races. Two horses in the grand sweepstakes caught her eye. Their names were Spurs and Wings. Both were owned by the same man and were very valuable, having won large purses in Tennessee and Kentucky. After the race, which Spurs won, Wings coming in third, Battle Axe followed the two to their stalls; and having seen that they were at the end of the row, she went back to her hotel for supper. Presently, by messenger, she dispatched a gallon jug of good corn whiskey to the boy who had charge of Spurs, and with it an unsigned note saying the snake poison came with the good wishes of one who had won on the horse that day. When she judged that the liquor would have been used for its intended purpose and produced its proper effect, Battle Axe quietly slipped into Spur's stall and led him out without waking the snoring stable boy, then did the same with Wings. Mounting Spurs bareback, she rode off with both horses. Ten miles out of town she changed to her business clothes, and from then on laid up by day and rode only at night, thus escaping with these prize horses to the camp near Broken Bow. Later she traded both of them to a man from Dallas, Texas, for two hundred head of steel-dust breeding mares. These were the foundation stock of the H E L brand, which Battle Axe ran for many years.

Her end was not spectacular. One day she picked up a Fort Smith, Arkansas, paper, and by pure accident came across a message in the "Personal" column intended for her. It said that her sister, with whom she had been out of touch for years, was very sick in Fort Smith, and wanted to see her. She climbed aboard a saddle horse, and with another following, made the hundred-mile ride to Fort Smith in less than sixteen hours. There she stayed, nursing the sick woman until she died. Battle Axe's sister left a five-year-old daughter, for whom Battle Axe felt a fondness and proposed to take home. The girl's father agreed to let her go. Since Battle Axe had now stolen enough to be well fixed, and had a good ranch, hundreds of good horses, and considerable cash in the bank as the wages of her crimes, she determined to turn over a new leaf, be respectable, and do the best she could for her niece. She had a talk with her ranch hands and friends, and spread the word that she wanted the girl to have the right kind of bringing up and a good safe home, so that she might grow up to be a lady and respect her aunt. So the old nickname, Battle Axe, was barred from that time forward. And while old-timers were welcome to a meal and a bed any time when they came by, the old life was out too. For many years Battle Axe continued to ride broncs and break them fearlessly on her H E L Ranch. One night she passed out peacefully in her sleep. She hadn't hesitated to take what she wanted, and she had shot to kill to keep what she got, and the lawyers have names for a lot of things she did. But who's going to stand up and say that she was all bad and completely rotted away with sin?

The old lady was buried at the forks of Little River under her right name, Helen Law.[14]

BILLY ("THE KID") BONNEY

Bustin' down the canyon,
Horses on the run,
Posse just behind them,
'Twas June first, seventy-one.

Saddle guns in scabbards,
Pistols on saddle bow,
The boys were ridin' for their lives—
The Kid en Alias Joe.

I

OF ALL the New Mexico "bad men," William H. Bonney, known as Billy the Kid, is by far the most famous. Sixty years after his sordid death, native women still scare their children by telling them "Bilito" will come and get them if they don't behave. Armchair adventure hounds halfway around the world scare themselves under their reading lamps over lurid accounts of his alleged exploits. His career has even been put in the movies, and from now on he will probably be pictured in the public mind as two-gun Robert Taylor.

There seem to have been about as many contradictions in Billy's character as in that of "Bad Man" Moore—he was part good and part bad, like most of the rest of us. But the most curious thing about Billy is not what he actually was, in the flesh, but the steps by which his reputation grew so that he is now transformed into the kind of person the thrill-hungry public imagines him to be. He is not history any more, but legend, romanticized out of all likeness to the gun-totin', rambunctious, carefree cowboy kid that his friends and enemies knew, and he has become a sort of super-hero. It is hard, maybe impossible, to separate the truth about him from falsehood, the facts from the fiction. However, that is what I have tried to do, and in this chapter I aim to examine some of the evidence concerning a very curious phenomenon in the history of the West.

Actually, Billy the Kid was just a little, small-sized cow- and horse-thief who lived grubbily and missed legal hanging by only a few days. He killed, or took part in killing, several people; but his killings were more often on the order of safe butchery than stand-up-and-fight-it-out gun battles. He took part in a range war on the losing side. He died, not in a blaze of glory, but like a butchered yearling, shot down in the dead of night in his stocking feet, when he was armed with a butcher knife and, possibly, though not certainly, with a six-shooter. Yet for all that, romance does cling to his name. Half a dozen books about him have been written and published. The town of Lincoln, New Mexico, thrives on his memory. And many people regard him as a sort of super-Robin Hood of the range, a daredevil of matchless courage, haloed by smoke wreathing upward from fogging guns. He makes a fascinating study in the technique and psychology of literary and national hero creation. Many have told the "facts" about Bill. Few have agreed about them. The heavy shadow of the "hero" tradition has made unconscious liars of some; others have lied about him on purpose, loading the public with tall tales to satisfy the appetites of listeners greedy for shudders and blood.

I, of course, did not know Billy. He died too young. His bones had been mouldering in the dust of old Fort Sumner for nearly ten years when I first laid eyes on the sunny flats and mountain ranges beyond the Pecos where the bloody events in which he shared, took place. But I knew Lincoln County intimately, and I knew many of those who knew him, including Sheriff Pat Garrett, who fired the shot that killed him; George Coe, who rode and bunked with him for months when matters were at their worst; Charlie Siringo who, although he knew Billy only slightly, wrote a small and highly-colored book about him; and many more. To most of those who knew him, Billy was no hero. To some, he was a good friend and a likable companion. Others considered him no better than any other brand-blotting thief, and a coward besides. The truth seems to lie somewhere between these extremes, as it usually does in judging the characters of people. But it is the growth of the hero myth that I am particularly interested to examine, thinking it might shed light on the deification of certain other "heroes" in our modern world, such as Adolf of Berchtesgaden and John Dillinger.

The Kid's background was certainly colorful. The years that made his fame were spent on or near the Pecos River, which well deserves its other name, the River of Sin.[15] The Pecos rises in the Sangre de Cristo Mountains at an elevation of ten thousand feet, and after cascading down rocky slopes wild with pine, aspen, and juniper, breaks out into the flat country near old Fort Sumner. Thence toward the south it threads the old cattle range of the Chisums, and on into Texas, finally entering the Rio Grande in a rocky gorge north and west of Del Rio, not far from Judge Roy Bean's town, Langtry. For several hundred miles the Pecos passes through a country almost destitute of trees, meagerly fed by five rivers from the west that have their origin in the Guadalupes, and by two from the east—Pintada Canyon, and Alamogordo Creek. The very name of the river came to stand for murder, for when the freebooters of the valley killed a man, they were said to have "Pecos'd" him, meaning, tied stones to his dead body and rolled it into the river. Three races, Indian, Spanish, and English, with a scattering of French and others, met, mixed, and fought in this valley. It is likely that the country that became Billy the Kid's playground, is richer than any other in the West in tales of lost mines, buried treasures, cattle wars, bloody violence, and mysterious happenings.

No one, for example, has ever explained the mystery of the three human skeletons found on the upper Pecos, together with their guns, saddles, and camp equipment, and a buckskin bag full of nuggets and placer gold. The guns were ancient cap-and-ball pistols, and two shots had been fired from one of the guns, one shot apiece from each of the others. Nor has anyone, presumably, ever found out where the bandits buried the gold they took when they robbed the stagecoach a few miles east of the Pecos River. The bandits, lost in a blind canyon, were overtaken promptly and killed near the river, but the stolen gold was not on them. Nor does anyone have an accurate record of the number of bloody battles that were fought at or near the site of the Pecos Pueblo, first between Plains and Pueblo Indians, and later between the Pueblos and the Spaniards.

A little to the west of the river stands the tragic Sierito Bernál, now called Starvation Peak, where a wagonload of emigrants fled when attacked by Indians. Besieged there constantly by the Indians, without food or water, all starved to death. This area, too, and the whole country from Las Vegas to Santa Fe, was the stronghold of *Vicente Silva y sus Quarenta Bandidos*— night riders who wore long white sheets with red daggers embroidered on the back, and who, when they rode into a town four abreast and a hundred strong, always left behind some victim of their vengeance, his corpse perhaps not being found for months.

Old Fort Sumner, on the east side of the Pecos, was founded in 1862, expressly to prevent bloodshed on the Bosque Redondo Indian Reserve, where thousands of bloodthirsty Apache and Navajo Indians had been placed. Two companies of cavalry had their barracks here.[16]

In the town of Roswell, further down the river, Sheriff Charles Perry, in order to keep the peace, had to kill three men in one day, while at Eddy (now Carlsbad) certain hard characters murdered the sheriff in broad daylight.

Two miles south of Eddy was a collection of saloons and dance halls, populated by the riffraff and outcasts of Eddy, the place being known as Phoenix. One of the houses here was run by a man named Barfield, who "fell from under his hat" when shot from the outside through the window. Across the street was a place run by Ed Lyalls and his wife, Nellie, frequented by a gang who paid for their liquor with stolen cattle. I stopped at Lyalls' place once for a few minutes on the way back to my ranch on Black River, and while I was there, two strangers rode up. They sat down at the faro table and proceeded to lose their money—maybe a couple of hundred dollars. One of them whipped out his gun and covered the dealer, the other covered the lookout man. They raked in the entire bankroll, backed out, mounted, and fled. I learned later that one of the two was the notorious John Wesley Hardin, who was afterwards killed in El Paso. The name of his companion I never learned.

Further south, at the junction of the Black River and the Pecos, was Red Bluff, near which the Butterfield stagecoaches were held up so often that the government finally established a camp of soldiers near the point of the Guadalupes to protect travelers.

These are only a few of many happenings that gave the River of Sin its reputation, and it was against such a bloody background that Billy the Kid played his part as a fighting cowboy and became a legend to scare the papooses. The man himself was a good deal less of a fellow than the legend; and it's the man himself I mean to try to put together from the authentic pieces that are left.

The original published source material about Billy is contained principally in five books, as follows: Pat F. Garrett, *The Authentic Life of Billy the Kid* (1882; 2nd ed., 1927); John W. Poe, *The Death of Billy the Kid* (1919); Chas. A. Siringo, *History of Billy the Kid* (1920); George W. Coe's autobiography, entitled *Frontier Fighter* (1934); Miguel Antonio Otero, *The Real Billy the Kid* (1936). It is significant that with the exception of Garrett's book, which appeared about a year after Billy's death, all of these have been published within the last twenty-one years, about forty years or more after Billy's death. For almost forty years the hero myth had little printed matter to feed on, and it was dormant or dying, and possessed only an antiquarian interest. Soon after the World War, however, the coals of interest began to show red again, and finally burst into flame. Old-timers, once given to obstinate silence about what they had seen, grew talkative, and began to tell what they remembered or thought they remembered.

The principal peg on which public interest was hung, of course, was the "fact," so called, that this beardless youth who died when he was little more than twenty-one, had killed "twenty-one men, not counting Indians"—a man for every

year of his brief life. Armchair appetites demanded good stories
about this matchless character, and supply has a tendency to
follow demand in the fiction business as well as in the cow business. The stories became better and better, taller and taller,
until maybe Old Truthful himself would be ashamed to own
an interest in some of them. Old Truthful, I might say, was a
character with a claim in the Guadalupe Mountains, who was
famous for handling facts in a free-and-easy style. One of his
stories had to do with a bear fight he allegedly fought with a
huge old silvertip with an eight-foot tail. Attacked by Old
Truthful himself, his little dog, and a swarm of bees all at once,
the bear took refuge in a fifty-gallon barrel that Old Truthful
had brought along to gather honey in. Her tail stuck out the
bunghole, and Old Truthful tied a knot in it, thereby attaching
the barrel permanently to her tail; and the bear left camp quick.
The next time Old Truthful saw that bear, he said, was about
a year later. She still had the barrel on her tail, and what's more,
she had two cubs with her, and each one of them had a gallon
keg on its tail.

"No, sir!" Old Truthful remarked after telling this yarn,
"I don't go to town often. I like ter live up here. Yer see, there's
a bunch that jest sets around the store with their feet wrapped
around nail kegs, an' they're always tellin' lies. They make me
so mad!"

Billy, the cow thief, the occasional killer, the buck-toothed
desperado, became more and more a "hero" in the stories. Final
deification came with *The Saga of Billy the Kid*, by Walter
Noble Burns, a book in which a cook-up of fact and fiction was
served with a literary sauce nicely calculated to please the
palates of thousands of readers whose only range-riding was
done in pipe smoke. There have been other publications claiming to give "the facts," which actually have only enhanced and
embroidered the legend. That legend has now grown to such a
size that it will not be ignored, even by those who know it to
be about nine parts fiction to one part fact.

To appraise the substance on which this shadowy hero
structure has been built, I have gone over all the evidence
again, and here present results and conclusions.

II

Authentic knowledge of Billy the Kid, insofar as we have it, is confined to the last four years of his life. He rides out of the shadows of a nomadic boyhood, into the sunlight of intense and recorded action, in the year 1877. What he had done in the eighteen years of his life up to then, is largely conjecture. There is some evidence that Billy himself knew how to spin a good yarn about his past, and was not unwilling to have people think that he had done some pretty bloody and impossible things in the course of his travels. Many a cowboy did as much. And Billy seems to have known, as some women know, that "a past" can often be an asset—if you are not too explicit about the details. Many of the killings attributed to him are supposed to have taken place in that unlighted past, beyond proof or investigation. The story of that period is told, allegedly, in the first seven chapters of Garrett's *Authentic Life,* and most later writers have blindly followed his account, without recalling all of Garrett's reasons for writing the book.

It's a tall tale, as Garrett spins it. Before he was eighteen, Billy is credited with having ended the mortal agony of (a) a man who insulted his mother, (b) three Indians on the Chiricahua Apache Indian Reservation, (c) a "soldier blacksmith," (d) a monte dealer in Sonora, Old Mexico, (e) a monte dealer in Chihuahua City, (f) about fourteen Mescalero Apache Indians who had attacked an emigrant train, and (g) an uncounted number of Apaches near a spring in the Guadalupe Mountains. The flavor of these episodes, admittedly largely imaginary, is shown by the words attributed to Billy just before the Guadalupe Indian killings. To his lone companion, he is supposed to have remarked:

"I believe a little flare-up with twenty or thirty of the sneaking curs would make me forget I was thirsty while it lasted, and give water the flavor of wine after the brigazee was over."

That might be the way dime novels talk, but not cowboys.

During this period of his life, Billy is pictured as dropping in occasionally at towns where he was known, just to jeer at officers

of the law who feared him, and "to watch their trembling
limbs and pallid lips as they blindly rushed to shelter." But the
author hedges occasionally on the authenticity of the events he
is describing, for he says of one killing, "Billy never disclosed
the particulars of the affair"; and of another, "The date and
particulars of this killing are not upon record, and Billy was
always reticent in regard to it." The truth is, of course, that
Garrett was building up this desperado for purposes of his
own. Sheriff Garrett, you remember, killed Billy in the dead of
night, when out with two deputies to capture and return him
to a condemned cell.

> A chance shot fired by Garrett,
> A chance shot that found its mark;
> 'Twas lucky for Pat the Kid showed plain,
> While Garrett was hid in the dark.

The West approved the kind of peace officer who gave even
a desperate gunman a chance, and Garrett was always a little
on the defensive in regard to the manner of Billy's death. His
claim was, "If I had not shot him when I did, I would not be
here to tell the tale." So he was interested in using any and
every device he could find, to play Billy up as a super-gunman.
In presenting an autographed copy of his book to Territorial
Governor Miguel Otero (later the author of *The Real Billy*),
Garrett said of his volume:

"Much of it was gathered from hearsay and 'made out of
whole cloth.'"

Garrett himself, be it noted, did not do the actual writing
of his book. That was the work of M. A. (Ash) Upson, an old
newspaper man who is said to have boarded with Billy's mother
in different towns. With a subject such as he had here, when
he was not held down to earth by facts of which either he or
Garrett had sober personal knowledge, Upson just loosed the
bridle and let old Pegasus sunfish and windmill. Billy's name, he
soaringly said, "will live in the annals of daring crime so long
as those of Dick Turpin and Claude Duval shall be remembered.
This verified history of the Kid's exploits, with all the exaggeration removed, will exhibit him as the peer of any fabled brigand

on record, unequalled in desperate courage, presence of mind in danger, devotion to his allies, generosity to his foes, gallantry, and all the elements which appeal to the holier emotions."

That's pretty loud screamin' for *any* eagle!

I think it is permissible to dismiss as unproved, and probably untrue because incredible, most of the killings supposedly done by Billy before he became a participant in the Lincoln County War. What remains? There is a list of eleven killings, more or less charged against Billy in that strange uprising which helped plenty to brand the Pecos as the River of Sin. Did Billy do these eleven killings? And if so, were all or any of them "heroic"? Let's see.

(1) The first two of the eleven killings charged to him were those of Billy Morton and Frank Baker. The exact truth of the Morton-Baker affair will now never be known. It was one of the earliest incidents involving actual bloodshed in the Lincoln County War. The history of that war is much too complicated and obscure to dwell on in a single chapter here. It's enough to say that it was born of range and trade rivalries and involved what is known as the Murphy-Dolan faction on one side, and the Tunstall-McSween faction on the other.

The Murphy-Dolan faction was the natural one for a gun-slinging tough like Billy the Kid to side with. Under the leadership of Jim Dolan, it represented political control and corruption, was allied with rustlers, grafters, and any who cared more about money than honesty. Such an outfit needed fellows who were prepared to steal cattle, blot brands, dry-gulch enemies, and otherwise do the devil's business on the range. And Billy did side with them. They were his first employers in Lincoln County. He played with their marbles, and maybe they paid him some wages. The big mystery is why he ever quit them for the other side. But quit them he did, and the reason may have been the personality of John Tunstall, the Englishman. Tunstall and Billy, somehow, seem to have been greatly attracted to one another right from the start, perhaps because they were such completely opposite types and their backgrounds were so different. Billy was a product of the raw frontier, and knew more about the inside of saloons, gambling halls, and *tendejons*

WILLIAM H. BONNEY

Aside from a scratched tintype, this appears to be the only known likeness of the curiously famous youthful bandit and cow-range tough known as Billy the Kid, who actually was just a small-sized cow- and horse-thief who barely missed legal hanging.

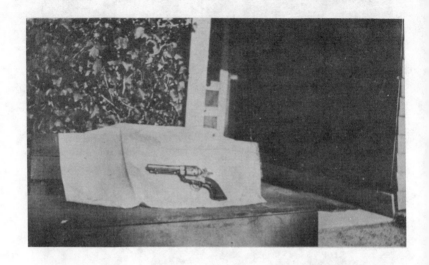

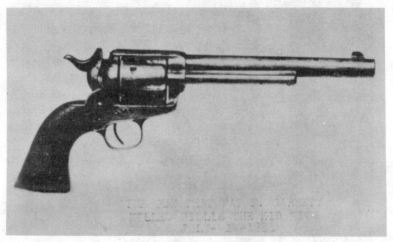

GUNS OF KILLER AND KILLED

The top pistol found a permanent resting place in the collection of the famous screen star, "Bill" Hart, because it was supposed to be the one with which Billy did a lot of his killing. The bottom pistol is the one used by Sheriff Pat Garrett in putting an end to Billy's criminal career.

than other kinds of inhabited buildings. Yet with it all he seems to have been possessed of a certain personal charm. Tunstall, by all accounts, was a cultured and educated Englishman of wealth. When they met, the spark of friendship was struck. George Coe tells of being in Lincoln one day, and asking Tunstall about Billy. He quotes Tunstall's reply:

"George, that's the finest lad I ever met. He's a revelation to me every day, and would do anything on earth to please me. I'm going to make a man out of that boy yet. He has it in him."

If these were not Tunstall's exact words, they undoubtedly reflect accurately his feelings, for Coe tells the truth about what he saw and remembers—and about what he didn't see, he keeps still. This remark of Tunstall's doesn't make a "hero" of the lad, but it does show him in a favorable light.

Now, the very first blood shed in the war was that of John Tunstall. He had come to Lincoln and opened a store which cut into the business of the store owned by the Murphy-Dolan crew, partnering in this and another enterprise with a man, Alexander A. McSween, who had displeased and defied that bunch. He had bought ranch interests and conducted himself on the range in an upright manner, which was calculated to bring him into conflict with their crooked operations. So, capping a series of events, Tunstall was waylaid and killed. Billy the Kid was working for Tunstall then. Just where Billy was at the time of this killing is a matter of dispute. He seems to have been just around the next hill shooting wild turkeys, but no one knows for sure. At any rate, the Tunstall killing was the shot heard round the range that set other Lincoln County guns to blazing.

Two days after the event, a group of Tunstall's friends carried his body to town. Four miles south of Lincoln, six Spanish-American workmen stood in a field of grain belonging to Señor Charles Fritz, and watched the procession pass. A youngster among them, Julian Chavez, listened to his elders (*hombres grandes*) discuss the event, and heard them express the opinion that it was an affair concerning American houses exclusively, and that probably the Mexican population would not be drawn into it at all. Many years later, in a naive longhand

narrative[17] recording his recollections of those days, Julian remarked that he himself of course had no opinion in the matter
then, since he was a youngster and a young boy did not have
opinions—*"Yo no tube opinion, pues estaba Joben, y las mucha-
chas no tienen muchas opiniones."* But he discovered soon that
the opinion of his elders was far from correct.

Bill Bonney and others swore vengeance on Tunstall's killers.
The Lincoln County War was on, and nearly everybody in the
region was drawn into it, either actively or passively, on one side
or the other.

An unofficial posse, of which Billy the Kid was a member
but not the leader, captured Morton and Baker, two men who
were connected with the Tunstall killing. The posse started
with them toward Lincoln, but the captives never got there.
The story usually accepted is that for some reason they made a
break to escape, presumably when one member of the posse, who
was suspected of favoring their cause, was shot. Pat Garrett
gives Billy the Kid all the blame for killing Morton and Baker.
In one of these highly purple passages of his book, he *(via* Ash
Upson) says:

"The Kid wheeled his horse. All was confusion. He couldn't
take in the situation. He heard firearms, and it flashed across his
mind that perhaps the prisoners had in some unaccountable
manner got possession of weapons. He saw his mortal enemies
attempting to escape. . . . . " And so on. "Twice only," Garrett
dramatically declares, "his revolver spoke, and a life sped at
each report."

Thrilling enough, if true. But it seems to be perfectly certain that Garrett was merely making up a good story, the way
he wanted it, out of an event of which he had no first-hand
knowledge, knowing that because of the peculiar circumstances,
his account was not likely to be contradicted publicly by any of
those who did have first-hand knowledge. George Coe, who
knew Billy the Kid more intimately than Garrett ever did, said
of the same event, "No one knows the details, but it is evident
that . . . . Baker and Morton . . . . put spurs to their horses and
made a desperate attempt for liberty only to fall, riddled with

bullets, a few seconds later." He says that all the mention Billy ever made to him about the affair, was:

"Of course you know, George, I never meant to let them birds reach Lincoln alive." "Billy," he adds, "did not seem to want to talk about it."

Let's sum up. There were eleven members of the posse. All of them, except the prisoners, were heavily armed; the prisoners weren't armed at all, and they died. It requires a pretty big stretch of credulity to believe that when they fell dead, the only bullets in their bodies were those of nineteen-year-old Billy the Kid, who was not even the leader of the posse. In any event, were those killings the kind to make a "hero's" reader proud of him? Did they reveal the dash and daring of a resourceful, courageous soul endowed with "all the elements which appeal to the holier emotions"? Or were they more on the order of butchering a couple of range steers?

(2) Another allegedly daring killing laid at Billy's door was that of "Buckshot" Roberts. Garrett did not witness this killing either, but his hearsay account of it has a fine air of gallantry, dash, and derring-do befitting a knight of the range, a cowhand with lance atilt. The encounter took place at Blazer's sawmill. Once again Billy the Kid was a member of a large posse, and Roberts, the victim, was alone.

"As the party," says Garrett, "approached the building from the east, Roberts came galloping up from the west. The Kid espied him, and bringing his Winchester on his thigh, he spurred directly towards Roberts as Brewer demanded a surrender. Roberts' only reply was to the Kid's movements. Quick as lightning his Winchester was at his shoulder and a bullet sang past the Kid's ear. The Kid was as quick as his foe and his aim more accurate; the bullet from the rifle went crashing through Roberts' body, inflicting a mortal wound."

That's the way a "hero" and his worthy opponent ought to meet and do battle to the death! The only trouble is, that's not what happened; in fact, it's nothing like what happened.

George Coe was there. He and Billy the Kid were temporarily members of the same gang. His shattered right hand from which the trigger finger is gone, is evidence to this day* of

---

* George Coe has died since this account was written.

his participation in the Blazer's Sawmill fight. Dr. Blazer ran a sort of roadhouse, and the party of twelve men, one of them being Billy the Kid, arrived and ate lunch there, two of their number standing guard because they were expecting some trouble. While the main bunch was eating, trouble arrived— Roberts on a bay mule. The fireworks did not start at once. Roberts dismounted and told one member of the party, whom he knew personally, that he wanted to speak to him. They walked around the house and sat down in an open doorway. Meanwhile, others of the party conferred and decided that Roberts, who was known to be after their scalps for a reward that had been offered by the opposing faction, had better be "arrested." Dick Brewer, the party's leader, asked who would go around the house and get him. There were three volunteers, Charlie Bowdre, George Coe, and Billy the Kid, *in that order;* and in that order they started around the house, guns in hand and cocked. Bowdre called on Roberts to surrender.

"Not much, Mary Ann!" he replied. All the accounts agree that those were his actual words.

Bowdre had the drop, but Roberts and he fired almost simultaneously. "Bowdre's bullet," says Coe, "struck Roberts right through the middle, and Roberts' ball glanced off Bowdre's cartridge belt, and with my usual luck, I got there just in time to stop the bullet with my right hand. It knocked the gun out of my hand, took off my trigger-finger, and shattered my hand." Bowdre's bullet, and his alone, was the one of which Roberts died. But he did not die at once, and before he finally passed out, he put up a very game fight. He took refuge in the room in the door of which he had been sitting, and from here he picked off and killed Dick Brewer, and wounded another member of the posse. Billy the Kid, according to Coe (who throughout his book tells only what he saw without elaboration), had slight part in the episode beyond being third in a party of three aiming to "arrest" Roberts.

Again the facts of a battle, in which one man was ranged against twelve, hardly seem to show Billy up as "hero" size.

(3) A third affair laid to Billy was a double killing—that

of Sheriff Brady and his deputy, Hindman, on the main street of the town of Lincoln.

Garrett, who generally makes out a case for Billy's daredeviltry and courage when he can, calls this "a crime which would disgrace the record of an Apache." It occurred a few days before the killing of "Buckshot" Roberts. The sheriff of Lincoln County at that time was a certain Major Brady. All events of the Lincoln County War were backgrounded against a relatively passive and pacific, but by no means disinterested, native Spanish population; and their judgments of the principal figures involved in the conflict are not to be disregarded. Many of the Spanish people, for example, thought highly of Billy the Kid, and he is said to have liked them too, and it has been claimed that of all the people he is supposed to have killed in New Mexico, not one was a pure-blooded Spanish-American. Many of the Spanish people thought well of Major Brady, too. To quote once more from the manuscript of Julian Chavez, this sheriff was held by the Mexicans to be an honorable citizen and very much the gentleman *(muy caballero)*, partly perhaps because he was married to a Mexican woman of the Bonifacia family. "I knew all of his family," Julian writes—*"yo conosi a toda su familia."* However, Jim Dolan is supposed to have undermined the Major's sterling character simply by giving him a paid-in-full receipt for eight hundred dollars, to clear off the balance of the mortgage on the Major's home, and thereafter *"el buen hombre se doblego, y se presto a serbir ordener"*—the good man became deceitful, and put himself out to obey Murphy-Dolan orders without question.

"Sabe Dios," exclaims Julian, *"Que tontas bacilasiones"*— God knows why men do such things!

Major Brady is supposed to have held warrants for the arrest of several of the alleged killers of Morton and Baker. So a group of the dead Tunstall's friends went to the town of Lincoln on April 1, 1878, and lay in wait for him behind an adobe wall surrounding Tunstall's store. They knew his habits, and expected him to ride along the main street at about the time they took up their positions.

How many lay in ambush behind the wall is reported vari-

ously. George Coe says there were five; others say there were
eleven. One of them, at any rate, was Billy the Kid.

The sheriff failed to come past as expected. Hence, a man
was sent to the lower end of town to pretend that he was drunk
and shooting bottles off the shelves. News of this speedily
brought the sheriff along Lincoln's one main street. With him
were his deputy, George Hindman, and the clerk of the circuit
court, Billy Matthews. As they passed the adobe wall, the ambushed "heroes" let them have it. Brady was killed instantly,
Hindman lived barely an hour, and Matthews, though wounded,
got away and lived to tell the tale.

Billy the Kid was credited with these murders. Garrett in
his book does not come right out and say whose bullets killed
whom. He does call the murder "a most dastardly crime on the
part of the Kid," leaving the hasty reader to conclude that Billy
did it all, or at least engineered it. But Governor Otero reports
Garrett as saying to him later that "he doubted if the Kid had
even fired at Brady," giving as his reason that he hated Billy
Matthews and would naturally have tried to get him first, and
Matthews was the one of the three who got away!

We shall never know the truth. There was no science of
ballistics then to measure bullet markings microscopically, and
photograph them, and to say past all doubt that a certain fatal
bullet came out of a certain gun. Did any bullet from Billy's
gun come anywhere near any one of the three victims? Nobody
can say for sure. Was his bullet only one of many that entered
their bodies? Was somebody else's bullet straighter and more
deadly? No one knows. But the nature of the crime speaks for
itself. It was butchery from the ambushed protection of an
adobe wall, and even a ruse was necessary to entice the victim
to the spot. If that's "heroism," maybe somebody will be erect-
ing a monument one of these days to every paid killer hired by
Al Capone.

(4) Next we come to the killing of Bob Beckwith.* I know

---

* According to the Chavez manuscript, which seems worthy of belief on this point, this
man's real name was Roberto Becues. Julian's spelling is never to be taken positively for
gospel; however, he knew the man personally, and declares him to have been a half-breed,
the son of a Mexican mother and an American father—"*misto hijo de Mexicana y de
Americano.*"

of no reliable testimony denying that Billy did this killing. Most people think he did. Probably he did. The blood was shed in the turmoil of a general conflict.

Consider the circumstances. A major battle was fought between the two warring factions in the town of Lincoln, and was the culminating action of that war. Fifty or more partisans were engaged on both sides. The United States Army got into it too, in the person of a certain Colonel N. A. M. Dudley, commander of neighboring Fort Stanton, who seems to have acted in a role unlike that usually adopted by the Army. He came with a detachment of soldiers and a gatling gun, parked the military in the main street, and saw to it that the "right" side (the side he favored—the Murphy-Dolan partisans) got the breaks.

The McSween residence, in which Billy the Kid and a number of others held the fort, was fired and burned. While attempting flight from the burning building, Alexander McSween, who never carried a gun and did not on that occasion, was shot and killed. Beckwith, or Becues, an enemy partisan, rushed forward waving a pistol and yelling, so it is said:

"I killed McSween. I've won the reward."

"Yes!" cried Billy the Kid, who was still inside the burning building, "you won the reward all right." And shot him between the eyes, "killing him dead."

Maybe almost anybody under the circumstances would have done as much. Still, give the Kid all the credit the deed deserves.

(5) Billy was supposed to have added another notch to his gun by killing a bookkeeper, Morris J. Bernstein, employed at the Mescalero Indian Agency.

As Garrett tells it, Billy and a bunch of his pals rode up in plain sight of the agency and began stealing some horses, which in the nature of things was a fool thing to do. Bernstein witlessly said he would go and stop them, and though warned, tried it, and that sounds like another fool thing. To Bernstein's order to Billy to desist, says Garrett, "the only reply was from the Kid's Winchester."

Siringo copies the story from Garrett, and embroiders it, calling the killing the Kid's most cowardly act. Gratuitously,

Siringo adds that the Kid's excuse for shooting Bernstein had a
strong Hitlerian flavor—"He didn't like a Jew nohow."

What were the facts? They seem to be perfectly clear.
George Coe again was there, and has told the tale. He says that
their party consisted of six or eight Mexicans, and four Americans—Hendry Brown, Billy the Kid, Fred Wayte, and himself.
Their object, he affirms, was not horse-stealing, but to discover
what had happened to the body of Dick Brewer, their former
leader, after "Buckshot" Roberts had shot him in the battle of
Blazer's Mill. When they were within a mile or so of the Indian
Agency, Coe says, he and the other three Americans decided to
go to the far side of the canyon for a drink at a spring. Now,
the spring was out of the shelter of the trees, and the Mexicans,
who were scared, refused to go. While the four were in the act
of drinking, shots were heard. The four Americans mounted
three horses, Billy's horse having run away at the first shot, and
raced for cover. When they reached cover and came up with the
Mexicans, they learned that a party of five riders had approached, and the Mexicans had desperately opened fire, killing
one. The dead man was Bernstein.

"It is a matter of record," Coe points out, "that the Kid was
accused of this killing, tried for the offense and acquitted. Several writers have attributed this murder to him as one of the
most blood-curdling crimes of his career. Since I was present
at the time, I can testify that he had nothing whatever to do
with it."

So passes another "notch."

(6) Now we come to the sordid saloon killing of Joe Grant.
Again the credit for the blood spilled, if it can be called any
credit, seems justly due to Billy.

Grant was a Texas tough who apparently had it in for Billy,
and Billy heard of his intentions and threats. One day Billy
entered a saloon in Fort Sumner with a group of cowmen whom
he had invited in for a drink. Grant was there already, and he
was mean drunk. He made a lunge and grabbed a fine ivory-
handled pistol from the scabbard of one of the men who entered
with Billy, putting his own in place of it. Billy, who was
ostensibly friendly with Grant, asked for a look at the pistol.

Grant stupidly handed it over. Examining it, Billy saw that there were only three cartridges in the gun, and he whirled the chambers so that when next fired, the hammer would fall on a blank. He handed the pistol back to Grant, who thereupon got noisy behind the bar, began breaking the glassware, called Billy a liar, turned his gun on him, and pulled the trigger. Of course nothing happened, since the gun had been "fixed." Meanwhile, the Kid deliberately pulled his own gun, fired, and Grant fell dead.

Was this a "hero" act? Heroes supposedly fight fair. And these dice were loaded, so that Billy could hardly lose. Maybe Grant needed killing. But to me, the manner of his killing looks more like butchery than heroism.

(7) Jimmie Carlyle was a young blacksmith who had "hundreds of friends and not one enemy," according to Pat Garrett. "He was honest, generous, merry-hearted, quick-witted, and intelligent." And Billy the Kid killed him.

With three members of his cattle-stealing band, the Kid had been trapped by a posse in the roadhouse of Jim Greathouse. The posse called for a surrender. There was a parley, in the course of which Greathouse went to the posse for a talk, and stayed as a hostage while Carlyle, who was a member of the posse, went unarmed into the roadhouse to talk to the outlaws. It was agreed that if Jimmie was harmed in any way, Greathouse would be killed. Several hours passed. The time when Carlyle was to have returned passed. According to one story, some member of the posse fired a gun, and apparently Carlyle thought that Greathouse had been killed and his own life was now forfeit. Anyhow, he made a rush for the window, and leaped through it, taking sash, glass, and all. Billy fired at him, wounding him, and while he was trying to crawl away on hands and knees, Billy deliberately polished him off. During the melee, Greathouse escaped.

Again Billy's gun was notched by the murder of an unarmed, desperate man. The act of a "hero"?

(8) And now we come to Bell and Ollinger, Billy's last two killings—if he killed them both.

Pat Garrett, in the course of events, had been made sheriff.

The main figures in the Lincoln County War had been killed off, and the "war" had degenerated into a ragtag-and-bobtail affair. Billy the Kid was now a notorious cow thief, a pest and a neighborhood blight, operating over eastern New Mexico and western Texas, and it was part of Garrett's job to get him and end the pestiferous pilfering. Garrett eventually captured Billy, very tamely, at Stinking Springs, and landed him in jail. Tried on the charge of murdering Sheriff Brady, Billy was convicted, and was sentenced to be hanged on May 13, 1881. He was lodged in an upper room in the old Lincoln County Court House, and because this building was a very poor excuse for a jail, Billy was leg-ironed and handcuffed, and was guarded day and night by Deputy Sheriff J. W. Bell and Deputy Marshal Robert W. Ollinger.

On April 28, a little over two weeks before he was to be hanged, Billy escaped. Both of his guards were killed.

How did it happen? Everybody knows the weaknesses and frailties of human observation. I read about a fatal automobile collision in which two newspaper reporters and a magazine editor, all trained to observe expertly, were passengers in the cars involved, yet there were seven different eyewitness versions of what actually happened, and no two were near enough alike to enable a jury to return a verdict placing the guilt. It is not strange that no one knows exactly how Billy made his escape, since the two guards were killed, and no one else is known to have been on the spot, and Billy, having flown, was not doing much talking for publication.

All stories, however, agree that Ollinger had taken some other prisoners across the road to supper, leaving Bell alone with Billy. Garrett's version is that Billy asked to be taken to the latrine, which was downstairs and outside in the jail yard. On the way back, he says, Billy ran ahead of Bell upstairs, broke into the room containing the jail's arsenal, obtained a six-shooter, and shot Bell who was coming up the stairs. Garrett doesn't say who told him that this was what happened—maybe he just "deduced" it. George Coe's version is that Bell and Billy were playing cards while Ollinger was away; that Billy dropped a card as if by accident, and when Bell stooped to pick it up, Billy drew Bell's gun from its scabbard and threatened him with it; that Bell made a lunge to escape, and Billy shot him. Charlie Siringo rather spectacularly claims that Billy had starved himself so he could get one hand out of his handcuffs, and that on the fatal evening Bell was facing him reading a newspaper; that Billy released his hand, swung the cuffs and stunned Bell, grabbed the deputy's gun, and shot him. Martin Chavez, a friend of the Kid's, is quoted by Governor Otero as saying that a line had been drawn down the center of the room and Billy had been warned to stay on his side of it; but he deliberately crossed over and taunted Bell, and when the latter was off guard, grabbed his pistol. Others, nameless, say that a confederate on the outside shot Bell, that Billy did not do it.

Be all that as it may, Bell was killed, and for lack of any eyewitness accounts, we can only guess and conjecture how it happened. Anyhow, Billy took advantage of his death. He next seized a double-barrelled shotgun, and fired both barrels into the body of Ollinger when the latter rushed across the street to see what was up. Billy then is said to have called for a file and a horse, and after freeing himself, made good his escape. No killings were credited to him after that. And less than three months later, on the night of July 13, 1881, he himself was shot to death in the dark by Pat Garrett in Pete Maxwell's bedroom in old Fort Sumner.

So the tale of the killings is told. What does it add up to? What must we conclude? Was Billy the brave lad and noble "hero" that he has been made out to be? Did he really kill as many men as he was reported to have killed?

I think not. Nowhere near as many. As I read the record, it is fairly certain that he killed the half-breed Beckwith, Grant, Carlyle, and Ollinger. Probably he killed Bell too. That makes five. I think some of his bullets may have lodged in the bodies of Morton and Baker, Brady and Hindman, but whether his bullets alone would have been enough to kill, no one can say. Definitely, he did not kill Roberts and Bernstein. Of the nine in whose killing Billy conceivably may have had some share, three were shot down when unarmed: Morton, Baker, and Carlyle. Two were killed from ambush: Brady and Hindman.

One, Grant, was murdered after Billy had tampered with his victim's gun to make sure of an easy killing. That leaves three, and three only, whom Billy met on tolerably even terms: Beckwith, Bell, and Ollinger, and he killed them when his own life was in deadly danger. Such an analysis certainly removes a good deal of the glitter from the "hero" halo.

III

How, then, did the "hero" legend grow? In large part, apparently, it grew spontaneously out of the public's never-ending desire for a hero, and the mists and shadows that gather over all persons and events with the passing of time. There's a glamor about the cowboy's life, that is heightened by the thoughts of risks and dangers boldly met. It's hard to dramatize events without actors. Every play needs a hero. Billy the Kid has been cast in that role, and with the passage of time the facts have been distorted to make him fit the role according to the way we'd like to have had him be. Maybe the Robin Hood legends grew in the same way. Maybe a lot of "heroes" were just as insubstantial stuff in actual life. The Lincoln County War was a pretty sordid chapter in the history of the range, but it was nevertheless backgrounded against romance and color. There were hard-riding cowboys who were not afraid to fight hell itself for the lives and property of their friends, and the thought of them has always stirred the blood of arm-chair adventurers. Billy the Kid, a cow-country tough, happened to be enrolled on the "good" side in the Lincoln County War. He was admired by the likable and upright Tunstall. Perhaps his own insinuations about the unproved notches on his gun helped the stories about him to circulate. The fact that he died young was in his favor. The stories grew by what they fed on.

An important factor, too, was Pat Garrett. Probably a psychoanalyst would have a highfalutin word for him. I believe that Garrett felt a need to justify himself to himself and to the world. Governor Otero in a casual paragraph remarks: "In spite of the money and prestige which Pat Garrett secured for his services in killing the Kid, Tom O'Folliard, and Charlie Bowdre, the author has always felt that he regretted it."

Garrett and Billy had been good friends. But Pat killed Billy, and he was on the side of the law when he did it. As I said before, he always claimed that he had to do it; that Billy would have killed him if he hadn't killed Billy. But did Billy have a gun when Pat shot him? Pat always maintained that he did have. And John W. Poe, one of his deputies on that occasion, who later became president of the Citizen's National Bank of Roswell, in the reputable brief account which he wrote of Billy's death, said that Billy was carrying a six-shooter. But it was close to midnight when they met. The seeing wasn't good. Billy was admittedly in his stocking feet and almost completely undressed. And the first people to enter Pete Maxwell's bedroom after the shooting of Billy the Kid—Jesus Silva and an old Navajo Indian woman named Deluvina—both declared positively that Billy had no pistol.

Once more, who knows? The facts are clouded and the reports differ. Was Garrett secretly aware that he had shot an unarmed man? Did he purposely build up his victim in the book he sponsored and the stories he told, in order to justify himself? I knew Garrett, but I can't be sure of the answers to my own questions. Certainly he did build Billy up.

I first met Garrett at a wagon camp at the point of the White Sands, in New Mexico, when he came over to arrest a fellow. That was in 1889 or '90, eight or nine years after the dramatic killing of Billy. Garrett was a tall, slim, rawboned officer, with a black mustache and a very pleasant manner. I met him often afterwards at Santa Fe, Tularosa, Las Cruces, and elsewhere, and got to know him well. He was a rough-and-ready customer, a great lover of poker, with a good enough record in a hard line of work. He was made sheriff of Lincoln County on the theory that he would clean up Billy the Kid and other outlaws and cattle thieves; and he did that. But I have the impression that the rest of his life was haunted by ghosts from the Lincoln County War. In fact, it may have been one of these "ghosts" in the flesh that finally ended him, for he too died of a gunshot wound, under circumstances never fully explained. I think secret doubts about his own actions troubled him, and I believe he was driven to make Billy the Kid a more-than-life-size villain in order that Pat Garrett might be able to look Pat Garrett and the world straight in the eye. It's a curious and not impossible thought that he may have made the Kid a "hero," in order that he, the "hero" killer, might sleep easy at night![18]

IV

If he was not a "hero," then, what sort of chap was Billy the Kid?

We have the testimony of a lot of people that in certain moods he was a friendly and likable lad, with a sense of humor and a good singing voice, that he was undersized physically, with hands little larger than a woman's, a graceful dancer, polite and respectful to women, generally neat in personal appearance, and that he neither drank nor smoked to excess. Charlie Siringo met him at Tascosa, in Texas, in the late fall of 1878, when the Kid was over there disposing of a bunch of stolen horses, and Charlie writes:

"I found Billy the Kid to be a good natured young man. He was always cheerful and smiling. Being still in his 'teens, he had no sign of a beard. His eyes were a hazel blue, and his brown hair was long and curly. The skin on his face was tanned to a chestnut brown, and was as soft and tender as a woman's. He weighed about one hundred and forty pounds, and was five feet, eight inches tall. His only defects were two upper front teeth, which projected outward from his well shaped mouth."

George Coe says that when Billy bunked with him, most of one winter, he helped with all the chores and domestic work— "And I could not have asked for a better friend or companion."

Was he a wonderful shot? The testimony indicates that he was pretty fast with a gun, and coolheaded in using one in an emergency. Siringo has this to say: "While loafing in their camp, we passed off the time playing cards and shooting at marks. With our Colt's .45 pistols I could hit the mark as often as the Kid, but when it came to quick shooting, he could get in two shots to my one.'"*

Garrett's testimony was somewhat similar. Asked by a newspaper reporter whether the Kid was a good shot, he replied, "Yes, but he was no better than the majority of men who are constantly handling and using six-shooters. He shot well, though, and he shot well under all circumstances, whether in danger or not."

George Coe, according to his cousin, Frank Coe, was the best shot among the Tunstall-McSween men. Frank Coe is quoted by Governor Otero as follows: "When he could take plenty of time for aiming, George hit the mark, and in hunting he always brought down more game than all the rest of the party put together. The Kid, however, was by far the quickest with a pistol; he could empty all six chambers of a revolver while an ordinary man was firing his first shot. He never seemed to take aim, but appeared to have an instinctive control."

George Coe, in the 220 pages of his book, makes little or no mention of Billy's shooting skill, except to say in one place that the Kid while spending the winter with him, did become quite expert as a deer slayer. Once at a shooting match, Coe tells, Billy was beaten by some buffalo hunters, and to get even with them, challenged them to a match with his friend—George Coe. Billy bet his last dollar on Coe, and won a dollar a shot until he banked eight dollars. If Billy had been a super-marksman, Coe undoubtedly would have mentioned the fact. His friends say he was good enough, but no wizard.

If he was likable, there are many things to show that Billy was not above saving himself at the expense of others, and in property matters he was shifty or worse. Siringo relates an exploit which he says was told him by the Kid himself. The government had given a gang of Mexicans a contract to put up a lot of hay at twenty-five dollars per ton. As they drew their pay, Billy who was an expert at monte, won it from them at cards. When the government contract was completed, Billy's source of money gave out, and he didn't like that. "With his

---

* In a personal letter written to me from Venice, California, September 22, 1927, Siringo said in part: "I have known a few men who could shoot two pistols at the same time with accuracy. But Billy the Kid was not a two-gun man. John Wesley Hardin was."—N. M. C.

own hands," Siringo says, "he set fire to the haystacks one windy
night." The government had to let another contract at a
higher price for more hay, and again Billy was on hand to win
the money from the haymakers. There seems to be some reasonable doubt whether sharp practice of that kind is altogether
"heroic." Also, there are records of occasions when stolen cattle
were sold, and Billy allegedly kept the bulk of the proceeds,
giving his partners little or none of it.

And it seems as though Billy's action was deliberately despi-
cable, or downright cowardly, on the night when his friend and
partner, Tom O'Folliard, was shot and killed by Garrett's posse.
Billy was riding to town with several friends. He sensed danger,
and ducked. As George Coe, reporting the incident from hearsay, put it: "By a clever ruse he avoided them (Garret and his
posse). He left his gang about a mile from town and rode in
by another route"—leaving them to "take it!" Garrett's account of that incident is different: "With all his reckless bra-
very, the Kid had a strong infusion of caution in his composi-
tion when he was not excited. He afterwards told me that as
they approached the building that night he was riding in front
with O'Folliard. As they rode down close to our vicinity, he
said a strong suspicion arose in his mind that they might be
running into unseen danger.

" 'Well,' I said, 'what did you do?'

"He replied—'I wanted a chew of tobacco bad. Wilson had
some that was good and he was in the rear. I went back after
tobacco, don't you see?' and his eyes twinkled mischievously."

A few minutes after going back for his chew of tobacco,
thus taking his own hide out of the zone of danger, guns blazed
out of the blackness, and the Kid's good friend, Tom, riding in
front, received a mortal wound.

Billy, according to Garrett's report, declared that if ever he
were taken prisoner by the law, it would be a dead man that the
law got. "The Kid," says Garrett, "had sworn that he would
never give himself up a prisoner and would die fighting even
though there was a revolver at each ear, and I knew he would
keep his word." Yet at Stinking Spring, after spending a cold
night and day in an old stone shack, Billy and his three com-

CHARLES A. SIRINGO

Cowboy detective and writer, author of "20,000 Miles on the Hurricane Deck of a Spanish Pony," and other books, "Charlie" Siringo knew and upon occasion hunted many of the men who went on the dodge in the old West. He worked at one time for "Bad Man" Moore, and shot at targets with Billy the Kid.

panions never fired a shot when Garrett and his posse built a fire and cooked supper outside. "The odor of roasting meat was too much for the famished lads who were without provisions. Craving stomachs overcame brave hearts."

No! Making all allowances, I think Billy the Kid was short weight for a hero. But the legend has grown past stopping. Even those who denounce him, now, merely add volume to his fame.

COWBOY HUMOR

I

THE COW business contributed a brand of humor as peculiar to the range and as characteristic of it as cowboy songs. When a cowboy took a tumble, moral or physical, the normal reaction of his friends was not shallow sympathy, but belly-shaking laughter:

> That time when Bob got throwed
> I thought I sure would bust;
> I like to died a-laffin'
> To see him chewing dust.
>
> He crawled on that pinto bronc
> And hit him with a quirt,
> The next thing that he knew
> He was wallerin' in the dirt.
>
> Yes, it might 'a' killed him,
> I heard the hard ground pop,
> But to see ef he was injured
> You bet I didn't stop.
>
> I jest rolled on the ground
> And began to kick and yell;
> It liked to tickled me to death
> To see how hard he fell.

Cowpunching was a hard old game, but always a certain number saw the funny side. The humor of the cowboys grew out of what they knew: the day's work, range and roundup happenings, human nature, cow nature, horse nature. It ex-

pressed itself in picturesque, pungent, imaginative, vigorous
speech; in practical jokes and pretty rough horseplay; in liars'
tales that grew and grew around the campfires.

"I told 'em the truth," said old Hank at the Bar W wagon
one night. "They didn't believe me. When they asked me for
more talk, I told 'em a plain lie. They believed that all O. K."

Cowhands could be terse in speech, especially with strangers,
and the conversation generally did not flow freely unless they
felt well acquainted and at ease with their listeners. But the
country they lived in was extravagant and vivid, their way
of life was extraordinary, and extravagance and vividness of
speech as essential features of cowboy humor were natural
results. "Man," said the cowhand of a horse thief he captured,
"was he boilin' mad! So hot, the starch was jest a-boilin' outa
his collar."

"Do you know the country north o' here well?" a sheriff
asked a strange cowhand.

"Yep."

"How fer north?"

"Long way. Up to where the timber grows so tall it gets
skybound."

If a cowhand was rawhided by the wit of his friends, he
might wait a long while to get his own back all in one bounce.
Bill Gaines was an old bachelor till he was forty and more, then
surprised his friends by marrying one of the prettiest and most
popular girls in the country, not over half his age, taking her
to live in his shack on the Palo Duro. Bill was known as a very
tenderhearted fellow who never could stand to see any animal
suffer. If any old lumpy-jawed or crippled cattle, or sick horses,
were found on his range, they were promptly shot to put them
out of their misery. For this reason he had been nicknamed
"Humane" Bill. When he got married, his friends had plenty
of comments to make about the big difference in age between
his wife and himself. One of the biggest talkers on the subject
was Tom Yates, who was a cousin of Bill's young wife, Letty.
Every time Tom saw Bill, he would say something about it:
"Ain't yo' feel kind o' 'shamed of yourself, bein' a cradle robber?" Or, "Why don't you send her to school?" Or, "An old

stag like you, marryin' a young girl like that—ought to know
better!" Bill took it in good style, but he didn't forget any part
of it.

He went away for several months to join the big roundup
of the Tumble A. Since he couldn't leave his young wife alone
at his shack, and since she was almost as good a cowhand as he
was anyhow, he took her along, and she helped him move the
wild brush stock down out of the mountains. But towards the
end of the summer Bill appeared once more on the streets of the
little town, alone, and after he had h'isted a few, he was spied by
Tom Yates on the sidewalk in front of the Lone Ace Saloon.
Tom greeted his friend joyously, and asked where Letty was.
Bill's face went long, and tears started.

"Why, what's the matter?" said Tom.

"Ain't you heard?"

"I ain't heard nothin'."

"Letty's dead."

"Dead!" Tom's jaw dropped. "How'd it happen?"

"We was ridin' the rimrock, Tom, tryin' to crowd a bunch
of mossy-heads down into the canyon. Letty was ridin' that
churn-headed horse, Two-Bits, you know—"

"Yeah, I know."

"Well, he fell an' broke her leg."

"She didn't die of a broken leg!"

"No, but she was sufferin' somethin' terrible, an' I jest
couldn't stand it, Tom—I had to shoot her."

Even the best cowboy humor, out of its setting, was not always sidesplitting. It depended for its effect, in part, on allusions
to characters and facts familiar to the special audience. It was
grounded in the basic attitude on the range toward life, namely,
the feeling that any man in pants had as much right as any other
man alive to breathe the free air and to strut his stuff the best
he could, and the conviction that stuffed shirts were made
mainly to be ripped open. Cowboys never developed a mythical
range rider on the order of Paul Bunyan of the lumber camps,
but some of their tales were as tall as the mountains in whose
shadows they worked cattle. On a deer hunt that became
famous in story and song, the deer climbed the mountains

"straight up," and the hunter dived under water "five hundred feet or more" to shoot them, and once bent his gun in circles "and fired round a hill." He got so much money for his venison and skin that he had "taken it all to the barn door and it would not all go in." Smut of the hole-in-the-corner, nasty-little-boy brand, never played any large part in rangeland humor. True, cowboy language might need plenty of expurgating for parlor use or publication, but it wasn't whispered with a smirk or spoken out of the corner of the mouth. It had a lusty, husky quality, as did the life that the cowboys lived.

Humor, indeed, was the cowboys' play—about all they had to play with. There were no movies, no radio, no telephones, no phonograph records, few women, little society. The only stage plays they ever had a chance to see were on the order of "The Black Crook" or "Uncle Tom's Cabin"; and these they seldom did see unless they were in town at Christmas. Once or twice a year there might be a big revival meeting offering some amusement as well as spiritual consolation for tough-skinned sinners. There would be a dance now and then, but not often. For musical entertainment cowboys had to depend entirely on home talent. So humor was a kind of safety valve that cowboys could always use to let off pent-up steam—a way of playing and amusing themselves, a way to keep from being too sorry for themselves for all the hard work and lonesomeness.

I have been around cowboys, sailors, and sheepherders most of my life, and all of them were more or less lonely men in isolated places, doing hard work, and it was humor, at bottom, that kept them all going. But the humor of all was different. I was born on the sea, and we had a summer home at Newport, and by the age of ten I knew every yard and sail on vessels coming through the port. One summer I shipped on a boat and went up to Newfoundland, and was gone three months. The sailors aboard that boat as well as the sailors I knew on the old clippers that had rounded the Horn, had a wonderful sense of humor, but the subjects of their humor all pertained to the sea.

I married a sheepman's daughter and have been with sheepherders quite a lot. They have a sense of humor too. But their humor pertains to happenings of the sheep camps, lambing time, and things like that.

The humor of cowpunchers had an entirely different set of subjects, different modes of expression, a different flavor.

Naturally, cowboys differed as much as other humans in their capacity for humor. There were certain men in every cow camp that the others liked to ride with, because they were good at telling droll stories and making you laugh and helping the time to pass agreeably. It was a gift with them, and some of them practiced it consciously and with considerable artistry. A puncher's story might be something he had seen or read. But it always had a certain individual fillip because of his way of handling the material. He would see it a certain funny way, and put his special interpretation on it, usually in cow terms.

II

A typical humorist of the range, an artist of his kind, unknown to fame except such as passed by word of mouth from cowboy to cowboy and from camp to camp, was Rip Van Winkle—"Old Rip," we called him. Nigger Add used to say of him, "He's the drolliest man I ever saw." There was a young Rip, the old man's son, who was apt to be rather quiet in his father's presence, but who, when he was alone, could sure string you along with some tall ones. Father and son often worked the cow camps together. I sometimes thought they were always welcome to a job, not so much because they were extra good hands, but because they kept everybody in a good humor.

Old Rip had this quality of the true humorist, namely, that he could always see a joke on himself. He was funny even to look at, and all his talk was salty. Once after he had been working in Arizona for a long spell, I asked him why he had come back to New Mexico.

"Well," he said, "out in Arizona, folks kinder got tired lookin' at me, but here, I'm a real curiosity."

I asked if he were going back.

"No," he said; "I aim to lay around here and lick salt till spring, anyway."

Two men rode up to the ranch one day and I remarked to Rip that they looked like brothers. "No," he said, being acquainted with them, "those two never came out of the same pasture. They just naturally think in different languages."

Nobody could tell by looking at him how old Rip was. One day one of the ranch hands came right out and asked him. "I'm hecked if I know," was the reply. "I runned away from home when I was just a little old baby."

Old Rip wore a long goatee, which cowhands were fond of giving a yank from behind. He always took after his tormentors with a quirt. But it was just in fun. I never saw him lose his temper. He had little or no education. I am not even sure whether he could read. One of his stories implied that he could not. It had to do with an eye doctor in Chicago who, according to Rip, was a holdup, a swindler, and a shyster. This is how Old Rip reached that conclusion. He went to Chicago with some cattle, he said, and while walking up South Clark Street from the stock yards, stopped to get a drink and heard two fellows talking, one of them saying to the other that he was having trouble with his eyes, and was going across the street to get a pair of glasses so he could read. Old Rip followed along, and this doctor put up a board in front of him with numbers of different sizes, then handed him a pair of glasses in a leather case and charged him ten dollars.

"When I got back to my hotel," Rip said, "I bought a nickel newspaper and went upstairs and laid down on the bed and held the paper up in front of me. And fellers, I couldn't read a word."

"Why, Rip," somebody said, "you don't even know how to read."

"Well," he said, "that's no reason for that doctor swindlin' me. He said plain as could be, he'd guarantee I could read with them ten-dollar glasses."

Literate or not, Old Rip had a natural gift for seeing the funny side of things, and it was often funnier to hear him tell about an incident than to be present and see it yourself. I was at the revival meeting the night Tom Jones, the notorious cow thief got religion. What I saw was good for a snicker, but that was about all. But when I heard Old Rip describe it afterwards, I realized how much I had missed. Rip described Tom's big open mouth and bulging eyes—how he held the baby in his lap during the oratory, how he started for the altar to heed the hurry call for sinners, how he tripped over somebody's wooden leg sticking out in the aisle, how the baby flew one way, Tom another, and how Tom,. hell-bent for salvation, gathered himself up and marched straight ahead with a holy glow, never minding where the baby went.

Old Rip went to Santa Fe with Buss Rogers to attend some kind of a convention. Buss, according to Old Rip, hired a hack to fetch a case of beer from a blind tiger a mile or so away, and what with the weight of the beer and Buss's big feet, the bottom fell out of the hack and dropped Buss in the middle of the road. The hack driver was kind of deaf, Rip said, and when Buss yelled at him to stop, he thought Buss wanted him to drive faster, and whipped up his horses. "Buss sure had a foot race," said Rip. "He got back alive but lost all the beer, and the next morning I had to pay his fine for punching the hack driver's nose. No more conventions for me, no siree!"

Old Rip's tallest stories generally ended with a reference to a mythical cowman, Bill Jones, whom no one on the range had ever seen: "You may not believe that, damn you! But I could prove it if old Bill Jones was only alive."

Old stories looked new when Old Rip told them. I once heard him tell about a "wonderful bad stammerer" he said he met on the Frio River seventy-five miles south of San Antonio, who would "paw just like a horse," he got so mad trying to say what he wanted to. Rip innocently asked this stranger how far it was to "San Antone." He imitated the poor fellow's futile efforts to reply, and his final "Aw hell! You can g-g-git thar before I can tell you."

And he told about a man who was sent to Phoenix, Arizona, as the representative of a big New Mexico cattleman, and who was enthusiastic about the hospitality he had received. Prominent citizens, he said, met him at the station with a brass band, and rode him in style to the best hotel, where they gave him "a regular Arizona breakfast," which, he declared, consisted of a big bologna sausage, a bottle of whiskey, and a yellow dog.

"What," he was asked, "was the yellow dog for?"

"To eat the bologna!"

And Bill Jones could prove it!

Young Rip was going to Deming on the train one time to watch Old Grey John run a race. The train was so crowded that the only seat he could find was one occupied by a priest, who had his grip on the cushion beside him. Young Rip walked up and down the aisle several times eyeing the priest, that being the first time he had ever seen a gentleman of the cloth, and finally he screwed up the courage to ask if he could sit beside him. The priest moved his grip and Young Rip sat down, but the cowboy, having already had a few drinks, couldn't keep his eye off the priest and the strange clothes he had on. In the next fifty miles Young Rip several times offered the priest a drink out of his bottle, which each time was politely refused. At length he could stand it no longer. "You can drink with me or not, as you think best," he said, "but you're drunk. Anybody could tell that. Why, even your blankety-blank collar is turned hindside foremost."

The embarrassed priest abandoned his half of the seat and Young Rip had it to himself all the rest of the way to Deming.

One night Old Rip was occupying a narrow bed in a hotel in Silver City. The town was crowded, and a big fat man came into Rip's room and started to undress. Hoping to discourage him from occupying the other half of the bed, Rip remarked that he was subject to fits and liable to have one any time. "I don't mind," said the stranger. "Confidentially, I got a sure cure for fits right here." And he carefully laid his six-gun beside him and climbed in.

Once when Old Rip was guiding a party of Easterners on a camping trip, they passed a lake bed which for some reason happened to be dry, while all the other lakes around it were full of water, and a woman in the party wanted to know why that was. There wasn't any reason for it that anybody could give, except the peculiarity of the rainfall that year, but that didn't stop Old Rip.

"Lady," he said, "last year a party of Dutchmen camped and fished here, an' caught a lot of fish. They brought plenty of grub along, also beer, and a barrel of pretzels. When they left, they found they had almost half a barrel of pretzels left, an' not carin' to haul 'em away, they dumped 'em in the lake. That's why that there lake is dry."

"I don't see—"

"Ma'am," explained Rip, "the fish ate them pretzels an' got so thirsty they drank up all the water."

Once both Old Rip and Young Rip, having two months' wages in their pockets, went to town, with the customary result that their thirst was flooded out completely. Somehow the two became separated, and Old Rip bedded down in a camp house to get over his spree. After he had been there sound asleep for two or three days, the owner of the campground, who was a good friend of Rip's, thought he ought to be awakened, for fear he would lose his job if he didn't get back to the ranch. But repeated efforts to pry him out of the bed, failed. Rip would answer his friend when he called or knocked, but he wouldn't unlock the door or get up. The camp man had a pet monkey and one of his neighbors had a big bear cub. With these two, and a pass key, the two men entered Old Rip's room. They lifted the bed covers, deposited the monkey and the bear on Rip, and made a hasty exit, locking the door again as they left. Nature took its course, and pretty soon a wild yell was heard inside the room. The door handle was given a twist, but the door didn't give, and two seconds later Old Rip himself shot out head first through the flimsy partition wall, having created a new exit in order to save himself from the imps that he believed the devil himself had sent.

Old Rip was a range type, a natural story teller, better than many a monologist I have heard on the stage. Nobody was expected to believe much that he or Young Rip said. They made the wildest exaggerations with perfectly sober faces, and that was the cowboys' way. It was part of the attitude, maybe something in the air, but it was grass-roots humor, often with a strong tinge of irony, though no cowhand ever used that two-ton word.

III

Humor, in fact, solved far more range problems than the six-gun ever did. Big talk, as a rule, wasn't pooh-poohed, ridiculed, or shot out. Instead, situations were invented where the big talker either had to put up or shut up. If a fellow bragged about how good a rider he was, maybe he would be given the gentlest horse in the pasture, with a cocklebur under the saddle blanket. When he got aboard, something happened right then! If the bragger really could ride, the cowhands welcomed him into the fraternity, and the laugh was on them. One of the favorite cowboy songs and situations dealt with the "educated feller" who talked bigger than Pikes Peak about ridin' 'em high, and who fooled everybody by riding even bigger and better than he talked.

Chronic soreheads were bad news in cow camps. If any showed up, Christians were soon made of them. The worst kind of sorehead was the average disagreeable cuss for whom nothing was right, or for whom nothing that *you* knew was as good as something that *he* knew. Maybe you told about your slick little cutting horse. "Aw," he'd say, "you ought to see" *his* much slicker little cutting horse!

Some of these pests were put into popular cowboy songs. "Top Hand," as sung in unexpurgated form on the range, was probably one of the "blisteringest" humorous pieces of poetry ever strung together anywhere. The song as I expurgated and printed it, and now accepted as the King James version, is very tame by comparison. Cowboys had direct treatment for soreheads when other methods failed. There was always the wagon tongue, for example. Somebody would give the "patient" a push when he was standing unsuspectingly near the tongue. Over it he would go, face down. A couple of the boys would jump on him and hold him, while others took his pants down and applied their leather leggings where these would do the sinner's soul most good. A few of the victims would get up from this kind of treatment ready to fight. But they had to fight the whole bunch, and that was a sobering thought. Generally one dose of this medicine taught a man considerable self-control and resulted in a mending of his ways, but soreheads who couldn't take it generally left the outfit, which was a cause of rejoicing for those who remained.

"That kind of a man," Pete Johnson of the Bar W used to say, "is bad for the *morrals*."*

Any fellow with unpopular habits made his own bed on the range, and generally it had cactus in it. Old Tom Mews made a pest of himself by chronic borrowing. One day after working for hours in the branding pens at the calf roundup, he went to sleep in his bedroll with his pants tucked under his head, the bottoms sticking out. Now the pants were crusted with salt from dried sweat, and an old steer, starved for salt, came along and started to eat them. That steer gnawed Tom's pants off clear up to the knees before Tom woke up and pulled what was left out of the steer's mouth. True to his parsimonious nature, Tom didn't have a second pair of jeans along, and he tried to borrow some. Not a soul in the roundup crew could (or would) let him have a pair, and everybody felt that strict justice was done when Tom had to ride to town to buy him a new pair, with his skinny old legs bare to view and all the breezes.

Tobacco was one of the things that Tom was always borrowing. No need for him to borrow, he earned as much wages as anybody, but he was just too stingy to lay in a supply of his own. At the end of one beef drive we were paid off in twenty-dollar bills. The cook was taking the wagon to town for a load of supplies, and asked if anybody wanted anything.

"Git me a little Duke's Mixture," said Tom.

"Gi' me your money."

Tom had nothing smaller than one of the twenty-dollar bills just handed to him for his pay. Grudgingly, he handed it over. When the cook returned, the first thing Tom did was to call for his change.

"Change?" said the cook. "You didn't say nothin' about change, Tom. I supposed you wanted to pay back what you been borryin'. Here y'are, fellers!" And he dumped out a *whole case* of Duke's Mixture.

---

* Pete knew what he meant, but was a little mixed in his terms. He meant "morale," of course; a *morral* is a nosebag used for feeding grain to a cowboy's horse.

Greenhorns had to be initiated on the range, the same as elsewhere. For them the badger game was an old cowland favorite. I understand some people still don't know how the badger game was played, though it was one of the cultural high lights of the Old West. Several cowhands, including the greenhorn, would be riding to town, and an air of mystery would be fostered by little remarks here and there. A couple of boys would be told to go ahead and pick up the fiercest looking dog they could find. Naturally the newcomer would be itching to know what all the mystery was, and sooner or later he would ask.

"Badger fight," he would be told, but he would be warned to say nothing about it to anybody, otherwise they might all find themselves in the *jusgado*. "Ever seen a badger fight?"

The greenhorn hadn't, of course. The other hands would grudgingly agree to let him take part in it, provided he'd be careful not to do any talking. It was always staged after dark in some old shed or stable. The badger, which was half-starved so he would be readier to fight, was kept under a weighted box with a rope tied around his neck. Everything was got ready, including the dog and the audience, then it was necessary to upset the box and give a hard yank so the badger would come out fighting. As a special favor, the task of freeing the badger was always assigned to the greenhorn. Of course when he yanked the rope, what came out was a nice white bedroom pot, an' the drinks were on him.

The sort of thing that tickled cowboys was the incident of the Englishman in the West who was found on the brink of a flowing creek practically dying of thirst, when a cowboy came along and asked him what the trouble was. "My word, my man," said the Englishman, "have you a tin cup about you?"

It also tickled them to think of another Englishman, Lord Lincoln, who, being new in the West and unfamiliar with the peculiar clarity of the atmosphere which makes the judgment of distances very deceptive for strangers, bet that he could easily walk in half a day from the railroad station in the town of Florida (pronounced Flor-ee'-da) to Cooks Peak, which looked to him to be not more than ten miles away. He started out strong enough early in the morning and in the middle of the afternoon was found by a cowboy on the bank of a little creek

about halfway to the mountain. He was stripping off all his
clothes. The cowboy wanted to know what in the name of a
mermaid he was doing that for. The Englishman replied that
he didn't want to get 'em wet while swimming the river.

"River!" said the cowboy, "why, mister, that's just one drink
for a dry steer. You can step across it."

"You can't spoof me, my good fellow," said the disillusioned
but determined Britisher. "I shall swim it, though I may be
an hour in the water."

And he dove in, head first.

Little spontaneous things were always happening. Pete
Johnson, foreman of the Bar W, gave Walker Hyde, one of his
hands, a kick in the bedroll, and said, "Get up, you little
shrimp!" Pete was five-feet-five, Walker six-feet-four.

A couple of cowhands were watching a *fiesta* parade in
Santa Fe. "Wonder what's the idea?" one said. "Dunno," said
the other; but drew on his knowledge of cow critters for the
guess that "they must be goin' to water."

A cowhand at a dance didn't like the way a certain girl was
dressed, and told some of his friends she must be a damn fool.
The girl's two brothers heard of the remark, and said the cowboy
would have to apologize. They walked him up to the lady, one
on either side, and this was his apology: "Excuse me for talkin'
that way; you ain't no damn fool."

Another cowhand at a dance thought he would take pity on
a homely girl who had been sitting alongside the wall all evening without a partner, and in the kindness of his heart, he
went up and asked her to have the next dance with him. She
looked down her long nose and declined. Naturally, he was
flabbergasted. "Why," he said, "you long-legged, sour-faced
old virgin!"

A cowboy told about the recommendation with which
Chuck Withers attempted to set up his daughter in the eyes of
a prospective suitor. The girl was getting a little "long in the
tooth," and her pa was anxious to see her married off. "Callie
ain't had much eddication," Chuck said, "but she sure can take
a calf by the tail and throw it over the corral fence."

Jim Brownfield, who ranched near me in the San Andrés
country, used to go to El Paso with his wagons once a year to buy

supplies. Jim was a natural dry as to liquor, and that was about the only time of the year he ever fell off the water wagon, but he would fall then, good and hard. After one of these trips he came home thoroughly plastered, and the next morning his daughter went in to see how he felt. He said he felt terrible.

"Could you eat somethin', pa?"

No, he said, he couldn't touch a bite. His daughter knew he was very fond of soft-boiled eggs, and she had some fresh eggs on hand, which in the cow country were about as scarce as tigers in prairie-dog holes. She asked Jim if he didn't think a nice soft-boiled egg would be good for him.

"Daughter," he said, "I'm feelin' awful puny. Just bile me up ten or a dozen."

Cowboys could play a hard joke on a man they liked very much. Three brothers, Len, Larry, and Will Jacobs, owned about twenty-five miles along the Frio River in Texas. They originally came from New York, but to look at them, you would have thought they were native Westerners. Len, the oldest, was naturally a very reserved man, and never got over it. He was the kind of man who never looked at a woman, and would turn pink if one looked at him. One year he was going home to New York for the Christmas holidays, and the boys decided to give him a blowout at the Brown Hotel in San Antone, and some of the young fellows thought they ought to do something. So, in the middle of the dinner, which was held in a private dining room, there was a loud knock on the door. Somebody yelled, "Come in!" A great big fat smiling colored mammy waddled in holding a coal-black pickaninny in her arms. She went straight up to Len.

"Mr. Len," she said, "we hears you is gwine away, so Ah thought Ah'd bring little Len in to kiss his pappy good-by."

Poor Len turned all colors and never did open his mouth.

IV

A favorite story-telling time on the range was after supper around the campfire. If it wasn't your turn on guard with the herd, or if you weren't catching up on sleep so as to go on guard, that's when you had a little leisure for cards or talk, and it was

then that song singers sang if they were present. That was the
time when the tall stories grew tallest. Anything might start
the storytelling, and it might end anywhere.

"Anybody seen old Hennery Gibbs lately?" some cowhand
might ask.

"Yeah," another would say, "I seen him. He was telling
about an air-o-plane ride."

"Hennery Gibbs? Why, he never even seen an air-o-plane."

Gradually the story would come out with all the explicit
details, a repeat of one of Hennery's own tall tales, for which he
was famous. He was one of the best game hunters in the state,
and a popular guide for hunting parties, but he rarely left the
high mountains where he lived alone. It seemed that Hennery
had been guiding a party of Eastern tourists in which there was
a little girl named Nancy. When they left for home, Nancy
made Hennery a present of a tiny pearl-handed knife of which
she was very fond. In gratitude, Hennery promised to send her
a little cub bear just as soon as he could catch one. One day he
was trailing a horse that had strayed, and came across a big
hollow pine stump twenty feet high. The bark was all clawed
by some animal climbing up and down, and Hennery saw it
was a bear tree with probably some bear cubs inside, just what
he had been wanting for his little friend Nancy. So he climbed
the stump and let himself down inside by his hobble rope. Just
as he thought, he found the bear cubs, and he wrapped one of
them up in his shirt and was all ready to leave, when suddenly
the daylight was shut out inside the tree. Looking up, Hennery
saw the stern end of the mamma bear backing down like
Hennery himself had done, and he knew at once that she
wouldn't approve of his taking one of her cubs. Also, he didn't
fancy being on the under side of a thousand pounds of fighting
she-bear. The storyteller would drag out the details here till
somebody asked impatiently, "How did Uncle Hennery git
out?"

"Air-o-planed out!

"Yes, sir! Uncle Hennery did things quick when he got
around to it. He grabbed hold of the bear's tail with his left
hand, and Nancy's little knife with the right, and began prick-

Photograph by New Mexico State Tourist Bureau.   STORY-TELLING TIME

After supper was a favorite story-telling time on the range. Then, if it wasn't a cowboy's turn on guard, he had a little leisure for talk, and tales grew taller and taller till they hit the moon.

SOLID RANCH COMFORT
Cigar, newspaper, rockin' chair, and all outdoors—and a wife to do the chores! This picture of Jack was snapped by "Blarney" (Mrs. Thorp) shortly after their marriage in 1903. Jack never approved of it because of the uncommonly heavy growth of catclaw and mesquite under his nose.

ing that bear in the tenderest part of her behind. An' when she
hit the top o' the stump, she just spread herself out an' sailed,
Uncle Hennery hangin' on by her tail till they come to a good
landin' field t'other side o' Hennery's horse pasture."

Any story that a cowboy heard or read might be given local
trimmings and told as if it had happened to somebody we all
knew. Tollie Sands was supposed to be the homeliest man without exception in the Guadalupe Mountains, but his wife Eliza
thought he was the last edition of some Greek god. She was so
jealous of a widow lady in town whom she suspected of having
unmaidenly designs on him that Tollie had a hard time keeping
any hair on the top of his head. The story was told that one day
a peddler came to the house and showed Tollie a mirror, a thing
which he had never seen or heard of before. Tollie looked in it
for a long time and admired what he saw.

"How much for this picture?" he asked. He paid the cash
the peddler asked and kept it.

Later, Eliza, who had been away gathering wood at the time,
was snooping in Tollie's things, and came across the mirror. "So
that's the sour-faced hussy you been chasin', is it!" she said, and
smashed the mirror over Tollie's head.

My one-time partner, Dan Grigsby, came from the mountains of Kentucky. He had a story about his Aunt Jane, who
was engaged in the moonshine business. She was finally caught
and taken to Louisville for court action. While staying in a
hotel there, waiting for her case to be called, she heard shots
one night and went out in the hall to inquire what had happened. She was told that a prominent citizen had just been shot
in the rotunda. "Ah! then the poor feller's a goner!" declared
Aunt Jane. Up in the mountains, she said, she had known of
people being shot in all sorts of places and getting well, but
never one that was shot in the rotunda. Dan told this story time
and again in the cow camps, and the fillip to it was the fact that
there was always some cowhand in camp who didn't know what
a rotunda was and sooner or later asked to be shown the exact
location of this vulnerable organ.

Troy Hale told the tragic story of John Cox and his brand
new wife, Eda May. Troy said he was on his way to Concho,

Arizona, and rode down from the Indian Mesa to John's cabin in the lonely salt lake region. He found John baking bread, which surprised him, because he knew his friend had been married not long before to a good-looking girl from Utah. After a meal shared by just the two of them, Troy couldn't hold in his curiosity any longer, and had to inquire about the absent bride.

"She got mad an' went home," John said, "after she was locked up."

It seemed that neither John nor his wife had ever had much first-hand experience of towns, and their reading knowledge of the crowded cities was very limited. In fact, there was no reading matter at all in their cabin except a book on saddles, a mail-order catalog, and a copy of a "wild west" magazine. Now in the magazine there was a story about kidnappers that impressed them both very much, and they read it over and over and discussed what they would do if they ever found themselves in similar circumstances. After they had been married several weeks, they saddled up and went to the county seat to see the circus and enjoy a delayed honeymoon.

Eda May never had stopped in a hotel, in fact, she had never been in a town with more than one street and a hitching post. She got to thinking about those kidnappers in the magazine, and when John said he would go down and get a haircut and shave, she fretted at being left alone, and John wasn't any too easy in his mind, so they reckoned the safest thing was for John to lock the door on the outside and take the key. Downstairs, a lot of his old cowpuncher friends jumped him and took him off to the bar. One thing led to another, till John found himself in a poker game facing the biggest winning streak he ever had run into. The game lasted all evening and all night and away into the next afternoon. John then had a stack of chips in front of him so high that he could hardly see over the top of them and one of the biggest jackpots of the game was lying on the table. He stayed with a pair of queens, drew three cards, and got the other two queens. It must have been the sight of so many female women in one hand, he told Troy Hale, that reminded him of Eda May. He jumped up, knocking over all the chips.

COWBOY HUMOR211

"Wait!" the others yelled. "You can't quit now."

"If there's anythin' left of me in fifteen minutes, boys," John promised, "I'll be back. But I done left Eda May locked up in a room for twenty-four hours, *an' I ain't neither fed nor watered her!*"

Cowpunchers had many sad experiences going to big cities and having their money taken by smart guys, so there was salt for them in the story Solemn and Squatty told when they came back to Hachita, New Mexico, after delivering six carloads of horses to New Orleans. They collected their return passage and some money, they said, then started out to see the town. They woke up in their hotel room next morning with empty pockets and no idea where the money had gone. Their only cash was a fifty-cent piece that had dropped through a hole in Squatty's pocket and landed in his boot. They were half-starved and decided they would go to the commission man and strike him for a loan, only to learn that it was Sunday and also the beginning of the "Mad Grass" (Mardigras) festival, and nobody would do a stroke of work for a week. Their problem was to get a full meal for two with the fifty cents. They walked, they said, till they came to a little restaurant with a sign in the window announcing roast turkey and all the fixings for thirty-five cents.

"How does that sound to you?" said Solemn.

"That's my kind of fodder," said Squatty.

"Foller me!" The restaurant man gave them a predatory look as they stalked in, but this gradually changed as the meal progressed. Over the soup Solemn remarked casually but in a carrying voice, "Don't you think I done right, Squatty, to shoot that restaurant man last night?"

"You couldn't hardly a done nothin' else," said Squatty soberly.

Big helpings of turkey replaced the empty soup plates. Solemn idly twirled the cylinder of his six-gun. "That fellar didn't treat us right."

"He was meaner 'n a sidewinder in a hot skillet."

The restaurant man asked if they would have anything more. Solemn said he believed he'd have the same meal, repeated. "That'll suit me, too," said Squatty. Two more big platters of turkey were brought, and these likewise disappeared.

"That there feller brought his troubles on himself," Solemn continued, "chargin' us more 'n a quarter apiece for a meal."

"Yeah, he brought 'em on himself."

The punchers had ice cream and cake, they said, and half a pie apiece, and they topped off with good cigars. Then they asked the restaurant man how much they owed him.

"W-would twenty cents apiece be about right?" he asked.

During the yearly roundup on the Closed-H range, we usually worked some ten cowhands, with a daily average of fifteen stray men representing other cow outfits that had cattle on our range. These stray men would bring news from distant points. We had plenty of augering, and it was an old custom that all the men working on the roundup should meet the first night at the chuck wagon and contribute to the general amusement by telling a story, singing a song, or doing a dance. Anybody who refused was sure to get a dose of the leggings over the wagon tongue. Most of the stories that were told were strongly on the order of the tall tale. From yarns told at different times by cowpunchers at the wagon, the following are a few of many that I collected and wrote down at the time or soon afterward in the lingo of the range as they were told.*

WAGON WHEELS

Ike Clubb told how, years before, he went over into Arkansas to buy cattle, as they were cheap over there in those days. He and his hands started out early in the spring with a chuck wagon and *remuda*. They crossed Oklahoma and the big river, and got into Arkansas, where the population, Ike said, consisted mostly of hillbillies and swamp angels. After a while the outfit worked out of the swamp lands and into the hills of the Black Mountain country, and everywhere they went, he said, they created a lot of excitement. In those days everyone living in Arkansas either traveled afoot or on horseback, or in a two-wheeled cart, with which it was easy to dodge the stumps. Mon Tate, who was the cook with Ike's outfit, noticed that when he

---

* I put these and some more in somewhat different shape in my little book, *Tales of the Chuck Wagon*. But as I published that book myself, and didn't hardly sell more than three million copies of it, maybe you didn't read them there.—J. T.

was driving the chuck wagon, folks kept watching every move he made. Most of them were ragged and barefooted, with snuff-sticks hanging out of their mouths, "plumb eaten up with chills an' fever, an' takin' quinine an' Black Draught as regular as their meals."

Finally, Ike said, he got quite a bunch of little swamp cattle together and started west, buying a few more from time to time as he went along. One evening he was bringing a little bunch up to the wagon to throw with the herd, when he saw someone dodge behind a tree. Not knowing what to think, he told Mon Tate to keep a close watch on the wagon and camp as the fellow he had seen might be wanting to steal something. Next day he again saw someone dodge behind a tree, and leaving the herd, he jumped his horse over to where he had seen the man disappear, but in the thick underbrush he couldn't find spit nor sign of him.

After buying all the cattle he could get, Ike's crew started for the river, and upon arriving at its banks, bedded down the herd and camped for the night. Ike said as he went on guard he saw a man running through the big trees along the river banks, but although he took after him, the man got away in the dark. Riding back to the wagon he told the boys about it, and warned them whenever they were on guard, to be sure and pack their six-shooters, as you never could tell what mischief these swamp hounds might be up to. However, nothing happened, and the next morning they swam the herd across the river and got into No Man's Land, as it was then called.

During the whole next week nothing happened, but one morning just as the herd was going off the bed ground, Ike saw a man afoot come out of a sand arroyo looking like the same fellow whom he had seen dodging around the camp. Ike jerked down his rope, took after him, and after quite a run, caught him. Ike said he was the skinniest feller he had ever seen, "so skinny he could a gone to bed and had him a good sleep in a shot-gun barrel." Ike marched his prisoner to the camp where the other punchers had just arrived with the herd.

"What have you got to say fer yourself?" he asked.

"Nothin', Mister. I ain' er-meanin' no harm."

"Ain't you the same feller that has been dodgin' around our camp ever since we left the mountains in Arkansas?"

"I be."

"What's the idea o' follerin' us? Are you tryin' to git away with somethin'?"

"No, I bein't."

"Look here!" said Ike, getting tough, "if you don't tell us what you mean by hangin' around out outfit. we're aimin' to shoot you full o' holes, and likewise murder an' kill you. Get that?"

"Please, Mister, I ain't a-meanin' no harm."

"Then why are you follerin' us?"

"Please, sir, I never did see a wagon with two sets o' wheels before, and I was jest follerin' to see when the big ones behind was a-goin' to catch up with the little ones in front."

A STACK OF REDS

Old George, who lived in the Estancia Valley, said he was getting fed up with drouth and bad company. "I tell yer," he said, "the whole valley's gone to the devil. Newcomers from the East come an' take up all the land—closes'-fisted bunch I ever seen, most of 'em from Illinois. I'm jest about as lonesome with this bunch as old Slabs Tyson said the cowpuncher was who died an' went to heaven. When he got there, all the men folks had dress suits on, their vests cut 'way down to their waistband, an' tails on their coats 'most to their heels. All the women had on lace clothes, an' not much o' them.

"Well, the old puncher was jest rigged out regular, and these high-toned folks turned their noses up at him an' wouldn't speak. This went on for some time, till at last one day he saw St. Peter and asked as a special favor if he couldn't get a pass to go down to hell for a few days and see some of the boys, as there wasn't anybody where he was that he was acquainted with. As he'd behaved pretty well, St. Peter gave him a round-trip ticket good for a week, and off he goes.

"Well, the very first person he met after he arrived was an old puncher from his home town, who takes an' leads him aroun' an' shows him the sights. Presently they come to an old barn, an' goin' in there, they sees about a thousand people all settin' 'round. They had candles stuck in old bottles and all of 'em was a-playin' poker; some of 'em the puncher did know and some he didn't.

"Pretty soon the old feelin' come over him, an' he jest got to itchin' to horn in, especially when he seen what a little some of 'em did know about the national game. As he didn't have any money, and all the boys he knew seemed 'bout broke, he was in a terrible fix. But at last, after gunnin' 'round among the different players, he noticed a feller that was dressed up fit to kill and seemed kind of out o' place in that bunch, though he sure had a swell stack o' chips in front of him. The puncher got to talkin' to the dude, an' told about gettin' a ticket from St. Peter, good fer a week, and after then he'd have to return to heaven. One word brought on another, till at last he swapped his return ticket to heaven fer the dude's pile o' chips, sayin' he'd rather live in hell with a bunch o' punchers than in heaven with them damn high-toned dudes."

THE PUNCHER AND THE NUGGET

Tom Beasley was given a gold nugget from the Klondike by a stranger for whom he did a favor, and the story of what happened to the nugget was told by Chalk, Tom's old side partner. Tom, by the way, had a good singing voice, and he was credited with the authorship of *Little Adobe Casa*, which he sang often in the cow camps, the chorus going as follows:

> The roof is ocateo,
> The coyotes far and near;
> The Greaser roams about the
>   place all day;
> Centipedes and tarantulas
> Crawl o'er me while I sleep
> In my little adobe casa on the plains.

"Spring," said Chalk, "comes on, an' Tom's back, I guess, commenced to itch. Anyway he got the movin' fever, drew his money an' pulled out fer El Paso, givin' the excuse that he'd got a letter from home and had to go—funny, how a puncher never will own up he jest wants to lay off an' get drunk.

"Well, the second night Tom rolls into El Paso, and it didn't take him long to hunt up the Wigwam an' Astor House. He lays around town for a couple o' weeks, playin' monte and drinkin' his share, attendin' all the Mexican *bailes,* an' takin' in the bull fights across the river, till his money began to get low. He was standin' one night in the doorway o' the Astor House, and overheard two men beside him talkin' about a man who was passin'. One, it seems, asks who the man was. 'Henry Heap,' says the other.

" 'What does he do?' asks the first party.

" 'Don't do nothin', but he gets well paid for it.'

" 'What's his graft?'

" 'Oh, he's just a private policeman an' bank watchman. He makes good money watchin' the bank, an' puts almost all of it in fool prospect holes. He's nuts about minin'.'

"A few nights after Tom had heard these fellers talkin,' and his pile had been cut down to a few dollars in silver, he sees this Henry Heap go into a saloon, an' directly Tom follows him. Tom was pretty drunk, but could still navigate both his legs and his brains. 'Come on, everybody!' he says, throwin' down on the bar what silver an' other trinkets he had in his pocket. 'Have a drink with me!'

"Henry, among others, stepped up and ordered his drink, an' noticed the gold nugget layin' on the bar among the change. 'Hello,' says he to Tom, 'what's this?'

" 'I don't know,' says Tom.

" 'Where'd you get it?'

" 'Oh, out between here an' the mountains. My horse got a stone in his shoe an' I got down to knock it out an' found this on the ground.'

"Henry got his magnifyin' glass out and looked the nugget all over, then called Tom aside. 'Say,' says he, 'my name's Henry Heap. Do you know where there's any more o' this rock?'

" 'Sure,' says Tom, 'there's acres of it out there.'

" 'Do you mind if I break a piece off and have it assayed?'

" 'Help yourself,' says Tom. 'Take all you want; I can get plenty more of it.'

"Next mornin' Tom just did have the price of a breakfast, and as he sauntered down the street, he runs into Henry, who says, 'Say, Tom, how much will you take to show me the place where you got that piece of rock?'

" 'Oh, I don't know,' says Tom; 'did you git it assayed?'

" 'Yeh.'

" 'Was it any account?'

" 'Jest pretty fair.' Henry never let on to Tom that it assayed over forty thousand dollars to the ton.

" 'Well, I tell you,' says Tom, 'I got to stay in town a few days longer, an' whenever I fix up to go it won't cost you nothin' to come along.'

" 'How are you fixed for cash?' says Henry.

" 'I'm about broke,' says Tom, 'an' I need a few things at the store.'

"Well, they go over to the Golden Eagle and Tom gets a whole new outfit, orderin' a pair of shop boots, and payin' up corral charges on his saddle horse for a week ahead, an' gettin' a twenty-dollar gold piece to boot to keep him runnin'. Tom told me he never did intend to hang it onto Henry, but when he wouldn't tell him how much the nugget assayed, and showed he was tryin' to get the best of him, Tom decided to make him pay. Every day or two, Henry would come through with five or ten, till at last he decided, on account of Tom's puttin' off the time of startin' so often, to quit. When the story got around town, everybody who'd meet Henry would pick up a stone, an' rushin' up to him (always waitin' till he was in a crowd), would sing out, 'Say, Henry, can you tell me how much this runs in gold?' An' to get rid of the joshin,' he would stand treat for the crowd."

WAYNE'S COURTSHIP

Wayne, who once worked for the Turkey Tracks outfit, was a cowpuncher who had lit out of New Mexico ahead of the sheriff on account of a little trouble he and some others had got into. The sheriff had lost his trail in the foothills of the Capitan Mountains. Wayne wasn't a bad *hombre*, but like lots of others he had been trailing with the wrong bunch. Since getting back to Texas where his kinfolks lived, he had been going straight, breaking horses and working cattle for his brother and brother-in-law, who weren't wise to what Wayne had been doing over the line. Naturally, he was kind of bottled up and looking for a way to express himself, an' it was about then that his brother, Doc, with whom he was living, made the long trip to San Antone in a buckboard and brought back a schoolmarm to teach his two kids, as there was no local school in the country. Ted, one of Wayne's old friends, told us the story of what happened between Wayne and the teacher.

"She was one o' them girls," said Ted, "brought up in a city with quite an idea of her own importance, you know—inclined to believe a man should propose to her before makin' any other advances. Very pretty, an' she had somehow safely arrived at the interestin' age o' twenty. Wayne saw through her veneer right off, an' hurriedly began to make violent love, in fact proposed to her on the second night after her arrival, which piece of information the schoolmarm, Christine, imparted to Mrs. Doc as soon as she got the chance. Mrs. Doc, not knowin' what to make of it, but hopin' Wayne was sincere, told Christine what a fine feller he was, thinkin' that marriage might tend to settle him down.

"Now Christine, wishin' to assist Mrs. Doc, who had a small child to take care of, offered to wash the dishes after meals, and Wayne gallantly came up to scratch an' offered to dry 'em. This arrangement threw 'em together away from the rest o' the household, as the sink was in a small lean-to kitchen which was off from the rest o' the house. This kitchen had a window without any glass in it, but a wooden shutter about two feet square instead, an' at night it was kept closed by an old-fashioned wooden button. Hardly a night passed while they was together out there that Wayne didn't propose, tellin' Christine that life without her was impossible, an' so on, an' she thinkin' him dead sincere an' refusin' him in her kind o' severe way.

"This continued till one night Christine told him he had proposed just fifty-six times, an' she hoped that was enough an' he'd quit. Wayne says that he'd give her just four more chances, an' that if she didn't accept him after he'd proposed sixty times, he'd do somethin' desperate, for he was bound to have her.

"Well, the night of the sixtieth proposal arrives, and that evenin' Wayne picks up all the used six-shooter shells he could find around the corrals, puttin' 'em in his left pants pocket, and a handful o' good cartridges in his right. After supper Christine and he adjourns to the kitchen to wash up the supper dishes as usual, an' she, recollectin' what Wayne had said about doin' somethin' desperate if she refused him the sixtieth time, with a woman's curiosity wondered what it might be. They had jest finished with the dishes, she standin' under the open shuttered window, and Wayne between her an' the door, when he again proposes, an' she again refuses him. Well, Wayne lifts the lid off the stove, blazin' with a hot fire, and divin' his hands into his pockets, pulls out in the right a handful o' cartridges.

" 'All right,' he says, 'we will both die together—'

"An' as she turns to jump through the window, he puts the used cartridges he held in his left hand into the stove, shovin' the good ones back in his pocket, and shootin' a couple o' shots out o' his six-shooter through the roof, to help things along.

"Well, Wayne noticed when the schoolmarm disappeared through the window, that her clothes caught on the wooden window-button an' came off, an' Mrs. Doc afterwards told him that when Christine got to her room all she had on was her B. V. D.'s And that's why Doc had to make the hundred-mile drive to San Antone in the buckboard again, an' was short one schoolmarm."

Baxter told us about his queer job. He was hired, he said, by old man Holspeill, to hunt for Holspeill's bagpipe-playing Scotch sheep boss, Dan MacLaw, who had disappeared in mysterious fashion without leaving a trace. Baxter said he stopped all night at a sheep camp and got filled up on tortillas and mutton, but couldn't find out anything from Juanito, the herder, about MacLaw.

"He go," said Juanito, "I no see more."

So, Baxter said, he rode to the town of Sunrise, where MacLaw had last been seen. It was a great mystery how the Scotsman could have gotten out of the country, for his horse and saddle were still at the sheep camp. In Sunrise, Baxter met the man who owned the trading post.

"An' I want to say right now," said Baxter, "he was full o' information and not afraid to pass it on. After I told him my business he began to laugh, an' instead o' gettin' mad, I laughs with him. I been in lots o' queer jackpots and on lots o' fool errands in my life, but never one that seemed as queer as this, for I've heard of a boss losin' herds o' sheep lots o' times, but I never before heard of a bunch of sheep losin' their boss.

" 'About a month ago,' this storekeeper says, 'was the Navajo fire dance, an' that same day the boss's sheep come in from the north, several flocks of 'em, an' they watered there at the creek jest in front o' the store, then drifted on down the canyon. Pretty soon up drives the chuck wagon an' this feller I guess you're lookin' for. Dan was his name, wasn't it?'

" 'Dan MacLaw,' says I.

" 'Well, the wagon stops, an' him an' the Mexican who was drivin' the chuck wagon comes in. He tells me he's sheep boss for old man Holspeill, and as I'd known the old man always I tells him he can have anythin' he wants, so he stocks up with a lot o' grub for the camp and grain for the horses. While the boys was loadin' the wagon, in comes old Tony who lives up the creek an' who used to work for this Dan, as I learned afterwards. Well, Tony had a bottle of this Navajo tis-win, and him an' Dan had several drinks and commenced to tell each other how much they thought of each other, an' Tony tells Dan that the Navajos are goin' to have a fire dance that night, and for Dan to let the wagon man make camp below town, and for Dan to go over to *his* house for the night. That seemed to just suit Dan, as he explained he never had seen an Indian dance before.

" 'So, gettin' his grip out o' the wagon he tells his driver to go a mile or two below town where the grass was good, an' make camp; to tie his saddle horse behind, and he'd be down in the mornin'.

" 'Well, there was all kind o' Pueblo Indians there, and some Apaches and Utes, with a big swarm o' Navajos, all camped up and down the creek. They'd been gamblin', drinkin', an' runnin' horse races for several days. They had a big cedar corral

built, and hauled stacks o' wood and piled it up in the middle all
ready to light when night come on. I had a big run o' trade that
evenin', and didn't see no more o' Dan, but I saw Tony several
times makin' trips across to the board shack fer tis-win, en
guessed he an' Dan was havin' a-plenty.

" 'About ten o'clock that night the Navvies began dancin',
an' you could hear the big drums an' singin' fer miles. So, as
everybody had gone to the dance, and my tradin' fer the day was
over, me an' one o' the boys who works in the store thought we'd
go too. They'd jest got to that point in the fire dance where
they're all trottin' around the fire with nothin' on but a cotton
breech-clout, an' everyone pokin' the man ahead of him with a
lighted torch, when we heard the worst noise you ever heard
in your life. No one knew what it was—sounded as if you had a
mountain lion in a shack and was chokin' it to death.

" 'Then out o' the dark into the light o' the fire came your
man Dan. He had a little short skirt to his knees, bare legs, an' a
pair o' low shoes, a funny little cap with a long feather in it of
all colors of the rainbow, an' he was drunk as a lord an' blowin'
on some kind of an instrument (yes, Holspeill told me he called
it a bagpipe) an' makin' an awful racket. Well, sir, the Indians
didn't know what to make of it; I overheard some of 'em
speakin' in Navajo, askin' each other what tribe he belonged to.
One would say Omaha, another Ogallala, another Sioux. But
anyway a Navajo is a good sport, an' wherever they find another
man who can out-dress 'em or make more ungodly sounds an'
call it music, they will follow him to the ends o' the world.

" 'Well, Dan with his bagpipe an' enormous liquid load,
marched solemnly through the brush corral an' out again into
the darkness, the band o' Navajos followin' in a line behind him,
an' where they went, young man, is your job to find out. But
one thing is certain, from that day to this, neither Dan nor
that bunch o' Navvies has ever been heard of!' "

TERRAPINS

When Hank McCall came to the wagon representing old
man Yost, Pete Johnson, the Bar W foreman, said he was reminded of an early episode in Yost's career in Texas. He prefaced

it by telling how Yost fell out with his partner, Larrimore, because they both loved the same woman. She preferred Larrimore, and married him, but the two men had a violent quarrel, and that quarrel was important because of later events. In the ruckus, Yost bit off a piece of Larrimore's ear, and Larrimore never forgot it or forgave, and he bided his time for revenge. Pete's story was that Yost went to San Antone for a trip, and there met a friend who took him to a high-toned restaurant for a feed. They sat down to a four-seated table where two men were already eating.

"I happened to be one o' them fellers," Pete said. "The other man looked like he might a been some high-toned Eastern drummer. He was settin' there sippin' his coffee, readin' his paper, an' a-twistin' his mustache. Jest about then in comes the biscuit-shooter and pours a fresh supply o' hot biscuits on the bread platter. Old drummer looks up at Yost an' says, 'Can you reach the biscuits?' Yost, who hadn't liked the looks o' the drummer any more than I had, carefully reaches out his hand, an' with the ends of his fingers touches the plate o' biscuits, remarkin' in his dry way, 'I jest ken.'

"Well, Yost's friend orders the grub, and they begins on soup. 'Say, Mac,' says Yost to his friend, 'what kind o' soup are we eatin'?'

" 'That's turtle soup,' says Mac.

" 'Well, it's sure fine,' says Yost.

" 'Ought to be,' says his friend; 'costs six bits a dish, and if you ordered it up north it would be about two dollars.'

" 'Go on!' says Yost.

" 'It sure would,' says Mac, 'and one turtle makes about twelve dishes.'

" 'That would make a turtle up there worth around twenty-four dollars,' says Yost.

" 'Bet your life,' says Mac.

" 'What kind o' turtles are they?' asks Yost.

" 'Jest plain dry-land terrapin turtles,' replies Mac.

" 'Well, I say!' says Yost—but it gave him an idea, and he got to thinkin.'

"A week in San Antone and Yost was glad to get back to his

ranch and get his idea to workin'. He got up a mount o' horses
an' shod them, and with the aid of a couple of his old niggers'
sons, started a little horse work, gatherin' all the stock-horses,
mares, and colts he could find in his brand. These they drove
to San Antone and sold, an' Yost found he had enough money to
gather and drive his famous herd o' turtles.

"Good luck was with him from the start with the rainy
weather settin' in, an' as fast as the water would run into the
holes that the turtles lived in, out they would come and sit down
to dry off, for down in the country I am speakin' of, the turtles
burrow holes in the ground in the sand hills, and live on flies an'
such. Well, old Yost and his punchers kept a-ridin' and a-ridin',
each with a gunny-sack tied to his saddlehorn, pickin' up turtles
an' bringin' 'em in to the ranch. There they put 'em into a big
corral made o' chicken wire, an' kept 'em till the rainy season
was over and they couldn't catch any more. Then they walked
'em through a chute and counted 'em, when they found they
had jest fourteen thousand nine hundred and eighty-six. John
takes the count over to the schoolteacher and asks him to figure
out how much they would come to at twenty-four dollars a
head, the price he expected to get for 'em up north. When the
teacher told him it amounted to three hundred and fifty-nine
thousand six hundred and sixty-four dollars, John like to have
died. The expense o' gatherin' the herd hadn't been so great, but
the feedin' of 'em while in the corral became a serious thing.
Old John had every nigger within ten miles o' the ranch catchin'
flies and bugs to feed 'em on, and it didn't ever seem as if they
got enough to eat. They always looked gaunt an' drawn, and
John thought the sooner he hit the trail with 'em the better he
would be off.

"From his experience gained gatherin' these turtles, he knew
he would have to keep the herd on high ground, for if he ever
struck a sandy flat they would be liable to stampede and try
to dig for themselves. He well knew if some fifteen thousand
turtles all began diggin' at once, they would be so much dust
a-flyin' that they couldn't see to hold 'em. Well, one mornin'
early the chuck wagon pulls out, and John turns the herd out
o' the corral, the nigger boys on each side, and old John on the

tail end bringin' up the drags. John says they sure was drags, and no use usin' your rope on 'em, for jest as soon as the turtles saw it comin' down, every head and their four feet would go into their shells, and the whole works would stop.

"About an hour before sundown, Yost had to lope on ahead and overtake the chuck wagon which he found camped some five miles ahead. Yer see, old Dread the nigger had always driven the chuck wagon for a cow outfit, an' he didn't know that a herd o' turtles couldn't travel over a few hundred yards a day, and consequently at the end o' the first day hadn't gotten outside o' the horse pasture.

"Now the trail drive that Yost aimed to make in order to bring him to where he could market his herd, was about fourteen hundred miles in length. Figurin' that if he made about a quarter of a mile a day, it would take him about five thousand six hundred days or some fifteen years, but still havin' that three hundred and fifty-nine thousand dollars in mind, he kep' a-goin'.

"When late fall came it began to freeze every night, and the herd got so restless they could hardly keep 'em on the bed ground, and to keep 'em from stampedin' when night came on they would turn the turtles on their backs. Unfortunately Yost found after a little experimentin', that when layin' on their backs they would kick their legs all night long, and would be so tired when mornin' came that they could hardly travel at all. Then one mornin' Yost had to leave several hundred turtles behind, as they had their feet frost-bitten; and the weather gettin' colder and colder, he decided to go into camp for the winter. Huntin' him up a nice sandy bottom, he hired a ranch-man who owned a big plow to plow him some furrows—and do you know, every last turtle when night come on crawled into those furrows an' layed down. After the turtles got all nicely bedded down Yost had the farmer drag the loose dirt over the top of 'em, and he now had his herd safe fer the winter. Yost next bought some hay an' grain fer his horses an' grub for his outfit, moved into a dugout, and prepared to spend the winter.

"He had a long wait before the spring opened up so he could again hit the trail. Wintertime on the plains o' the Panhandle in

CORNUDAS TANK

"If you were looking for . . . . the last home of desolation, you might pick the Cornudas."

Texas is liable to be cold—in fact, always is. Comin' out o' southern Texas where it was warm, old Yost and his darkies like to have froze to death. Somehow they managed to tough it through, though old Dread remarked, 'Boss, dis is de out-freez-in'est country in de whole world.'

"When the frost came out o' the ground in the spring, green grass soon appeared and the buzzin' o' insects told 'em they would soon be on the trail. After plowin' out his turtles Yost put 'em on the trail; but they traveled very slow, for he found that the herd, owin' to the innumerable number o' small turtles which had arrived durin' the winter, had doubled in size and consequently was harder to handle. This, although a seemin' drawback regardin' drives, meant a much larger return when the herd was marketed. The herd had already swam several rivers without any loss, and the great Red River which was the next one to be met with, held no terrors to old Yost.

"The news concernin' Yost's herd o' turtles bein' driven up the trail had o' course spread all over Texas and preceded him as far north as the Kansas line. Now it happened that old man Larrimore had settled on the banks o' the Red River and had heard o' Yost an' his herd o' dry-land turtles, and that they not only was on their way but was daily expected to arrive on Red River. And Larrimore after all these years had never forgiven Yost for havin' bit off the top of his ear, even if he had won from Yost the girl they was both courtin', and had shot off the end o' Yost's nose in the scrap. Followin' receipt o' the news o' Yost's expected arrival, Larrimore schemed how he could get even with him for the loss of half of his hearer.

"On July the Fourth Yost found himself and herd on the banks o' the Red River with the turtles all nicely strung out for the water. I know the Fourth was the date, as for years after-wards Yost would never go to any Fourth o' July celebrations an' always cussed the day and the man who invented it. Well, one o' the boys who had been workin' in the lead o' the herd rode up to Yost and reported that he had seen a man monkeyin' about a log or a stump that seemed fast in the middle o' the river. As he watched the man in the boat, he noticed him lean over the log and place a pan on it and afterwards somethin' round an' black which looked in the distance like a turtle. However, as the man and the boat had disappeared towards the other bank o' the river he could not positively say what he *had* been doin'.

"Presently the herd o' turtles in a long line enters the water an' swum along fine till the lead turtle come abreast o' the log in the middle o' the stream. Suddenly Yost, who had been watchin' 'em close, saw somethin' dive off o' that log, and every last turtle in the herd dived after it.

"Well, with their increase, somethin' over a half a million dollars' worth o' good turtles was lost fer all time. And as Yost expected to be fourteen years more on the trail, he had lost also the turtles' natural increase for that time, which Yost figured would be worth at least sixty million dollars that he could count —jest because Yost's old partner, Larrimore, had put a *divin'* mud-turtle on a log, an' lured the herd away, to get even with Yost for bitin' off his ear."

V

Some nights there were no stories at all around the camp-fire. Other nights they got taller and taller till they knocked the eyes out of the man in the moon. One story, to my mind, was more characteristically humorous than all the rest. It was funny because it was so common on the range and cut so deep into real cowboy character. It was told about like this, and very soberly:

"Jack, I been savin' my money all year. This fall, as soon as the last critter is shipped out o' here, I'm goin' to sell my saddle an' quit cowpunchin' for good. That's all they is to it."

> I'll sell my outfit just as soon as I can,
> I won't punch cattle for no damned man.

I remember old George. "Estancia Flat's what they call the place where I live," he said, grouchily—"but it ain't even flat. With the salt lakes and sand hills, it never was intended for a white man anyway. Sha'h! when a cow brute ain't dyin' from the thirst, they're boggin' down in some alkali spring. I'm a-goin' to leave jest as soon as grass gets big enough to travel on, see if I don't."

That's the way many another cowboy talked. Old George had lived so long on the flats, which he said he hated, that his hair was whiter than the alkali in a dried-up buffalo wallow.

This story always had a sequel. Maybe the teller of the story actually sold his saddle as he threatened to do. Maybe he actually thought he meant it when he said he was through. But next spring, come green in the grass and roundup time, he was back with a new saddle, huntin' the old job, ready for the old grind, the old dust, dirt, and struggle, the old fights with steer critters and with horses that went up straight and came down crooked. Let a cowboy once get the range in his blood, its sunsets and its dawns, its stars that told him the hours for changing guards, its loneliness and the whisper of winds, and the crawl of clouds around the peaks and the howl of coyotes—let him get all that into his system, and he was pretty likely to keep at it till he died or faded away. Yes, that was real cowboy humor. And true as the grass roots, too—if old Bill Jones was alive, I could prove it.

DEATH AT CORNUDAS TANKS

I have always wished to be laid, when I died
In the old churchyard on the green hillside,
By the grave of my father, oh, let my grave be;
Oh, bury me not on the lone prairie.

I

COWBOYS could see the funny side of most situations, but some situations sobered them, and made them wonder just how the Big Boss brings things to a balance in his stock book of human critters. If a man in a card game or a saloon brawl picked a fair fight and ate lead and went over the range for it, that was one thing. He'd had his fighting chance, at least, before he cashed his chips. And if somebody like Little Joe, the wrangler, rode the stampede down and his horse fell and he was trampled to death, at least he died like a good soldier, facing the hazards of his work, and in the midst of exciting action. But when a man or a woman, not quite knowing where from or where to, and with the deck of cards stacked wrong from bottom to top, passed out with no more notice than a blind worm stepped on by a stray horse, it made a cowboy push back his hat and scratch his head.

Often and often I wondered,
At night when lying alone.

After a prairie fire the grass always grew green again. Life smooths out the wrinkles somehow, after sorrows and heartbreak. The grin comes back. The bitter was a far smaller part of range life than the sweet, but the range did have its share of pathos, sometimes masked under a show of humor, but sometimes as naked as the needle peaks of the Organ Mountains slashed across the sunset. About as somber an occasion as I remember was the time Bill Muggridge and I made a funeral for the frail mother whose last home, if you could call it such, was a shack in the shadow of the Cornudas Hills, in the vicinity of the Cornudas Tanks.

II

The Ray family came to New Mexico from a little place called White Rock, east of Dallas. They were tumbleweed people going nowhere, blown here, back, and yon by all the winds. Or maybe it was only Joe Ray, the father, who, being a worthless no-account, dragged the others on his trailing rope. There were four in the family when we first knew them—father, mother, six-year-old Joel, and Tommy, aged eight or nine. The mother was white-faced, wispy, and tubercular. These four had drifted out from Texas in the vague hope that a higher altitude and sunshine would be good for the sick woman's health. But discouragement and failure circled like a buzzard over everything they tried. One day Joe, the father, came down to see Bill and me.

I have mentioned Bill Muggridge before. He was my English partner. Bill and I first met one time when I was riding home alone from a trail trip. Topping a rise in the Black River Valley, I saw a fellow, drunker than the seven deadly sins, driving a pony hitched to a sulky. He brought the pony to an unsteady halt.

"H'lo!" he said. I returned his greeting, and he said thickly, waving a bottle, "My name'sh Edgar Knowles. What'sh yours?" I told him. "Pleased to meetcha, Jack," he said. "Come on down 'n visit me 'n Bill."

"Bill who?"

"Yeh, Bill." He waved vaguely toward a ranch house ahead.

I didn't know what sort of a chap Bill might be. But I was hungry for human company after three months with cow critters, trail grub, and night-guard duty, so I accepted. Edgar, on closer acquaintance, turned out to be just one of those lads from England who were often temporary guests in the Far

West, to the great relief of their families back home. He was the son of the high sheriff of Manchester, whose dignity, I was told, entitled him to a carriage with four horses and outriders. Edgar was a wild child, and had been sent to New Mexico to become a reformed character, a job at which he was making a complete failure. He was "batching" with Bill Muggridge, another Englishman, but a very different sort of person. Bill also got remittance checks from England, but he was making an honest effort to learn the ways of the West, do a job, fit in, and make his own way. He succeeded, and became a substantial citizen of Eddy County.

When I first met him, Bill was the most innocent farmer west of the Atlantic Ocean. He owned a few acres along the Black River, which he had planted to alfalfa. He kept some chickens, and was trying to fatten hogs on his alfalfa. He had been warned that alfalfa wouldn't fatten hogs, and that his pigs would get higher and higher, not wider and wider, on that diet, but he stuck it out, being built that way. And the hogs fulfilled the prophesy, developed into regular racers. A Dutchman who lived up the road a ways, had planted a patch of corn. When the wind was in the right direction, Bill's hogs used to get the scent of it, and they couldn't resist breaking out of Bill's alfalfa patch and heading for the Dutchman's corn. They were so long-legged that they could sail over almost any fence like antelope, and Bill would have to ride over and fetch them back. A lane connected the two places. His old mare was fat, placid, and middle-aged, but she could sometimes be prodded to a lumbering lope, and Bill rode her as if he were master-of-the-hounds and she a famous hunter. As he came down the lane, the hogs ahead of him would fly over the top of the five-foot wooden gate while I stood waving my hat and hollering "Tallyho!"

Old Bill was no farmer in those days, and was not even used to the country. He had absolutely no sense of direction. I could lose him in a round corral with the gate shut, and he was even a complete innocent about looking after himself in any emergency. I remember coming back to his place one time after a long trip, to find him smoking his pipe and reading the *Illustrated London Times*. "Hello, old chap!" he said.

I gave him a hail and asked if he had anything to eat.

"We'll see." We went out to the cupboard and foraged around together, and the one and only thing in the house we found that might be called food was a small bit of tea. "I didn't get my check," Bill explained sheepishly. And not having it, he was going along, chin up, starving. What else was there to do?

I went out the next day and mavericked a beef for both of us—picked one that wasn't branded, and "borrowed" him. After butchering, I took one quarter to the store and traded it for a batch of supplies. I took another quarter to an old lady who kept bees and traded it for a big can of honey. Then Bill and I sat down and ate like lords.

Under all his innocence, however, Bill was pure wool and would do to ride any river with, and he and I teamed up on a proposition to open up a large ranch in the San Andrés Mountains. You have probably heard of the fellow who owned fifty thousand head of cattle and eleven acres of land. That was possible in those days in some parts of the West. The whole country was open range, no homesteads or fences, splendid grazing country, with grama grass up to your knees, but you had to have water to control it. If you had your waterings, you might control the use of half a million acres. Bill and I had dreams of (a) controlling endless acres of range by (b) getting all the water we wanted by (c) drilling a deep well. We never got enough water to amount to anything, but we got clean winds from off the mountains, golden sunsets, memories of songs and riding and wide spaces.

Our well-drilling location and temporary ranch headquarters made us the nearest neighbors of the Ray family, who, as I said, lived in a shack near the Cornudas Tanks. If you were looking for a bit of scenery to represent the last home of desolation, you might probably pick the Cornudas. They are not very high, just three old volcanic cones, and big tumbled hunks of lava and porphyry, rising out of an outwash plain where nothing much thrives except ocatillo and rabbit brush. They are lonely, yet they have had a long human history. In places the giant boulders are covered thickly with the sign writings of a vanished race, and there are caves whose walls are blackened with the smokes of savages' fires. When the Butterfield stages ran this way, the company had a station at the point of the Cornudas, because there was a spring of pure water here, the first in fifty miles or more of dusty travel. But the ghosts of history had quit haunting, the ancient race had vanished entirely, the stage coaches long since had quit running, and nobody now but the tumbleweed Rays lived in the desolation of the Cornudas.

Joe Ray came down to pay Bill and me a call. He had a shifty eye, and I didn't take any kind of a shine to him at all, even less when the purpose of his visit finally came out—he wanted to borrow twenty-five dollars. He had some flame-in-the-skillet reason for wanting it. Now the old West, if it was nothing else, was free with its hospitality, generous to its friends, open-handed and willing to share, and I never knew of anybody who went hungry because people wouldn't divide their food, or cold because they weren't welcomed at the hearths of people who had fires.

> Let me be easy on the man that's down;
> Let me be square and generous with all.
> I'm careless, sometimes, Lord, when I'm in town,
> But never let 'em say I'm mean or small.

Food and help are one thing, cash money is another. Neither Bill nor I inclined to the idea of giving money to Joe Ray without the best of reasons. As a matter of fact, Bill didn't happen to have twenty-five dollars, because, as usual, he was waiting for his check; and if I had it, which hardly seems likely, I was probably saving it to buy toothpicks for my pet tarantula. Anyhow, we said "No!"

We never saw Joe Ray again. Two or three days later he just skipped clean out of the country, all by himself except for his conscience, leaving his sick wife and two little boys to fight and fend for themselves the best way they could. That gave us a line on the color of the fellow's backbone. Of course the neighbors one and all would have seen to it that the Rays didn't starve, but there was no need of that, for the three of them helped themselves and somehow scratched along. Although we were their nearest neighbors, we lived many miles away, and didn't see much of them.

III

One morning just as Bill and I were finishing our breakfast, we heard hoofbeats outside. A little bay horse, blaze-faced, stopped at the door. Astride him was Tommy Ray, the older of the two Ray boys. Bill went to the door to find out what was wanted. The boy didn't say good morning or give any other greeting. His face was all sad, and he was tight-lipped, holding onto himself to keep back the tears, and when he spoke he clipped off his words few and short.

"Mr. Bill," he said, "Ma's dead."

That was all. We got it. A frail little woman, never gifted with beauty or brains, fortune, or anything else much, deserted and cast adrift at last by her weak stick of a man, sick, with nothing stirring to live for or with, fighting her last losing battle dumbly in a shack not fit for pigs, with nobody to help but two tykes hardly old enough yet to realize what anything meant— just a blind worm in the pasture, stepped on by the stray horse, death.

Bill and I didn't say much, either to Tommy or to each other, but saddled up our horses and rode up to the Ray place with the boy. The house they lived in was built of the loose *malpais* which was scattered all over. It had only one room and three built sides, the fourth side being a cliff of rock. Not much of a place to die in. Not much of a place to live in. Not for a woman who at least was gentle-born and certainly knew about decent things back East. God-forsaken at the best of times, it looked dreary past belief when we went in with bared heads and saw the white-faced woman, her eyes not yet closed, lying dead on the disorderly bed, and the six-year-old Joel, white-faced and scared, sitting in the corner watching.

There wasn't much to be said. I asked Bill if he would try to dig a grave, saying I would ride over to Uncle Johnny Root's and see if he had any boards—there wasn't a stick of loose lumber in the Ray shack.

Uncle Johnny's place, the Alamo Ranch, was about twelve miles away. It didn't take me long to cover the distance. Uncle Johnny was an old bachelor, deaf as a post. I thoughtlessly rode up behind him without warning, scaring his horse; he was nearly thrown, and the accident started a stream of profanity that would have been a joy to listen to at any other time. He sobered down as soon as I told him what the trouble was, and what I wanted. He said he had no lumber—all his buildings were made of adobe—but he did have a wooden chicken coop. After looking at it, I saw that some of it could be made to do, so Uncle Johnny and I set to work and tore down one side of it, saving all the nails. What we made from these salvaged materials had the shape, and would serve the rough purpose, of a coffin. Ransacking an old trunk that he had in the house, Uncle Johnny found some clean white shirts. We tore them up to make a lining for the inside of the coffin. He also found a box of brass-headed tacks, and we used these to fasten the shirts to the wood. It was the best we could do, lacking satin and soft plush, but we reckoned the dead woman might rest a little easier than on bare boards or with nothing at all.

Uncle Johnny had no wagon, but he did have a double-seated surrey with a fringed top. We tied the coffin securely on top of this, that being the only place where it would fit. Next we had to find animals to pull the surrey. Uncle Johnny owned plenty of saddle horses and mules and, like most ranchers, he had a few horses broke to harness, but none of these were in the pasture at the time, and where they might be out on the range, or how long it would take to run them down, we had no idea. So I borrowed one of his saddle horses, and to complete a team, used the horse I had ridden over. Neither of these two had ever been in harness before, and I had no idea what might happen when they were hitched up. To prevent their running away and smashing everything, if possible, I mounted to the top of the surrey, and sat astride the coffin, getting a good grip on the lines. I gave the word, and with Uncle Johnny riding alongside a ways to help calm the excited animals, away they went at a mad run. I have ridden sky-bumping broncs, but I never rode rougher than on the coffin atop that surrey. By luck and providence I managed to hold the team steady enough to keep the surrey right side up. But they cut such a rapid hole in the atmosphere that it was hardly any time at all after leaving Uncle Johnny's before they reached the Ray shack.

Bill had succeeded in digging a grave. We unroped the coffin and carried it inside the house. The dead woman wasn't much of a weight to lift. We put her in and smoothed out her dress a little, Tommy and Joel standing by wide-eyed and sober. I nailed down the lid. We lowered the coffin into the grave with the ropes from our saddles. Bill said a few words of prayer. We filled in the grave and built up a little mound of *malpais* for a headstone. The shadows were beginning to be long by this time, and it was starting to get chilly, as it does in New Mexico when the sun goes down.

"Come with us, boys!" said Bill.

They mounted their pony, and we all rode down the hill, none of us talking.

In time the door sagged and fell off the hinges of the little rock cabin of the Rays. Wild cattle or burros, stopping at the tanks for water, sometimes sheltered inside; sometimes a cowboy did the same. Today it looks more like a ruined stable than a home—no sign at all of any woman fixings such as make four walls cheerful. Unless you were told or knew just where to look, you would never notice the little unevenness in the *malpais* that marks a woman's grave. I took Uncle Johnny's surrey back, and Bill later moved the few cattle belonging to the Rays down to his Black River ranch, letting them increase for the boys. He arranged for Tommy, the older one, to go to school in the town of Eddy, paying all of his expenses. Joel, the younger one, was taken for a while by a family named Jeffords, and later was sent back to his mother's folks in Tennessee. And that's how the winds blew the tumbleweed Rays in all directions.

CALENDAR OF THE HERD

Such is life upon a cow-ranch and the half was never told.....

I

THE infallible sign of spring and the active start of another year's work on the range, was the arrival of the cowpunchers who had been away for the winter. Drifting in to the different outfits' headquarters ranches, hunting work, they were the perennial "spring vi'lets," as faithful to the season as boys with marbles.

Most of the large outfits, which worked ten or more men during the season, cut their force in winter to about three riders, plus a foreman and the ranch cook. The other men went home if they had homes, or housed up in town, or stopped with some other hand at a line camp, or teamed off with somebody who trapped till spring work opened up again, or rode the chuck line. Riding the chuck line was applied to a cowhand who, though out of a job, had an outfit of his own, including saddle, pack horse, and bedroll, and rode from one ranch to another hunting work—in the winter, of course, his chances of finding it were slim. But all the ranches made the rider welcome for a night or so and then he moved on. He brought news of the surrounding ranch country, and entertained his hosts with accounts of marriages, weddings, deaths, horse-thief hangings, and other dog fights, or sang songs or told stories that he had picked up en route, and the new ones he acquired during his stay, were of course carried along to provide entertainment at the next stop. Chuck-line riders were really the wandering minstrels or troubadours of the range.[19]

Each season in the cattle country had its special jobs. The

calendar of the herd was bound to differ somewhat on different ranges and ranches, and in different years, but the general pattern of work was pretty much the same all over, and in this chapter I propose to give a systematic account, season by season, of the principal jobs and how they were done on those ranches in Texas and New Mexico that I was most familiar with.

Winter, of course, was the off season, and as I said, most big outfits kept only a skeleton crew of two or three riders then. These winter hands would have a mount of two saddle horses apiece, and would feed them hay and grain to keep them strong and fit. The other saddle horses, numbering anywhere from a hundred up, depending on the size of the outfit, were turned out on the range to hustle for themselves. Winter hands were expected, among other things, to keep a lookout for cattle rustlers; and if the loose saddle horses showed any signs of wandering they had to turn them back on the home range; and then there were many chores for them to do, such as making a supply of *jaquimós* and rawhide hobbles for next summer's bronc-busting. On the whole, winter was a lazy season compared with the strenuous spring, summer, and fall months.

Spring work commenced with the gathering of the saddle horses, in preparation for the big spring cattle roundup. Sometimes this gather was easy, sometimes slow and tedious. If the grass was good, most well-broken saddle horses on the open range tended to keep pretty much in the same locality until wanted again, and it was no great job to round them up and throw them into the horse pasture at the home ranch. The ones that gave most trouble were the little bunches, two or three head to the bunch, mostly young horses, which had been broken out and ridden only a few saddles the year before, and then when turned out, quickly went back to their old wild bunches, or followed a stray mare off their own range and pretty well out of the country. Sometimes such horses would not be recovered until some distant outfit on general horse work picked them and sent word for the owner to come and get them. The spirit of do-unto-others-as-you-would-be-done-by was pretty general in those days, and comparatively little stock was lost.

While wintering on the range, saddle horses grew long coats

and looked to be in better condition than they were. Actually, few of them could stand up to a half-day's ride when first brought in. So if the owner had any prairie hay cut and stacked, the horses were given that, and were kept away from the little short grass of early spring, which weakened them. If the winter had been a hard one, they might be fed grain night and morning at the home corral, either in troughs or in *morrals* (individual nosebags). Later, when the new grass was up good and strong, they would quickly fatten on it.

Next came the task of selecting mounts and shoeing the horses. The foreman naturally had first pick of the *remuda* in choosing the horses he wanted for his mount. Old hands had next choice; and then the new hands in the order hired were given their pick of the animals that were left. Every hand had to shoe the horses in his own mount, and the horse wrangler shod the chuck-wagon mules, though he was usually helped by some of the other hands if, as was often the case, he was just a kid. I might mention here that the wrangler's job, though usually held by a boy and considered as a sort of apprenticeship, was not quite as easy as eating tomatoes out of a can. The tenderfoot (in the song) who went out one spring for the fun of it to see how cow-punching was done, struck the cattle king for a job, and got an easy one from Foreman Brown:

> He put me in charge of a cavyard;
> And told me not to work too hard,
> That all I had to do was guard
> The horses from getting away;
> I had one hundred and sixty head,
> I sometimes wished that I was dead;
> When one got away, Brown's head turned red.
> And there was hell to pay.

The first thing a wrangler had to do was learn the name of every horse in the *remuda*; this wasn't quite as hard as it sounds, for, though there might be a hundred or even two hundred horses in a *remuda*, they were usually named for some distinguishing characteristic of looks or disposition, and any wrangler worth his salt soon got onto each horse's peculiarities. Besides knowing their names, he also had to know to which rider each horse belonged, and the order in which that rider rode it. A puncher usually rode two horses a day, so the wrangler had to know and keep in his head just which horses all the different riders were going to saddle next. Quite often the boss or a cowhand would need to know which horse some other rider was riding in order to locate him quickly, and the wrangler had to be able to tell.

On the trail, the wrangler moved the *remuda* from camp to camp. At night, after the night horses had been caught and staked out, all the horses in the *remuda,* if they were working on the home range, had to be hobbled before they were turned out to graze—and they must all be started off in the same direction. After this, the wrangler could turn in and sleep; but when the last guard went on the herd around three o'clock or so, he had to roll out again, find every horse in the dark, take the hobbles off, and bring them in to the wagon so that each rider could have his fresh mount by chuck time. And if any horse was missing, look out wrangler! Other than these tasks, the wrangler had little to do. A wrangler who was really a hustler, and smart, though his job was accounted a humble one, could help a lot to make any roundup or trail trip go smoothly.

And sometimes something interesting happened even on the wrangler's job. Once when I was out riding on the hunt for cowboy songs, I spent the night at a ranch where the horses packed the JL brand, and the foreman's name was Clabe. They had just butchered a yearling beef. As I unsaddled, I noticed the carcass hanging in the open shed. Next morning I offered to help wrangle the *remuda,* and saddling a horse of the outfit, pulled out at daylight to gather the pasture. There was a heavy Gulf fog, and I had to hug the east pasture fence to keep my direction, another hand riding to the west. We got to the end and started what horses we had back towards the horse corrals. When we had almost gotten back, I saw the horses split in two bunches to go around something, and there, sitting in the trail like a priest, with his back to me, and not a hundred and fifty yards from the ranch house, was a big lobo wolf so full of fresh butchered beef from Clabe's shed that he paid no attention whatever to the horses. I didn't have my gun with me, but I did have my rope down, hazing the horses along, and I just snapped the little dog lop over the lobo's head and made a run for the ranch, taking him to the country with me. In front of the house I threw the slack of the rope over the hitch rail, and pulled the lobo's head tight against it and hollered for help. Clabe ran out with his six-shooter and dispatched him.

When I was leaving, Clabe handed me a twenty-dollar gold piece.

"What for?" I asked.

"The lobo." All cowmen around there, he said, were glad to pay well for any lobo killed on their range.

Once the horses were shod, the next big undertaking was overhauling the harness, collars, and chuck wagon, which included tightening all bolts and greasing the wheels. If the outfit was to start work on the treeless plains where the *cocinero* would have trouble finding wood for his cook fire, a green hide was stretched underneath the wagon, so that any wood picked up along the way could be thrown in and saved. A set of wagon bows and a wagon canvas sheet were put in place, then the all-important chuck box was fastened on the rear end. This box was made with shelves and drawers, and held knives, forks, spoons, tin cups and plates, and all the small groceries. A coffee mill was fastened on the outside. Underneath the chuck box was bolted a rack containing the dutch ovens, coffee pot, and frying pans, while on one side of the wagon was a keg for water. All the heavy grub, such as flour, beans, sugar, coffee, lard, and dried fruit, was loaded in the front end of the wagon, together with extra horseshoes, the shoeing outfit, and an axe, hammer, and saw.

If the outfit was of medium size, and it was not expected that very many stray men would work with them, the bedrolls were all piled into the one wagon. If a good many extra hands were expected, the ranch would furnish a second wagon, known as the bed wagon.

In good time notice was sent to all the neighboring ranches, some of them as much as seventy-five miles away, that the So-and-So wagon would leave the home ranch on a certain day. The others were invited to send men to represent their brands and work with the wagon. These representatives were called "stray men," not because they were lost, but because they were hunting critters in their brands that had strayed. They were expected to furnish their own mounts and bedding, and to work under the direction of the ranch foreman or wagon boss, but the home chuck wagon furnished all the grub. It was customary, however, for the stray men to kill an occasional fat calf in their brands to renew the meat supply, particularly if a great many of their stray cattle were found. Day by day these stray men with their mounts would show up, and it often happened that a wagon that started out with only ten men and fewer than a hundred horses, in a few days was the headquarters for as many as twenty-five men, and the *remuda* might have grown to number a couple of hundred horses or even more.

II

> When early dawn is breaking and we are far away,
> We fall into our saddles, we roundup all the day.

"Come on, boys, let's go!" the wagon boss called. It was just beginning to get light, and twenty of us set off at a high lope from the wagon. The cook had routed us out of our bedrolls half an hour before, and we had downed a hasty, sleepy breakfast, and were off to a day's hard-riding grind. The calf round-up, first important event in the calendar of the herd, was getting under way. On this roundup, as in fact on any spring roundup, it was usual to start at the extreme southern end of the range, the wagon camping at the last watering and staying there maybe two or three days, until that part of the country was cleaned up of all the cattle which watered there.

All of the cowhands rode out to the rim of a big circle, with the wagon roughly somewhere near the center, and from there we started driving in anything on four legs that we found, heading them for the wagon. The foreman would distribute the men, usually in pairs, assigning them to the different areas—two men, say, to the cottonwood watering, to start everything high-tailing towards the wagon, two more to the Niggerhead Springs and Box Canyon, another two to the Work Mound Springs; three or four to clean out the foothills and waterings near Salt Creek, two to Mound Springs, two to Star Springs, and so on. The size of the big circle was determined partly by the nature of the country, and partly by the number of men present to work it. Riding circle took a horse with plenty of bottom, for in the course of a day's work he was sure to cover a lot of miles. On the out trip, it was the smart thing to save your horse, maybe loping awhile, jog-trotting a few miles, and walking some, in order to have him in good shape when you actually started hazing animals out of the brush or the canyons and headed them towards the wagon. You did plenty of riding then, and gave your horse plenty of work. Sometimes in a rough terrain it practically took a crazy man and a race horse to turn the critters and keep them turned.

Now if you happened to be at the chuck wagon watching the roundup, you would soon begin to see clouds of dust rising in all directions on that big circle as the cattle started out of the hills from different quarters towards the flats. Presently some of the bunches began meeting. Whenever a couple of bulls met, they usually had a great time horning and pushing one another around, while the other cattle bellowed and seemed to cheer them on. As the sun got higher, and hundreds of cattle had struck the flats, the dust clouds got bigger and thicker, and came nearer to the wagon. The first two men out would usually be the first two in, and they would hold their cattle near camp and get them contentedly grazing. This bunch would be added to as other cattle appeared from the drive. When all were gathered, they would be held under herd that night and calf branding would begin.[20]

Most of the principal waterings had large corrals for the branding, and the procedure was to cut off a small bunch of cattle from those under herd, and corral them. A fire was built to heat the branding irons, with two men tending it. With them at the fire were two punchers to do the bulldogging or flanking —that is, to throw the calves on their sides, and "hog-tie" their four feet together. Also at the fire was a tally man, who kept a record of all the calves branded. Two men on horseback would ride through the cattle in the corral, and with little dog loops (small-size loops in their ropes) would catch and drag the calves up to the fire for the branding. Each calf, of course, was given the same brand as its mother. If there were any doubt about the ownership, the mother cow would be sorted out of the herd and driven up to the calf to see if she would own it. Generally this was not necessary, as the mother cow was likely to follow her calf and be full of business when it was dragged bawling up to the branding fire—in fact, quite often she would go on the prod and keep the punchers dodging to stay out of her way.

As soon as every critter picked up in the roundup at that camp was branded, all cattle belonging on the home range were cut out and turned loose. They were shoved in the opposite direction from the roundup's direction of travel, so that they would not be picked up again on the next day's drive. The strays were held under herd.

The wagon boss would designate where the next night's camp was to be. At daylight he would start off the cook with the chuck wagon, the wrangler with the *remuda,* and as many men as necessary with the stray cattle. He would spread the rest of the riders out, fanlike, in a big half circle for a distance of perhaps fifteen miles on each side of the just-abandoned camp, with orders to hold everything and drive it in that evening to the next camp, which would usually be about ten miles ahead.

This procedure would be continued for a month or six weeks, depending on the size of the range, the branding proceeding daily, and the stray herd increasing in size till the home ranch was reached. Here the strays were held under day herd, but were corralled at night to avoid the disagreeable duty of standing night guard.

The next job was to sort out (cut) the different brands of strays. One man was assigned to hold the cut of a given brand as it accumulated, most of the other hands holding the main herd. The stray man representing the brand that had the most critters in the herd, would ride in and commence cutting. He would see a cow and calf in his brand. Slowly and with great patience he would work them towards the edge of the herd, then, *pop!* he jumped his horse after them, one of the hands usually giving them a scare, and he hazed them towards the spot where the cut herd was being held. Then he immediately went back for another cow and calf. Cutting was hard, wearying work, keeping man and horse constantly on the alert, and the man doing the cutting would be relieved occasionally while he changed horses. Quite often some bull-headed animal, after being headed for the cut, would whirl around and dash back to the main herd; then the work had to be done all over. If the same critter tried it again, some puncher would probably "forefoot" him—that is, rope and throw him so hard that he would be half stunned and would listen to reason. This was called "busting" him.

After the first man to enter the stray herd had trimmed it— that is, cut out everything in his brand that he could find—the roundup boss would ride through the herd to see if he could find a head or two that the other man might have missed. If he found nothing, that stray man would then pack up a horse with his bedroll, throw his mount of horses in with his cattle, and start for the home ranch, which might be several days' drive away. He would usually plan to strike ranches on the way home, so as to have a place to pen his cattle and to eat and bunk for the night.

In the main herd, cutting continued till every stray man working on the roundup had gotten his own cattle, and left.

After the work, there probably would be a few head of strays left, which nobody claimed. These were put into a corral and roped, one-by-one, in order to determine the brand more readily. If the ownership were in doubt, due to illegibility of the brand, the hair was picked, pulled out, or clipped. The rightful owner was then notified, and meanwhile these strays were held in a pasture. If the owner lived too far away to make it worth his while to come after them, he would notify the ranch to include them in the first shipment and sell them, remitting the money to him. Nowadays an inspector of the Cattle Sanitary Board takes charge of such cattle; but in the old days, thanks to good will among owners, very little stray stock was lost.

As soon as the calf roundup was over, the chuck wagon was pulled up to the ranch house and unloaded. The hands at this time usually took a day or so off, going to town to do any necessary trading—in either dry or wet goods.

III

We rope, we brand, we ear-mark, I tell you we are smart.

Now came an interlude in the calendar of the herd. Calf branding continued, but in a different way.

A few days found all hands back at the ranch again, relating their experiences in town, shoeing up their mounts afresh, and rigging up packsaddles (one for every two men) to carry a month's grub. The boss would send them out in pairs, with their bedrolls on pack horses, to camp and work at different waterings, some of which, 'way off in the mountains or the most isolated places, might have been missed during the roundup. The job was to brand all the calves that had escaped before, as well as the little fellows that were too small for branding when they were rounded up at the wagon. Usually there was some kind of a shack at each watering; it might be merely a place where salt for the cattle was stored, or maybe it had once been the home of a former owner of the watering who had sold out. Anyhow this shack now became the temporary home of the two cowhands doing the calf branding at that location.

For working convenience, most of the waterings had corrals built around them. The cowboys at this stage of the work would keep the corral gate closed, and when a bunch of cattle came in to water, they would open the gate and let them in, then close it again. If there were any unbranded calves in the bunch, the boys would build a fire and brand them, then turn the whole bunch out, repeating the operation until they were pretty sure that all the calves watering regularly at this point were branded. Then they would pull up stakes and go on to the next watering and do the same.

On account of the overflow from the tanks, many of these waterings had bog holes, and the cattle that came a long way to water and were weak, sometimes got stuck in them. If not

pulled out soon, they would die. "Pulling bog" was a regular
part of a puncher's job. The boys would rope the bogged critters, then hitch the ropes around their saddle horns and haul
them out. The grade of intelligence of the average range critter
was shown by the fact that after one of them had been pulled
out by main strength and horsepower, and had rested for a while
in the sun, then, if you "tailed" it up (gave it a lift by the tail),
as like as not it would either dash straight for the bog from
which it had just been rescued, or would turn and try to hook
its rescuer.

One of the regular jobs on every good-sized ranch was
operating the trouble wagon. Usually two hands accompanied
it. Their duty was to see that all of the pipe lines leading from
springs to watering troughs were kept in order, and wherever
there were windmills and wells, the pumps had to be kept
greased and in repair. The hands on the trouble wagon also
hauled salt, and saw to putting it in the salt troughs which were
located at every watering. On some ranges the owners never
did salt their cattle, and it was a steer from such a range, crazy
with craving for even the dried salt that had collected on an
old pair of jeans from sweaty work at the cattle pens, that
chewed up the pants of old Tom Mews when he didn't have an
extra pair along on the roundup:

> Now I ain't goin' to moralize,
> Or give you no advice;
> When you burn your fingers in the fire,
> You ain't goin' to try it twice:
> So it's always salt your cattle
> When the grass is comin' green,
> And never go on a trail drive
> 'Thout an extra pair of jeans.

Calf branding continued as a rule until the start of the beef
roundup. The time for this differed in different places and seasons, but it usually got under way sometime in July.

The beef roundup was worked in about the same way as
the calf roundup, as far as gathering the cattle was concerned.
Many outside men joined the wagon at this time. All steers from
yearlings up would be held. Usually a few two-years-olds would

be picked up, these being left over from the year before, either because they had been missed on the roundup or had been too poor to travel on the trail drive. Occasionally, too, we would pick up an aged steer. This might be a critter that had been started up the trail several times, but each time had sneaked off the bed ground at night and returned to the home range. These old roustabouts were known as scalawags, and unless they were held with the trail herd until it had gotten several days' drive from the home range, they would go back. I have known old steers when they escaped from the herd, to go over two hundred miles back to their home range. The old trail drivers had a sure cure for confirmed scalawags. They would neck them two-by-two, sometimes sewing a gunnysack over their heads, leaving a slit over one eye for each steer to see through. That usually did the trick.

On the beef roundup, the gather was trimmed of all stock except what was to be trailed to market. A beef herd of good size that still could be managed handily might contain twenty-five hundred head. Eight or ten men could drive such a herd, allowing one man to each two hundred and fifty or three hundred animals.

And now the trail boss was selected (he would be either an old ranch hand, or somebody hired from the outside especially for the job) and it was time for the beginning of the long trek to market.

IV

We had no little herd—two thousand head or more—
And some as wild brush beeves as you ever saw before.

Romance has come to gather around trail driving and trail drivers, and the story of the great trails that led north across endless unfenced country is a vivid chapter in the history of the West. Viewed in one way, it was a life calculated to suit self-reliant free men in love with big open country, horses, and the skills of an industry that wasn't exactly farming and certainly wasn't manufacturing, but was just as important and necessary as either. Viewed in another way, life on the trail was a

grind of hard work, dull enough a good part of the time, and
sometimes downright dismal—

> No chaps, no slicker, and it's pourin' down rain,
> And I swear, by God, I'll never night-herd again—

but exciting enough when the herd stampeded or there was a
dangerous river to cross, with swimming water and quicksands.
All in all, what with starry quiet nights and clean clear air by day
(if you weren't in the dust of the drags!), there was something
lazily fascinating about it, and right down to this day, if
"progress" and barbed wire hadn't happened, there would be
plenty of men willing and glad still to join a trail crew and do all
the hard grinding work of it, counting as their chief gain the fun
and the talk around the campfires and by the way, and grub that
the *cocinero* tossed up at the wagon tail, incidents that were
experienced and never forgotten, and friendships that were
made and treasured.

There were three kinds of trail herds. One, called a wet
herd, was made up entirely of cows. It was started when the
grass showed up in the spring, and calves were dropping every
day. It traveled slowly, and took along a calf wagon to carry
the very little calves that were too weak to keep up the first day
or so. At night these youngsters were let out of the wagon and
quickly found their mothers.

A second kind of herd, known as a mixed herd, was made up
of all classes of cattle. It was usually the cleanup herd which
contained every critter found on the range when some outfit
sold out.

The third kind of herd, commonest on the long trail drives,
was the beef herd, which contained nothing but steers, and
usually was headed for some place on the railroad where the
critters could be shipped out in cars—though sometimes they
were sold to other outfits that trailed the animals to a different
range to be fattened and finished for market.

The trail crew consisted of a boss, a cook, a wrangler, and
whatever number of punchers was needed to handle the herd.
The cook might have been the wagon cook on the roundup, but
he was seldom the regular ranch cook—the latter, along with

the range foreman, usually stayed and took care of things at home. A typical trail crew might include eight punchers. If the boss had never been over the trail, he was pretty sure to select at least one puncher who had been over it, and who knew the waterings. The disposition of the eight punchers during the day's drive would be as follows: two "on point," riding abreast of the lead cattle to hold them up when necessary and to point them in the right direction—point position was usually given to a competent and reliable puncher who could act as a sort of assistant to the trail boss; four "on swing," riding along either side of the herd to keep the cattle strung out and moving; and two "on drag," riding with the slow cattle, called the "drags," at the rear end of the herd. Under a good trail boss any man working with the drags was forbidden to have his rope down to haze them along, for the secret of successful trail driving was not to try to make the drag cattle keep up with the leaders, but to hold the lead cattle back and govern their pace by the speed of the drags—walk them slow, let them graze, and still make distance.

An ordinary day with the trail herd began with the calling of the horse wrangler. He would be routed out by the early-rising cook or by one of the men on the last night-guard trick, and would set off to bring in the *remuda*. Often the trail boss, since he did not have to stand night guard, went along and helped him. On a still dark night with no stars or moon showing, it was not so easy to find the horses, especially if the grass was short and the horses had had to graze over a lot of ground to get their bellies full. A competent wrangler, however, seldom had any serious trouble. He mounted the horse which he had staked out for himself the night before, and rode off in the direction in which the horses had been started. Usually one horse had a bell on him. But sometimes the horses would have grazed so far that the wrangler couldn't hear it, or the bell horse might have gone to sleep. If it were too dark to see any trail or sign, the wrangler would stick one finger in his mouth and wet it, and hold it up. The side that was cold would show him the direction from which the slight breeze was coming —that was the direction to take in search of the horses, for in warm weather they would always graze against the breeze. Presently the wrangler would hear a horse nicker and he would overtake one of the drags of the *remuda*. He would unhobble him and tie the hobble rope around his neck, and straight ahead, in the direction that first horse was pointing, he would find the others. As he unhobbled them, he counted them, and when all were accounted for, he would head the bunch back towards the wagon.

By the time he got there, the punchers would be waiting with their ropes stretched out to make a rope corral. This was done by tying the end of one rope to the front wheel of the wagon, and another to the rear wheel. If the *remuda* were large, it might be necessary to tie a couple of ropes together in order to make a corral big enough to hold all the horses.

Now each man in turn roped out the horse he meant to ride that day, and the night horses were turned loose in the *remuda*. As soon as two men had finished eating breakfast, they would ride to the herd to relieve those who had stood the last night-guard trick; and these men rode to the wagon to change horses and eat breakfast.

Each hand as he got up, rolled up his bedding and carried it close to the wagon, where it would be handy for the cook and wrangler to load it. The boss gave the cook the day's directions, and all hands pulled out for the herd, which by now had been started off the bed-ground, grazing in the direction they were to go. The drags were not moved at once. Riding to the lead of the herd, the punchers would ride *back* on each side of the cattle and string them out. Cattle are contrary. If you rode from the rear of the herd towards the lead, the cattle you passed would slow up or stop, but if you rode "against" them, that is, from the lead towards the rear, they would begin following their leaders again and keep moving.

As soon as the whole herd was on the move, the trail boss gave the point men the approximate direction to go, and then rode on ahead to see about the next watering. He might have to ride anywhere from five to twenty miles to find a watering place with plenty of water for a big herd. Cattle on a long trail drive needed water every day if possible, and every second day without fail, if the hands were to succeed in keeping them quiet on the bed-ground at night.

Slowly the herd would graze along. Much of the time the boys would just sit their horses and keep a lazy eye on the cattle as they drifted. Anybody impatient to get somewhere in a rarin' hurry, had no business to go on a trail drive. If the grass were good, the leaders would stop, and a few would hunt the shade, if any, while most of the others would lie down. There was nothing to do now but wait for the boss to return and report on what was ahead.

Presently he would appear. Maybe he reported that the lake where he intended to water was brim full. It would be along towards noon now, and all but two of the men on herd would go back to the chuck wagon, unspan the mules, and rustle wood for a fire, while the *cocinero* pulled down his chuck-box lid for a table and commenced making biscuits. Some of the boys built the fire and put the coffee pots and skillets on to warm; others cut steaks off the carcass of the fat yearling that was wrapped in canvas in the wagon. This is a good place to mention that the cook when making camp, always headed his wagon in the direction from which the wind was coming. Since the chuck box was on the rear of the wagon, he thus had the wagon as a shield to break the wind from his fire. Anyone riding up to the wagon was supposed to approach behind the fire so that no sand would blow into the skillets and ovens. Any green puncher who, not knowing this law, violated it, was likely to learn it soon enough, by being told the names of his ancestors and kinfolk.

Dinner over, the *remuda* was driven in, everyone catching up a fresh horse for himself, and somebody tying up two for the men still on herd. These two men were now relieved and came to the wagon for dinner. Next the wagon and *remuda* pulled out, circling wide to get ahead of the herd, in order to fill the water barrel and water the horse herd before the cattle got to the lake and riled it all up. In riding ahead with the wagon and the *remuda*, the boss would tell the men on point about how far off the water was, and would warn them, when a mile or so from it, to send two boys ahead to cut all stray cattle away from the lake, so that they would not get mixed with the trail herd.

When the lead cattle were still maybe two miles from water, they would commence poking out their noses and snuffing, walking faster and faster, stringing out till they might be a full mile ahead of the drags. Finally the point men could no longer hold them. With tails up, they'd run bucking and jumping down to the lake, wading in, some going so deep that they had to swim, but since the bottom was hard from the packing of many hooves, none bogged down. They would drink their fill, then climb out and lie down. It was the habit of thirsty range cattle to drink, then leave the water and lie down. In a couple of hours they would drink again, then pull out to graze.

As the cattle finally left the lake, they were headed towards the chuck wagon, which would have been camped a mile or so ahead. About sundown, the herd would be checked up on a side hill some distance beyond the wagon. Supposing that the critters had had a good fill, one by one they would begin lying down, the boys riding around them until they were all bedded in a loose circle, contentedly chewing their cuds. When the last old steer had been bedded down, all the hands, except two left on herd, would ride to camp. Here the wrangler would have the *remuda* in a rope corral, and the men would catch their night horses. It was at this time that all the horses which were not going to be used would be hobbled and started out to graze for the night.

Night-guard duty was generally divided up into two-hour shifts, two men to a shift. It was their duty to ride around and around the herd in opposite directions, and to turn back any stragglers that got up in the night and showed signs of wanting to leave the herd. Unless they were full and contented when bedded down, sometime during the night the cattle would get up and quit the bed-ground to start grazing. After the morning star came up, most of the cattle became restless and began to get up, and they didn't need any alarm clock to waken them! By then it was the start of another day, and the monotony and grind were all to be gone through again, the new horizon looking just about the same to the boys as the old one, the sun shining just as hot, the dust you ate having about the same taste today as yesterday, and the critters in the herd acting according to their cantankerous lights about the same as usual.

Eight or ten miles a day was good traveling for a beef herd, and if the drive were a long one, the herd might be sixty or ninety days on the way. You never slept in a bed or pulled a chair up to a table to eat the whole way, but if it were your disposition to feel that way, you had a sort of a notion that you were taking part in a job of work that needed doing and that somehow was better for you than sitting in a cage in a bank or at a desk in an office somewhere, just counting dollars.

Arrival at the railroad corrals marked the beginning of the end of the drive.

> We rounded 'em up and put 'em in the cars.
> And that was the last of the old Two Bars.

Thirty head of four-year-old steers would fill a car, and the herd was cut into bunches of about that size, each bunch being put in a separate pen as the loading proceeded. One man on horseback and two on foot did the cutting. The cattle inspector, standing at a gate by the loading chute, read the brand and earmark of every critter going by, to see that no strays from near or far got included in the shipment. There was a general feeling of relief when the last car and the last steer had been loaded without a critter crippled or lost.

Some of the punchers would make the train ride with the cattle to destination. This was a chance to see a big town and bright lights, altogether a broadening experience for a cowhand with a naturally very narrow education, also a chance for a man to spend all the money that was coming to him. Transportation both ways was free, and on a full trainload of cattle (a "stock run," as it was called), the train would make almost as good time as on a passenger run. Each puncher making the trip carried a lantern ("hay burner") and a prod-pole that looked something like a rake handle with a short spike in the end. Whenever the train stopped to take a siding, or for water, or for orders, the punchers walked along the cars and prodded up any animals that might be down.[21] Cattle in transit, according to law, had to be unloaded every thirty-six hours or less to be rested, watered, and fed. This was done by attendants at the different feeding yards along the railroad, and the punchers at such times usually took the opportunity to hunt up a bed and get in a good sleep, for the amount of rest obtained from bumping along in a caboose was very casual.

At destination, the commission-house man to whom the cattle had been consigned, took charge. When the boys got ready to go home, he was the fellow the boys came to for their return transportation, also for rescue from any scrapes they might have gotten into because of high spirits and unfamiliarity with the regulations on a range as crowded, say, as Kansas City or Chicago.[22]

V

> The scream of the outlaw split the air
> As we tied him hard and fast
> To the snubbing post in the horse corral,
> For his turn had come at last.
>
> To learn the feel of spurs of steel
> As they graze along each side.

Back at the ranch, while the herd was on the trail, work was still going on, with usually two or three riders and the foreman and cook on the job. One task that they were likely to undertake at this time was a little horse roundup and some bronc-busting. This was not done to give anybody a thrill, but for the purpose of having some more horses broken to ride. There is a good deal of misunderstanding in some places about the process of bronc-busting. In romantic writing it is often pictured as a battle of wills and skills between an unbeatable bronc and an unthrowable cowboy. As a matter of fact, bronc-busting was really a case of man and horse getting better acquainted and making friends, and learning not to be afraid of one another.

Western horses raised on the range were practically wild from birth, with little or no contact with human beings, not pasture-raised and hand-fed, as in the East. So when it came time for them to be broken to ride, they had two sets of fears to overcome—the natural fear of wild creatures for man, and the fear of those strange and disquieting things, the saddle and the bridle. The bronc-buster who really knew his business was one who played the part, not of a bully, but of a teacher. He wasn't supposed to break the bronc's will, but to gentle it, overcome its fears, so it would be willing to carry a rider, and at the same time not get the idea of misusing its powers against riders. With teeth, heels, muscle, speed, and sufficient dynamite in their dispositions, cow ponies could be more than a match for almost any man, and a spoiled horse knew this and took advantage of it. A competent bronc-buster gentled them without spoiling them, and the process was one requiring a good deal of patience and understanding of horse psychology, as well as riding ability.

The first step was to round up the stock horses and cut away the three- and four-year-old geldings that had never yet been ridden, putting them in the horse pasture. As needed, a bunch of five or six would be brought from the pasture and put in the horse corral, which generally was a round corral, about thirty feet across, small enough so the roper could stand in the middle and always be close enough to the horses to "fore-foot" them, that is, as they circled around, to catch the fore feet of the bronc and set back on the rope, so that he "turned a cat" (somersaulted). The roper's helper immediately piled on the fallen horse's head, turning it back across his neck. While in this position, the horse couldn't get up, and the roper now tied all four feet of the fallen animal, and slipped a rope halter on his head. During the slack winter months, as mentioned before, some of the hands would have made up a good supply of rope *jaquimós*, or halters, and rawhide hobbles, so as to be ready for bronc-busting work. Into the back side of the *bosal* (the noseband of the halter) the roper now tied a good heavy thirty-foot rope. The feet were untied, and the animal was allowed to get up.

This first handling would not have tended especially to allay the bronc's natural distrust of human beings, particularly cowboys, and he would be all excited and bound to run, but for the first time in his life, he would find himself running on a rope. One of the boys now mounted his horse (a trained saddle horse, that is) and took a couple of *dalebueltas* ("dallies"— wraps of the halter rope) around his saddle horn, and allowed the bronc to run at will.[23] After a while, finding that he couldn't get away from the rope, he would stand. At this point, the rider maneuvered his saddle horse so as to take in the slack of the rope, and drew the bronc's head up close to his saddle horn, then headed for the corral gate, half-dragging his charge, the helper meanwhile waving a gunnysack or saddle blanket to assist in scaring the colt along.

Outside the corral, at some spot where there was grass, the cowhands would already have hauled logs and scattered them about a hundred feet apart. The end of the bronc's thirty-foot halter rope was tied to one of these logs, giving him plenty of room to graze. Now the log had to be heavy enough so that the bronc could not run off with it, but light enough so that when he did run it would give some and not jerk his head down, perhaps rupturing the cords of his neck. If that happened, he was useless, and would probably have to be shot.

When all six of the young horses in the corral had gone through the same process and had been staked out to their separate logs, they were left to themselves. Quite often they would get twisted up in the ropes to which they were staked, and some of the skin would be barked off their legs, but this experience was instructive to them, just one of the incidents of a bronc's elementary education. The first night they would be too excited to graze much, but they would have learned at least one thing, namely, not to run too hard on the rope, for every time they did, it hurt, most of the pull coming on the sensitive brain area just behind the ears.

The next morning, having gotten over their first scare and learned that the logs to which they were tied would not hurt them, it was easy to lead the broncs back to the corral to be saddled. When the *mansador* (horse-breaker) led a bronc inside the corral, the first thing he did was to put a blinder over the animal's eyes. How this was done, depended on the disposition of the horse. If fairly gentle, the *mansador's* helper got hold of the rope, the lead man working his hand up toward the bronc's head, talking to him all the while to calm him, and usually he could soon be rubbing the animal's nose and forehead. If the colt were one of the gentle kind, the lead man would soon have a blinder (a neckerchief, gunnysack, or old piece of

RANGE CRITTER—OLD STYLE

Cattle when Jack Thorp first came West were no-good old Spanish stock, like this longhorn survival photographed by J. Frank Dobie in southern Texas in 1937. These wild cattle could outrun a jack rabbit. They lived on cactus and rattlesnakes, and satisfied their thirst by looking at a cloud once a week. They were well fitted for survival under hard range conditions; but the number of good beefsteaks per animal was negligible; so their day was numbered.

Photograph by New Mexico State Tourist Bureau.

RANGE CRITTER—NEW STYLE

When cowmen sought to improve their herds they introduced bulls like this prize-winning gentleman from a modern New Mexico ranch. Born to luxury, these blue-blooded cattle couldn't fend for themselves as well as the old Spanish stock; but they made up for it by the quantity and quality of beef produced.

WRANGLER AND REMUDA

The horse wrangler usually was a boy or green hand, but his job, for all that, was no bed of geese feathers. He had to know the names of as many as two hundred horses in the *remuda*, and be able to pick out in a corral full of milling horseflesh, the particular animal that a rider was calling for right then.

Photograph by New Mexico State Tourist Bureau.

CHANGE OF HORSES

Cowboys usually rode at least two horses in the course of a day's work, and sometimes more. When it was time to change, the wrangler drove the *remuda* into a loosely-held rope corral. Here the horses wanted next by the different hands were roped and saddled.

RANGE WORK

One of Jack's riders "flanking" a calf (throwing it and tying its legs) on the range preparatory to branding it. This animal escaped the iron at the earlier general roundup.

Photograph by New Mexico State Tourist Bureau.

THROW THAT CALF!

Branding was hot, hard, tedious, dusty work. In a well-organized branding crew, however, where each man knew his work and was expert at it, several operations, including roping and throwing the calf, branding, ear-marking, castrating, and (in later years) vaccinating for blackleg, could all be done and a calf turned loose in an average time of thirty seconds.

ROUNDUP

A gather of cattle belonging to Jack Thorp and his partner, J. Hurt, in 1919, on the Ojo dela Espiritu Santo Grant, northwest of the Rio Grande.

Photograph by New Mexico State Tourist Bureau.

MANY IRONS IN THE FIRE

To make a permanent brand mark in a beef animal's hide, the branding iron had to be heated red hot. Irons used once were immediately put back for re-heating; and if the roundup had brought together cattle belonging to several owners, the branding irons were likely to be numerous.

Photograph by New Mexico State Tourist Bureau.

THE BAWLING HERD

Unforgettable on the range was the sound made by a herd of hundreds of head of cattle assembled for cutting-out, branding, or a drive to market. At a distance of a mile or so, it resembled the singing of a great choir.

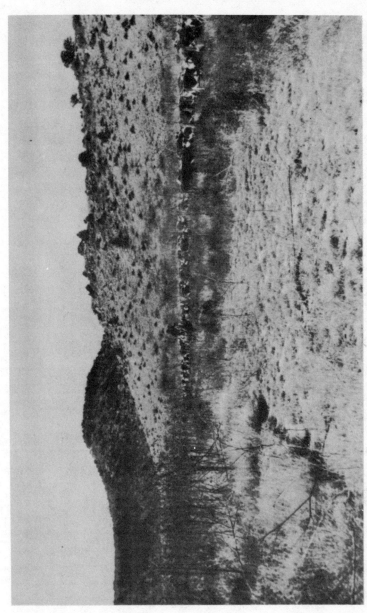

Photograph by New Mexico State Tourist Bureau.

RIDING "SWING" ON A TRAIL HERD

The job of the men "on swing" was to ride along the sides of the herd, at intervals, and keep the cattle strung out and moving, and also to prevent any of them from breaking away to freedom.

blanket) over his eyes. If the animal were mean, or badly frightened, he might have to be snubbed up to the post which generally was planted in the middle of every corral. If he were inclined to bite and strike, it might be necessary to fore-foot him again and lay him on his side in order to get the blinder in place. There were no set rules. Each horse to be broken was an individual, just as every child in a schoolroom is, and each one presented a different problem in handling.

Once the bronc was blindfolded, the lead man rubbed his head, neck, and back gently, to quiet him down. Presently he would take the saddle blanket and stroke the bronc's back with it, to acquaint him with the feel of it, and eventually he left it in place. He next picked up the saddle, which his helper would have placed conveniently beside him on the ground, with all the gear, cinches, and stirrup leathers pulled over on the left-hand side. Gradually, so as not to frighten the bronc by any sudden and unexpected move, he would ease the saddle onto the animal's back. He now dropped the two cinches into place, and with the cinch strap reached under the horse and placed it through the ring. After passing the strap through the ring a couple of times, he drew it up till it was tight. He then went through the same performance with the flank cinch, and the saddle was firmly in place.

If, when the saddle was on him, the horse showed signs of pitching, usually the buster pulled the blinder back off his eyes without unfastening the ends. He would then give the animal a little scare and let him romp around the corral carrying nothing but the saddle. After he had had his play, the buster pulled the blinder down over his eyes again.

Using for a line either the thirty-foot rope that was fastened to the *bosal*, or a shorter one, the buster now eased himself into the saddle, his helper at the same time mounting his saddle horse to guide or herd the man on the bronc and keep him out of trouble, for a young horse unaccustomed to carrying the weight of a man and a saddle, was liable to fall or run into things or do almost any crazy thing, hurting the rider and himself in his excitement. Remember, this was all new to the bronc and threatening. He had probably never had anything bigger than a cottonwood leaf on his back before, and to him the saddle with a man in it was probably a wildcat or some other equally undesirable alien. His first thought as a rule was to get it off of there as fast as possible, and if he couldn't dislodge it, to run away from it.

After riding the bronc for a while in the corral, the gate was thrown open and bronc and rider, herded by the helper, hit the flats. The helper had to be constantly on the alert, riding between the bronc and barbed wire fences, arroyos, or other danger spots. At the beginning the buster could do very little in the way of guiding his mount.

A young horse, unaccustomed to weight would tire easily, so the first day's ride (called a "saddle") was usually not more than three or four miles. He was returned to the corral, unsaddled, and tied again to his log after it had been moved to a fresh grazing spot. Except for watering, he was left alone for at least another day.

Another bronc was now put through the same performance. Usually three broncs were ridden in a day, but the number varied according to the nature of the broncs and the ambition of the rider. If three of the six horses were ridden each day, that gave a day's rest between saddles, allowing the bronc a chance to recuperate and fill up. During the time they were being broken, most young horses fell off in flesh and looked drawn and gaunt.

Some horses broke out very easily. They just wanted to run —it seemed as if they had an idea that they could run away from the man and saddle on their backs. Others would pitch and run both, usually, after a few seconds of pitching—"breaking in two" was the term the cowboys used when a bronc quit pitching and started running. Still others would rear and fall backwards. These were dangerous horses since they were liable to fall on the rider. Another dangerous kind were the hard, high buckers, which changed ends with the rider, and if they happened to throw him, kicked at him as they ran away. These were the horses that learned their own strength and were spoiled rather than broken and after they had thrown all local riders, they were condemned as outlaws. Unless they happened to be bought by some rodeo outfit, as old Brown Fox was, they would likely spend the rest of their lives in the roughs, as far as possible from the haunts of man.

Many a horse was spoiled in the breaking, even though naturally of a good disposition. Some busters in the early days had the idea that breaking really meant breaking, and they would hang their spurs with wrapped rowels on each shoulder and with a quirt would start whipping the young horse over the head if he acted up. To them, "education" meant "you do as I tell you, or else!" When ranch owners began appreciating how many horses busted out that way were ruined by having stiff shoulders and being crazy-headed, the old-fashioned "bronc fighter," as he called himself, found himself out of a job.

I have now enumerated the main events in the calendar of the herd on typical Southwestern cow ranches in the days before barbed wire and "progress" wiped the old order off the map. Come another winter, the boys would mostly be paid off and drift away, here, yon, and elsewhere, and everything would be pretty quiet till spring, those hands who were kept not having much to do except lie around and see if they could eat the cook out.

VI

> He began to put thorns in all of the trees,
> And mixed up the sand with millions of fleas;
> And scattered tarantulas along all the roads;
> Put thorns on the cactus and horns on the toads.

There was one job, not on the regular cowpunching calendar, that cowhands in the Southwest indulged in to quite an extent, which was liable to be as dangerous and exciting as the wildest sport you could think of. This was the hunting of unbranded wild cattle, mavericks, that sought refuge and lived in the matted thickets that extended in some places for miles along either side of the Rio Grande. These thickets were of two kinds. In one, the brush was mostly mesquite and catclaw. Such thickets were called the *matorral*. In another, the prevailing brush was the *tornillo*, and these thickets were known as the tornial. In some places these tornial thickets were extremely dense. *Tornillo* grows from ten to fifteen feet in height, the branches are thorny, and at certain seasons of the year the bushes bear screw-shaped pods which contain the seeds. The tornials are found in clumps, or motts, varying in extent from a few acres to several square miles. Horses as well as cattle were often lost from the ranches when the animals took up with wild ones and sought refuge in these natural havens.

The tornial was a regular clothes snatcher, and in working it, an ordinary outfit wouldn't last a mile. The men wore leather leggings (*chaparejos*), taps (*tapaderos*) on their stirrups, heavy canvas brush jackets, leather cuffs and gloves, and the *barboquejo*, or chin strap, on their hats. We protected the horse's breast with the *reguarda*, or shield of rawhide. We also tried using rawhide leg coverings, but these were always getting out of place, and were of little use.

The wild cattle were caught either by roping or by driving. Either method made a wild and exciting game.

Parallel with the Rio Grande, at distances from it of one to ten miles, are ridges known as *sejas*. The wild cattle and horses would lay up in the tornial during the daytime, and at night fed towards the *sejas*. If the weather were cold, some of the cattle would lay out in the roughs of these *sejas* for two or three days, and graze back to the tornial at night. In the fall, when the *tornillo* beans were ripe, the stock would get as fat as on mesquite.

Roping the mavericks was usually done on moonlit nights. We would make our camp at one end of a tornial, so as not to scare the animals, and in the moonlight we would watch the trails leading out of the thickets. When the cattle showed up on the flats, we would wait until they were at least a quarter of a mile from the brush. Then, riding like hell-a-beatin'-tanbark, we would go after them, building our loops as we went, and dabbing our lines on anything we could get to that had a long ear—and that was 'most any of them. The ones we caught we hobbled so they couldn't get far away from us.

We usually worked from one camp for about four nights before moving on. By that time, the cattle we had caught would have to have water. Shortly before moving camp, one of the boys would go to the ranch and bring back some gentle work oxen. We would neck up our mavericks to them, using twisted rawhide neckings made up during idle times, then turn them loose. There was no need to ride herd on them. The gentle ones would graze along towards the ranch, leading the captives with them. Sometimes it would take them three or four days, grazing and watering at different pot holes, to make the ten- or twelve-mile trip; but eventually they would enter the home corral and when we returned we would find them there, licking salt.

Some maverickers lost many of their catch by necking two wild ones together. These would usually get to running, tug- ging, and fighting, and would keep it up till they were over- heated and killed themselves. If we were short of oxen, we sometimes used burros, especially with the yearling mavericks and "muleys"—critters without horns. Often when the animal necked to a burro refused to lead ("sulled" was our word for it), the little canary would blaze away with his heels at the steer, who after one or two lessons realized that it was smarter to obey the orders from the burro's headquarters than from his hind- quarters.

Rounding up mavericks by a drive meant working right in the tornial, and this was very different from roping steers on the outside. For this job we would split up. If there were twenty men in the crew, about half of them would go to the end of some big tornial and start driving everything toward, say, the north. The rest of us would ride ahead maybe a couple of miles and take up stands about a quarter of a mile apart, and on the side of the thicket to where we wanted to turn the drive out into the open.

Most of the hands rode mules for this work, though many rode horses. Those little mules whose mammies were burros and whose daddies were horses were apt to be very smart and for some obscure reason were usually better reined than those bred from a jack and a mare.

> His mammy's a burro, his daddy's a horse;
> Of course you'll all think it's a mighty queer cross;
> He's got brains in his eyes, he's nary a fool;
> And smart as a cricket, my little brown mule.

These mules had smaller heads and ears, and as the Mexicans said, could outdodge their own shadows. They would save themselves from thorns and brush-swiping whenever possible, but they would get as wildly excited as any old brush horse once the chase began. Some of the riders on these mavericking roundups ("brush-poppers," as we used to call them) took a lot more chances than any other riders going.

Imagine that you have taken your stand along about where you think the drive will pass. Your brush horse seems to be asleep in the drowsy heat, and you can't hear anything except the drone of flies or the hum of mosquitoes. Presently one of your horse's ears commences to point forward—then his other ear. For all his seeming to be asleep, he has heard something that you, alert and listening, can't detect. Soon, rousing himself, his head raises up. Maybe now, 'way off, you too are able to catch a high-pitched yell that sounds something like the whoop of an Apache Indian. Your old brush horse works his bit with his tongue, and sort of fishes for it, tightening his reins. Another yell—the drive is coming closer now. Pretty soon, without warning, your horse is off. And so are you—to a wild, hair-raising ride. Somehow, swinging from side to side, you dodge the limbs. With an arm you ward off the thorny brush. *Rip!* goes a pocket of your brush jacket as a stiff limb tears it off. Buttons and buttonholes are yanked out. The tail of your slicker is left on a bush. Your fast-flying horse lands you beside the racing cattle, and you and the others who have taken their stands, try to crowd the bunch out in the open. But you have crowded them too close: they split on you. You dodge in behind the split and head them again toward the main bunch. If you are not side-swiped off your horse or forked in a tree, you stand a chance of throwing them together again.

Some of the old experienced brush horses depended less on dodging and more on breaking their way through the brush. By "riding Indian" all over such an animal, topside and underneath, provided he didn't take the bit in his teeth or go cold-jawed on you, you might, though full of thorns, and scratched and bleeding, find yourself still on your horse when the run was over. Your horse's front legs and flanks might be full of thorns, but he would seldom fall with you.

A drive like this was real excitement, as good as any hunt, better than most. Pigsticking, polo, steeplechasing, and fox hunting are tame sports compared to it, and I have tried them all. The horse you rode might not be quite as pretty as some of the well-groomed Eastern hunters, and his knees would likely be covered with bumps from past bruises and from the sores of old thorns that had entered and broken off; and for the first few miles after saddling he might go stiff. But when he was warmed up, you had a horse under you—none better for the job to be done. He would go fast, in fact, you'd often seem to be flying, brush whipping you at every jump, and half the time he was in the air clearing badger holes or big branches that he couldn't break through. At full speed he might jump sharply to the right to avoid a tree. You'd throw your weight and swing low in the same direction, and before you could swing back, the next jump would be sharply to the left, the whole maneuver being something like a corkscrew leap. It was then that your blood was up, and fine electric needles played up and down your spine, and the short hair at the back of your neck turned into boar's bristles an inch long. Riding a good brush horse gave you more thrills than bulldogging steers for the rest of your life. In the prairie country you would find many cowhands tying a knot in their bridle reins, but never a brush hand; if a limb should catch the lines above the knot, it would be liable to jerk the horse over backwards or break his jaw.

After a hard day in the brush, your chief pleasure would come when riding towards camp at night. You would sight the pot rack, and smell hot coffee, Dutch oven biscuits, and frijole beans, and hear the old cook's yell, *"Vengan a comer!"* And that food would make you just about the finest meal you ever put under your belt.[24]

VII

We fellers don't know how to plough,
Nor reap the golden grain.

The use of barbed wire on a large scale marked the beginning of the end of the big roundups and of trail driving. All along the Kansas line, in Oklahoma and the Panhandle of Texas, and in northern New Mexico, miles of drift fences and huge pastures began to appear. In time, this trend towards fencing completely changed the former aspect of the cow business. And before long it became apparent that the long-legged, long-horned old Spanish cow was doomed too.*

One of the early enormous pastures created by barbed wire was that of the XIT outfit on the Llano Estacado, or Staked Plains. This was so large that a trail herd headed north would take fifteen days or more to drive across it; the tract was acquired from the state of Texas by the owners as pay for building the state capitol in Austin. Another tract west of the XIT, the Maxwell Grant, at one time claimed over two million acres; while still farther west, bordering the New Mexico-Colorado line, was the Tierra Amarillo Grant, with over a million acres.

Before the advent of barbed wire, a blizzard from the north would start the cattle drifting south, like buffalo, tails to the storm. A succeeding blizzard might drift them still farther south, and often by spring cattle that belonged in northern New Mexico or even in Colorado, would be found clear down in Texas. Especially along the Pecos River Valley, where the country was wide open, with no mountains or other barriers, and there was practically no protection against storms, cattle drifted a long way. In bad storm years, cowhands from northern New Mexico would be sent as far south as Horse Head Crossing, in Texas, to start the spring work. Along the way they would find plenty of their own cattle to reward them for their efforts. It was not unusual for men with their mounts of horses, covering these great distances, to leave the home ranch in April, not returning with their bunches of strays till October or later. Once in those early days a few hands around Pecos Town rounded up a herd of those blizzard-driven cattle from a distance, and with no inspector present, shipped them to New Orleans and got cash money for them. The lone inspector who was supposed to work the territory between Big Springs and El Paso, at the time of this occurrence was in El Paso, being royally

---

* Several of Jack Thorp's stories about the bellicosity of these old longhorns are to be found in J. Frank Dobie's book, *The Longhorns*, published in 1941.

entertained by friends of the boys who were shipping the herd.

When the Pecos country was still open range, it was probably the greatest cow producer, and started out more trail herds than any other range district in the West. It was not unusual for from thirty to forty chuck wagons to be working at one time, either along the mountains west of the river, or in the plains country east of it, or on the Pecos River proper; and during the spring and summer months a trail herd would be made up and started out almost daily from some point along the river. The works, drives, or roundups, as they were variously called, starting some hundred miles south of Pecos City, Texas, usually broke up or ended either in the vicinity of Fort Sumner or Anton Chico, in New Mexico, where the last trail herd was formed, and the different bunches of cattle that had been held on the drive were started for their home ranges. During those days Roswell and Eddy (now Carlsbad) were the principal trading posts for the cowmen, and they were wild and woolly.

The first fences that appeared were used to make saddle-horse pastures, which usually contained just a few hundred acres. Presently you would find a cattleman fencing a small piece of bottom land which was overflowed whenever flood waters discharged from some canyon up in the mountains. Being extra fertile or well watered, it produced a lot of grass, and was fenced as a meadow, from which hay was cut for feed for the winter saddle horses. Next, fences began to appear around the large tracts leased or otherwise obtained from the state, like the XIT, and around the old Spanish grants. By a gradual process, which really was not so slow when it got rolling, the open range was transformed into fenced pastures—enormous pastures, some of them, but fenced. The old order changed.

One feature of the new order was the introduction of improved grades of cattle. Through many generations the old Spanish longhorns had adapted themselves to conditions and fitted themselves to survive in a country where grazing critters often had to rough it out and hoof it over big distances. In parts of New Mexico, what with barrancas and arroyos, waste sand hills, timbered uplands, and areas where for miles there is nothing growing but snakeweed, it takes from eighty to a hundred acres (the size of many fair-sized farms in the humid East) to support one cow. The old Spanish cows, when there was no grass, knew how to live and even thrive on mesquite, *tornillo,* cottonwood bark and shoots, and every form of cactus. When drought came for two or three years in succession, and everything for a distance of ten or fifteen miles from the waterings was eaten off, it did not bother those Spanish cattle if they had to go fifteen miles or more for water, lay out two or three days (especially if they could find a cactus thicket), travel all night to water, and be back to grass again in the early morning.

It cost Southwestern ranchers a lot of grief at first, trying to stock up with the hand-raised cattle that some of them brought back when they went East to visit the livestock shows. Those fine bulls hadn't been trained to the hard way. Born to luxury, they would not thrive without their hay and grain, which they had been accustomed to since calfhood. If they failed to get their rations, they would hang around the waterings till they got so poor that they were useless. It was like transplanting a soft-living family of human beings to a hard, grim land, with nobody to wait on them. The cow newcomers didn't know how to make out unless they were pampered more than any cowpuncher with good sense ever pampered long-horns. New ways of ranching had to be developed.

One curious and unexpected effect of fencing the open range was that it tended to reduce the amount of surface water in a region already half a desert. A newcomer starting a ranch, say, bought a tract of land in one portion of which was a large lake that old-timers told him held water practically the year 'round. He proceeded to fence and cross-fence, leaving only a limited number of cattle watering at that lake. And presently the new owner noticed that the water level in his lake was going down and down, and soon the whole thing was dust dry. It would hardly hold water at all. He thought, of course, he had been swindled and everybody had lied to him. Actually fencing was the cause of the trouble. There weren't enough cattle wading and tramping in the lake to make the muddy bottom and sides hard so they would hold water like a jug—that was how the old buffalo wallows were made, and they often contained water even in severely dry seasons. Hundreds of lakes on the plains and mesas of New Mexico were dried up in this way.

With the passing of the open range and the coming of new methods, the cowpuncher's job as we knew it, passed too.

CHUCK AND GEAR

It was chuck-time on the roundup, and we heard "Old Doughy" shout—
"You had better come and get this or I'll throw the whole thing out."

I

THE chuck wagon was not only the cowboys' social head-quarters; it was also the place where eating was done. And food was one subject that was invariably interesting to all cowhands. Josiah Gregg a century ago noticed that appetites and altitudes seemed to go up more or less together. "The insatiable appetite acquired by travelers upon the Prairies," he wrote, "is almost incredible, and the quantity of coffee drank is still more so. It is an unfailing and apparently indispensable beverage, served at every meal—even under the boiling noonday sun, the wagoner will rarely fail to replenish a second time, his huge tin cup. . . . . "[25]

There was considerable monotony about the usual diet on the range. Morning, noon, and night the meals were all the same, or substantially so, but there was always plenty. The rule among cowboys was to eat all you could hold every time you had a meal, then you were safe. Breakfast was liable to be the sketchiest meal. But if you could make it to the chuck wagon for any meal, it was sure to be hearty. The cook gave you all you could eat of what he had. As soon as an outfit began to skimp on food, everybody quit it. The cook generally kept a pot on the fire all night, so if any rider came in late and hungry, he could help himself to something hot.

Old "coosie," the cook, was naturally a very important member of the working crew. Few camp cooks had any fancy training for their job, and none of them, as far as I know, ever thought of wearing white chef's hats. Every cowboy had to know how to cook a little, and many of the ranch and roundup cooks were cowpunchers who had been crippled in some way so it was hard for them to ride; but a good cook might have any kind of background and come from anywhere. One of the best cow-camp cooks I ever knew was our own H. Benjamin Franklin. He called one of the Carolinas home, and he was a real master of the cooking art. His first name was Howell, but somebody had once accidentally made it into "honorable," and he liked that and insisted forevermore on being called the Honorable Benjamin Franklin. My partner at the time was a kind of comical mountaineer from Kentucky, a chap named Dan Grigsby. One day Dan announced that he had three cousins from Kentucky coming to pay the ranch a visit, and he warned old Ben to do us proud on the meals.

Ben said yas suh! he sure would—and he sure did. He had big platters of beef and chicken, with all the trimmings, done to make your mouth drool and your eyes ache.

Dan's cousins solemnly ate the vegetables and nothing else. They never touched the chicken or the beef, and though we wondered about it, we didn't think it was polite to say anything.

But next morning when Ben served another bang-up meal, with stacks of thick, juicy beefsteaks done to a turn, and Dan's cousins again turned them down, we asked them what we could have Ben cook up that they would enjoy eating. It didn't look as if they would ever fatten up on just biscuits and coffee.

"We'd like some *meat*," they said.

Back in their part of Kentucky, it seemed, "meat" was pork and nothing else. They had never tasted beef, and being so far from home, didn't mean to do any experimenting.

Most cow-camp cooks were cranky, and had plenty of excuse for it. A cook with a roundup or trail crew, for example, might have to work pretty nearly any and all hours. He had to be up by four in the morning, at least, so as to have breakfast ready before the wrangler brought the *remuda* to the chuck wagon and the day's work began. His work was done with equipment that was none too efficient, and half the time he was short of wood or other fuel for his fire. Some thoughtless puncher, or a horse or stray critter from the cow herd, was always kicking dust in the food he was preparing. Ants got in his biscuit dough. He usually was paid more than anybody else in the outfit except the foreman, but even so his life was not a happy one, and if he took it out by being wrathy, that was no more than any puncher expected. In fact, a gentle-tempered cook would have been such a surprise to everybody, that probably no cowhand would have survived the shock. Still, when it came to serving up ample and good-tasting food under unfavorable conditions, I never saw anybody to beat the average cow-camp cook.

John Patten was probably the fastest-working cook I ever ate under. Once when he was cooking for the Diamond A at a roundup on the Rio Grande, we kept time on him. In the morning before he moved the wagon, he peeled and cut up enough potatoes for the noon meal. He sliced his meat and rolled it in flour and put it in a pan in the chuckbox. Then at noon, from the time he put his Dutch ovens on the fire to heat, till dinner was cooked for forty men, less than twenty minutes had passed. Besides meat and potatoes, he had gravy, hot bread, and coffee.

McKinney was another cook I'll not forget. He was an old Irish sheepman who lost all his sheep because in order to satisfy his prodigious thirst, he couldn't afford to take the time to look after them properly. After a whole winter of practically continuous drinking in Albuquerque, he was broke and in pretty bad shape physically, and some of his friends thought they could straighten him out by getting him out on the range and giving him a job as a cook. In his shaky condition he was having a pretty hard time of it, talking to himself a lot, and "seeing things." It began to rain hard and steadily, and as we couldn't work, we took shelter for a couple of days, while it lasted, in an old abandoned adobe house where we were at least able to keep dry, and where Mac had an open fireplace, long out of use, to cook over. Crowded in as we were, a dozen or so of us, and idle, there was a lot of banter, a good deal of it directed at Mac and his cooking, mainly along the lines of giving him advice and suggestions about fancy dishes that different ones wanted, all

of the dishes of course requiring ingredients that Mac didn't
have. He took it in good style.

One morning he was cooking bacon for breakfast in a long-
handled camp frying pan. It sent out a pleasant odor, and the
rest of us were anticipating sopping our biscuits in the bacon
grease—this was considered a range delicacy. Just then a big
house snake fell out of the chimney and dropped squirming
right into the frying pan. We all yelled at Mac about it. Now,
he had doubtless been seeing plenty of snakes that weren't there,
and he had been taking plenty of joshing, and he probably
thought the snake wasn't really there at all. At any rate, he paid
no attention at all to it, but turned to us and said very soberly:

"Boys, let me advise ye earnestly hereafter to stay away from
the hard liquor!"

The staple range diet, three times a day, day after day, was
fried beef with thick gravy, biscuits, and coffee; and "lick" to
go with it for sweetening—corn syrup, in fact, though it was
never called anything but "lick." About the only thing we got
in the way of vegetables came out of cans—corn and tomatoes
mostly. Once in a great while we got some potatoes. If he had
an accumulation of dry bread, sometimes the cook would mix
it with water and a few raisins and a little sweetening, and make
up a pudding. For our beef we'd usually kill yearlings. Even if
the weather were pretty warm, the cook would wrap the carcass
in canvas and cover it with the bedding, and the meat would
keep sweet till we ate it up. Of course one yearling didn't stay
very long with a hungry roundup crew. Immediately after a
beef was killed, all the insides were cut up—heart, liver, brains,
practically everything—and stewed. This was an especially
appreciated dish. In the camps we called it "s.o.b.," but if there
were any ladies present, it was politely referred to as son-of-a-
gun." Whether or not the name is derived from slumgullion, a
somewhat similar dish, I don't know. Another dish was "prairie
oysters," but it isn't polite to talk about it.

Hot biscuits three times a day were the doctor's orders for
cowboys. When I got married I kept right on wanting them,
but my wife, who knew all about such things, said they would
ruin my digestion. One day old Tom Livingston rode by and

dropped in for a meal or two, and I prodded her to consult him about hot biscuits.

"Tom," she said, "do you eat hot biscuits three times a day?"

"Sure do," he said.

She said she didn't believe it was a good thing to do.

"Why, you know my father," said old Tom, "he's about ninety-five years old, and he lives out on his little ranch six miles or so from Brackett, Texas, and he drives into town every day. He's justice of the peace, you know, and he holds his court and drives home, and I know, Mrs., that he eats hot biscuits three times a day and has all his life, and if they don't hurt him, I don't see how they'll hurt Jack none."

The regulation hot biscuits of the range were sourdough biscuits, and this is how you prepared them. You had a one- or two-gallon jar in which you put some flour and water—about a quart of flour, say, to a pint of water. You stirred the mixture and made a fairly thick paste of it, then set it close to the fire for a few hours, not so it would cook, but close enough so the heat would sour it. A good cook always kept his sourdough jar full. When you wanted to make bread, you filled the bread pan about half full of flour, and mixed in a little soda and salt; and in the middle of that you poured just enough sourdough out of the jar, then kneaded the mixture till it was right for baking. Pinch it off into biscuits, and jam them tight into a big bake oven with grease—the tighter you jammed 'em, the higher they'd rise and the lighter they'd be. First-class biscuits were four inches high at least. That's what they called larrupin' good food, biscuits like that, dipped in the gravy, kid of mine! The first four or five would sort of whet your hunger, they were "moreish." After that, you could begin to enjoy 'em.

When a man was on the trail alone with a pack horse, or just riding, his meals were likely to be rather haphazard and promiscuous. I once wrote up an account of a ride I made on the trail of some horse thieves, in which various actual meals along the way were mentioned, and a few excerpts from that account will give a fair idea of what a puncher on such a trip made out on: "I shoots me a jackrabbit, and with some *tortillas* and coffee that I brung along, I made out fine for supper. At crack o'

Photograph by New Mexico State Tourist Bureau.

THE "DRAG"

Slow cattle bringing up the rear of the trail herd were known as "the drag." Riders here got plenty of dust and action, but in the book of good trail driving it was against the rules to haze the slow cattle to greater speed with the rope.

MAKING CAMP

Where the chuck wagon stopped for the night was the cowboys' home, often for months at a time, while they were on the roundup

Photo by Pinto.

HOME FROM THE ROUNDUP

Chuck wagon and hoodlum wagon homeward bound at the end of the beef roundup. Riders will sleep in the bunkhouse tonight and eat off a table for the first time in weeks.

RIDIN' FENCE

A routine but necessary ranch job was connected with keeping up fences. The coming of barbed wire on a large scale marked the end of universal open ranges and the passing of old-style cowpunching.

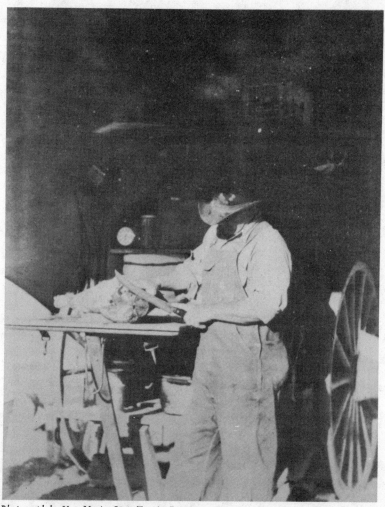

Photograph by New Mexico State Tourist Bureau.

"COOSIE," THE COOK

On every working crew in the cow country, the *cocinero*, or cook, was one of the hardest-working and most respected members. He didn't offer a great variety of food, but of what he had he never stinted.

Photograph by New Mexico State Tourist Bureau. COOK'S HEADQUARTERS

The cook's pot rack was the center of all social and eating activity on the range. His first job on making a new camp was to get the fire pit dug and start a pot of coffee a-boilin'. When an outfit had too much gear to be carried in the chuck wagon alone, part of it was carried in an extra "hoodlum" wagon, shown here in the background.

Photograph by New Mexico State Tourist Bureau.

WHAT COWBOYS ATE

The staple range diet, day in and day out, was fried beef with thick gravy, sourdough biscuits, coffee, and "lick"—corn syrup—with an occasional treat of s.o.b. when a fresh beef was killed. Once in a while an ambitious cook would whip up a pie when he had the makings; and sometimes he would serve dried fruit and vegetables out of a can. In his universally useful Dutch ovens he could make an appetizing mess of 'most any materials he had on hand.

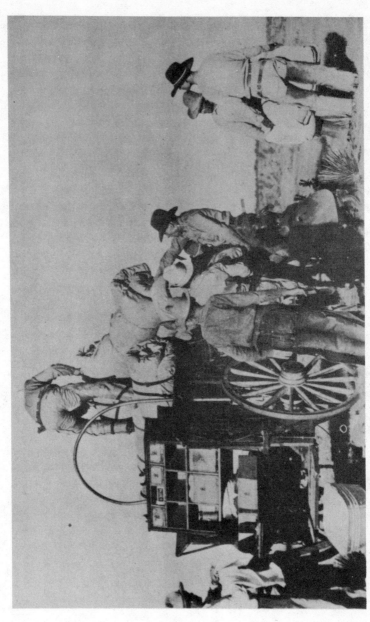

Photograph by New Mexico State Tourist Bureau.

BAGGAGE AND DINING CAR IN ONE

The chuck wagon was driven by the cook, and carried not only cooking and eating equipment, but also the bedrolls and other heavy equipment of the roundup hands or trail crew.

CHUCK WAGON ACROSS

Fording rivers was part of the day's work for a cow-camp cook. But he generally had willing helpers if he needed them. Jack Thorp, riding here just to the left of the team, has tied his line to the wagon and is giving it a "lift.".

Photograph by New Mexico State Tourist Bureau.

A COWBOY'S WAR BAG

Personal belongings such as tobacco, snakebite medicine, and clean socks went into the "war bag." This might be made of a twenty-five-pound flour sack, or from the tail of an old shirt.

day I gits kinder cold, so I starts a fire, and after a couple cups o' hot coffee and a few bites, I pulls out on the trail again. About noon I pulls in to old man Renfro's ranch and gets a good feed for myself and old Rocker. That night I sleeps at a sheep camp and fills up on chili and mutton. It was easy to take. Then I ambles over to the Shoo Fly Restaurant and I'm jest finishin' a third helpin' o' ham and eggs, when..... About a mile outa town I goes ahead makin' a little fire, and fixin' some bacon, bread, and coffee," and so on.

There was one staple item in the Southwestern cowboy's diet which it would be sinful to overlook, and that was the lowly *frijole* (free-holy) bean. It was guaranteed by reputation to break a strong man's digestion plumb in two, but just the same it was eaten with relish by the rich and the lowly, especially when "sow" and chili were added to the pot. It had a certain savor, "such a muchness, such a taste .... a particularly satisfying flavor," and humble though it surely was, it inspired me once to break out into appropriate song:

> I've cooked you in the strongest gypsum water;
> I've boiled you in water made of snow;
> I've eaten you above the Arctic Circle,
> I've chewed on you in southern Mexico.
> In the campfire, on the stove, or in the oven,
> Or buried in the ashes overnight,
> You've saved my life on more than one occasion—
> Oh, frijole bean, you're simply out of sight.

Once in a while the cooking on the trail wasn't much to a beef man's liking. I went down to Old Mexico one time to get a bunch of cattle during the Villa trouble. The Mexican cook I took along on that trip was named Filleberto Carillo, and the chuck he fixed up may have been his idea of food, but it wasn't mine. He would mix up cornmeal, grease, and salt, making a batter, which he would spread out very thin on a hot stone over the fire. These Mexican cooks didn't bother to tote a frying pan or bake oven, but relied on picking up the right kind of flat stone when they needed it. When the mixture was cooked into a big flat crispish cake, thinner than a pancake, Filleberto would throw the flaps over to make a sort of roll, and then hand it to

us, and we ate it that way. He called it *guayave*.[26] It was their
principal diet; they practically lived on it. I had it for a good
many days, and when I struck Tucson, drawn and gaunt like
a bronc that's being busted, I headed straight for a restaurant,
and the woman asked what I'd have. I said:

"Just give me a double order of everything, I don't care
what it is, an' a gallon of coffee, an' I'll make out somehow."

II

You could have bought his whole darned outfit fer a yearlin' steer or two,
Hat, boots, overalls, en chaps—there was nothin' that was new.

Nowadays when Easterners and other tourists come to the
cow country, they like to "dress like the cowboys," and they
sure do rig themselves up in some funny outfits. To see some of
the women who strut around in pants on the streets of Santa
Fe would be quite a sight for old-timers like Jim Brownfield or
Old Rip Van Winkle. Cowhands had a good reason for everything they wore or carried, and their object was not to be
"picturesque."

Equipment different with different individuals, and with the
kind of work a cowhand happened to be engaged on. He
wouldn't wear chaps unless he was working in a brushy country,
like the tornial or some of the south Texas ranges. If he were
just out for a few days' fence fixing, of course his outfit would
likely be a good deal less than if he was to be gone for several
weeks or months, as on a trail drive. But no matter where he was
going or what he was doing, he generally made do with a minimum, and that all useful, because of the difficulties of transport.
If he were with a wagon crew, he could throw his bedroll and
other fixings in the wagon, but if he were away for a long time
alone, as when hunting stray horses or on some similar job, he
would generally take a pack horse.

My outfit when I was away on my first trip collecting cowboy songs, was more or less typical. The first and principal items
were my two horses, Gray Dog, my riding horse, with a heart-L-
connected brand, and Ample, the pack horse, which I had roped
out of a half-wild bunch as a two-year-old and had made a pet

of and never branded. The pack horse wore his rope hobble on his neck during the day and on his forefeet at night; and he carried a sawbuck packsaddle on his back, with two *maletas* containing grub hanging down on either side.

The "soogan" was an essential pack item. I was once called as a witness in a lawsuit to tell the court and jury the meaning of a soogan. No old-time cowhand had to be told. It was what kept you warm in your bedroll at night. It was a kind of quilt or comforter, often patched and sewed together from parts of old overalls and shirts, and stuffed with cotten batten. Sometimes a cowboy stuffed his soogan with sheepskins, but that made it too warm for me.

My "war bag" was a catch-all made from a twenty-five-pound flour sack, with both ends sewed shut and a slit cut in one side. I would throw this over the packsaddle with the two closed ends hanging down. It was always handy there and easy to reach into through the slit. In it I carried tobacco and other little tricks, such as an extra pair of socks when I was wealthy enough to have a second pair.

The tarpaulin ("tarp" for short) was seven feet wide and fourteen feet long. It was tied over and around the pack when I was moving, and at night was spread both under and over the bedroll. About the only unusual item in my outfit was my mandolin-banjo in a heavy leather case, which I stuffed into one *maleta* and roper over with the tarp.

The riding horse had bridle and hobble, saddle and Navajo saddle blanket, and a slicker tied back of the saddle. In New Mexico the saddle was nearly always a double-rigged, or double-cinch, saddle. It had a horn in front, strong, and generally made of steel and nickel-plated; and a high cantle behind. It weighed from forty to forty-five pounds, and on the average cost anywhere from forty-five to a hundred dollars, though with special trappings the cost could run up to any amount. I have seen a saddle at the Miller Brothers Ranch, covered with silver and kept for show purposes, that was valued at seventeen thousand dollars. A cowboy ordinarily would never let anybody else use his saddle, because the stirrups would need readjusting. Anyway, that was his own outfit, bought with his own money, and he didn't want anybody monkeying with it.

The cowboy's catch rope, too, was a private and personal possession. He was so particular about it that generally he would put it under his pillow at night, to keep it dry; and he never used it for a stake rope or anything like that. The ordinary catch rope in New Mexico was about thirty-five feet long; in California it was longer, commonly as much as fifty or sixty feet. These ropes were made of sisal, manila, rawhide, or hair. The "maguey" was a coarse kind of rope used mostly by Mexicans, made from the fibers of a plant somewhat like the century plant. Hair ropes were usually used for hackamores. They were pretty, and there was an old superstition that if you put a hair rope around your bed, no snake would cross it. Lots of cowhands really believed this. A hair rope was too light to throw, and was seldom used as a catch rope.

I wore regular cowboy riding boots, spurs, blue denim pants or jeans, a wide-brimmed hat, cartridge belt, and six-shooter. This might be a good place to say something about guns and shooting. Guns were as natural a part of a cowhand's equipment as, say, a jackknife is of a boy's pocket kit, and only a few didn't carry them. A favorite kind was a Bisley Colt's .45 short, on which the barrel was no longer than the extractor. Many had a .38 built on a .45 frame; a gun like this didn't have as much kick as a .45, but was very heavy for the reason that there was so much more steel in it than in a regular .38. A single-action gun was favored by many because it could be shot faster than a double-action gun by "fanning" the trigger, that is, you held the trigger back and raised the hammer with the right hand. With practice you could move the hand faster than you could move one finger.

If a cowboy carried a gun in an inside holster, it was usually a .38, because it was lighter, about what you'd call a police pistol now. Sometimes a bad man had a special leather pocket sewed inside his *chaparejos*. He would have it sewed with buckskin, using the same stitching as for the outside pockets, so it didn't show. He would carry a small gun in this hidden holster, and if he were expecting trouble, he could stand with his hands inside the chaps, looking innocent, but actually with his hand on his gun. One of the tricks I sometimes used when out alone was to sleep with my gun in my hand between my doubled-up knees. Another trick was to hold the gun in the crook under the knee when hunkered down cooking supper; it was handy there in case somebody suddenly spoke up out of the dark, telling you to reach both hands for the sky—you could reach all right, but with the gun talking on the upward arc. Once or twice I was mighty glad to have it there.

There has been a lot of overemphasis on how cowhands used their guns to shoot up other people every chance they got. That was actually a rare thing. The attitude of cowboys toward shooting was that it was a good thing to know how to do, because it might get you out of a tight sometime. I've often shot up a box of cartridges as I rode along, aiming at cans and rabbits. Almost anybody on the range could shoot a little, and now and then a man would practice a lot and get to be an expert. I have heard of a blacksmith's son in Jackson County, Texas, who could fire two powder-and-ball Colt's pistols (one after the other) and do great execution. He once won a bet of two hundred and fifty dollars that he could kill six quails out of a flock sitting on the ground before they could get away. Some he killed on the wing after they had raised to fly. But the two-gun man, so-called, was a rare specimen and lived mostly in fiction. Sometimes when you were all tanked up it was considered great sport to shoot out the coal-oil lamps in a dance hall; and sometimes a cowboy would shoot at a tenderfoot's heels to make him dance—and usually he danced, too! But this was thought of more as a bully's trick than anything else, and was mentioned in the blistering cowboy song, "Top Hand," as an example of the sort of thing that might be expected of a windy:

> When he meets a greener he ain't afraid to rig,
> Stands him on a chuck-box and makes him dance a jig.

The main reason for carrying a gun, and it was plenty legitimate, was the lonesomeness of the country and the need a man had to take care of himself in case of accidents. If he were off by himself, say, and took after a calf, and his horse stumbled and fell and broke its neck, and he was partly underneath, the dead horse might lay on him for four days and the worms eat him up before anybody would find him. With a gun in reach, he had some chance of summoning help. Or if an old cow got on the prod and came for him when he was afoot, he might have to kill her to save himself from her wicked horns. Sometimes there was a coiled rattlesnake right where he wanted to bed down the cattle; they wouldn't settle down while the snake was there, and it was easier to move him with his head shot off than with it on and working. If there was a stampede, sometimes he could head it by shooting his gun a few times in front of the running animals. So most cowboys carried guns, but not primarily for purposes of homicide.

The above was about the size of the average cowboy's equipment for a long ride. When you were away from headquarters for a considerable length of time, with no five-and-ten-cent stores to shop around in at the lunch hour, it was a good idea to have extras of some things. An extra pair of jeans, for example, would have been a great source of comfort to old Tom Mews when the cow ate his pants.

I never carried water when I was in the saddle. In fact, if I ever saw a canteen hanging on a saddle horn, I was inclined to jump to the conclusion that the rider was a tenderfoot. Some way or another, an experienced man could usually make it to water. Very seldom did we have to make a dry camp. Of course the water we found wasn't always crystal clear, in fact we sometimes had to chew it pretty thoroughly before swallowing, and it sometimes tasted anything but sweet, and handkerchiefs were sometimes handy for straining out the wrigglers, but if it was wet, it was water.

III

My books are the brooks, my sermons the stones;
My parson the wolf on his pulpit of bones.

You might also ask what was the cowboy's mental equipment and what he did with it as he rode the trail or the range, often alone. Well, that naturally differed a lot.

A cowboy was pretty apt to think what anybody thinks— how rich he's going to get to be, about the day after tomorrow. Generally a cowpuncher's thoughts weren't what I would call profound, but I have seldom known professors who were profound for any big percentage of the time. Maybe he would think what a big time he had the last time he drew his wages and went to town, and what a big time he was going to have next pay day. A principal occupation for any cowboy's thoughts was his saddle horse, for a cowboy was a rider first, last, and always. Would he look at the scenery and think about it? Well, maybe. But after all, they have the same stars in New Mexico and in New York, even if they do look better in New Mexico, and you get used to looking at mountains and flats after a while, and don't think much about it. Each fellow would naturally think most about what interested him. When riding, he would generally have his eye on the ground a good deal, looking for any sign of animals or human beings that might be of interest to him. One great source of entertainment with some punchers was thinking what might be done to certain brands with a running iron. Not everyone who thought along those lines was aiming to be a rustler. It was just something to occupy the time. For instance, the first cattle I ever owned was a little bunch of about two hundred head that I ran in the San Andrés Mountains under the Slash SW brand, written /SW. It wouldn't take a brand-figuring cowboy long to see that you could very easily make that over into cross-eight-double-diamond.

Many cowboys were hopelessly ignorant, of course, as far as book learning went. I remember once when I was working on a wagon with eighteen or twenty men. It was close to Christmas, and one night by the campfire I got out some paper and envelopes I had and wrote a letter home. Next day one of the boys sided me purposefully when we rode out, and after beating around the bush for a while, said, "Jack, I seen you writin' a letter last night." I nodded. "I ain't got my writin' things along with me," he went on; "I was kinder wonderin' if you'd mind writin' a letter for me." The fact was, of course, that he couldn't write. But he didn't like to come right out and say so.

Of course I wrote his letter for him. And before I was through, *every man* at the wagon had asked me the same favor, in private. In that whole outfit, I was the only one that could write. That was one time in my life when I was made to feel like a smart man.

But a majority of the cowboys, even if they had no book learning to speak of, were keen-minded and eager to learn about things that interested them. They asked questions, observed, put two and two together, and in their own special field of work were the best educated people in the world. Many cowboys had a special curiosity about the meaning of words. Old Tom Beasley, for example, hero of the gold-nugget incident in El Paso, was an old puncher with no education at all, but whenever he heard new words he always was wanting to know what they meant. He was one of those who helped to drill the well that Bill Muggridge and I put in. I had my horse Ample at that time, and Tom asked me one day what the word "ample" meant. I tried to explain it by saying that it was "plenty" or "fast." Tom's interpretation of my explanation, I suppose, was that it meant about the same as "some," as that word was used in the West— "That horse is running *some!*" He stored the word in his mind and remembered it, and some time afterwards while we were at work, Old Lady Harris rode past at a good clip on one of her horses. Tom watched her cut the wind, and then remarked:

"The old lady's sure ridin' an ample pacer this mornin'."

Hundreds of sheepherders in New Mexico shared the open range, sometimes peaceably, with cowhands, and not one out of a hundred of them could read, or figure past ten. Still, they could all count sheep correctly, and this is how they did it. They would count *pares* (pairs) on their fingers; ten *pares* of course meant twenty sheep. For each twenty sheep so counted, the herder would cut a notch on a stick which he carried for the purpose. When he was all through counting, he would turn the stick over to the boss, who could count the notches and multiply by twenty. Sometimes an ignorant herder would count a flock containing several thousand head, and never miss a one. I have also seen herders count five sheep at a time as the sheep were going out of a chute as fast as they could go, and the herders were never off-count.

Cowhands for the most part, I'd say, were well enough educated to know that all the learning isn't in the books, and that's something that some of the professors don't seem to know. The range, by and large, bred full-size men who knew their jobs and hated nothing quite as much as pretense. Partners of wind, sun, horseflesh, and the ground they slept on, they lived constantly close to bedrock things, and respected facts, not appearances. It was at a roundup in the Mogollon Mountains that I first heard the cowboy song, "Crossing the Divide." It was sung by an average-ignorant puncher named Freckles, and all the boys who listened to him sing it that night, knew what the words meant. A few lines will serve to bring this book to a close and convey the average puncher's ideas about what he actually was and what he wanted others to think he was:

> Tell 'em, when the Roundup comes for all us human critters,
> Just corral me with my kind an' run a brand on me;
> I don't want to be corralled with hypocrites an' quitters;
> Brand me just for what I am—an' I'm just what you see.

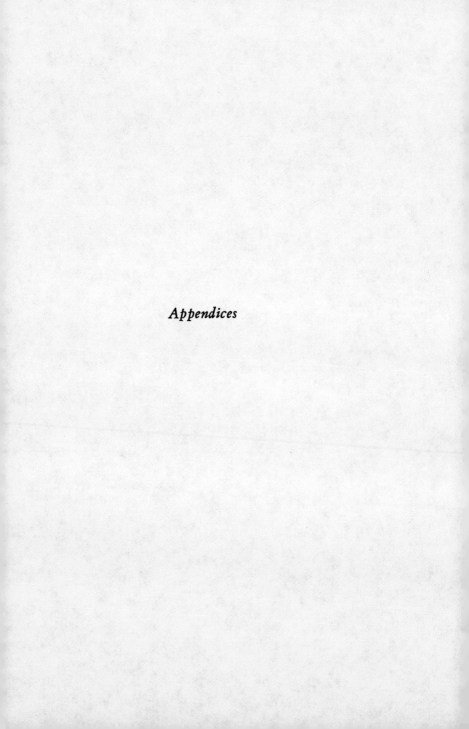

Appendices

APPENDIX I

NOTES ON THE TEXT

1. The title of the song is, "Whose Old Cow?" (see Thorp, *Songs of the Cowboys*, page 166), and concerns a critter found in one roundup and claimed by no one. Nigger Add was a dictionary on earmarks and brands, but this one was a puzzler even to him. He read the tally of the brands:

> "She's got O Block an' Lightnin' Rod,
> Nine Forty-Six an' A Bar Eleven,
> Rafter Cross an' de double prod,
> Terrapin an' Ninety-Seven;
>
> Half Circle A an' Diamond D,
> Four-Cross L an' Three PZ;
> BWI, Bar XVV,
> Bar N Cross an' ALC."

Since none of the punchers claimed the critter, Old Nigger Add just added his own brand—"For one more brand or less won't do no harm."

Late in life Add got himself engaged to a colored girl and told a few friends he would be married on Christmas Day. The news spread. Every cowman or outfit wanted to send a present, but ranches were far apart and nobody knew what the other fellow was sending. So on his wedding day, Add and his bride went to the Roswell freight depot to claim gifts which they had been told were there, and found *nineteen cookstoves!*

2. In summertime, the mule star would go to sleep at about four o'clock. For cowpunchers, a different star goes down and comes up every hour of the night; for example, at twelve o'clock "Old Peckerneck" raises up in the East, and at two o'clock "the Horseshoe" shows—five stars around in a circle, a familiar sight, but I don't know by what name the astronomers would call it. That's the way the punchers told the different watches.

3. It was in this gypsy camp that I first learned the odd meaning of a common enough word. An old gypsy woman saw me headed toward the creek, and asked if I was going to the "branch." I said I was. "I wish you'd bring me a toothbrush," she said. Not meaning to show my ignorance by asking her what she meant by a toothbrush, I cornered a gypsy boy on the way and asked him, and found out that in gypsy argot a "toothbrush" was a snuff stick. They put the snuff under the upper lip, and the stick held it in.

4. My first little book, published in 1908, was followed by the publication of a bigger book, under the same title, in 1921, under the imprint of Houghton Mifflin Company. In the meantime I had collected many more songs, the new book containing exactly one hundred and one. I submitted forty or fifty additional unpublished songs, but the publishers wanted a smallish book, and left the extra ones out. Among those omitted was "Home on the Range," then almost unknown, but now one of the most frequently sung of them all.

5. Cowboys in New Mexico hardly ever carried water.

6. Edwin Bryant, *What I Saw in California: Being the Journal of a Tour. . . . in the years 1846, 1847* (New York: D. Appleton & Company 1849), p. 109.

The Arabians were naturally small, but it is my judgment that a physical adaptation to environment had probably also taken place in the dry Southwest, where pastures frequently dry up and are seldom lush as in the rainier East. The burro of the Southwest, friend of prospectors and burden-bearer extraordinary for slow-moving people having an infinity of time as well as of space and patience to move around in, is nothing but a donkey, though much smaller than the European donkey. He also, I think, has adapted himself physically to his environment, a fact on which I once had some rather interesting evidence. I took two tiny burro colts back East for a little friend. They grew up there with all the feed and water they could ever eat. In later years when I went back and saw them, I was astonished at the size they had grown to. They were regular man-size donkeys. Had they grown up in the West where they were born, I am satisfied they would never have gotten any bigger than any other Southwestern "mountain canary."

H. H. Halsell, author of an interesting book of personal recollections, *Cowboys and Cattleland* (privately printed for the author by The Parthenon Press, Nashville, Tennessee), furnishes interesting testimony along the same lines. "It seems unreal," he says (pp. 213-14), "but a Texas horse four to five years old, when taken to northern and colder climates and kept there, will grow larger for one or two years more. When wintering for the first time in the North, I was surprised to find our horses grew larger."

Josiah Gregg, author of *Commerce of the Prairies,* remarks on how the traders returning from Santa Fe in the 1830's and '40's, were generally astonished at the size of Eastern horses when first encountered again at the settlements:

"Accustomed as we had been for some months to our little mules, and the equally small-sized Mexican ponies, our sight became so adjusted to their proportions, that when we came to look upon the commonest hackney of our frontier horses, it appeared to be almost a monster. I have frequently heard exclamations of this kind from the new arrivals: 'How the Missourians have improved their breed of horses!' 'What a huge gelding!' 'Did you ever see such an animal!' This delusion is frequently availed of by the frontiersmen to put off their meanest horses to these deluded travellers for the most enormous prices." (page 208).

7. Loco weed, or "crazy weed," is one of the first green plants to make its appearance on the range in the spring. Horses crave it, and once a horse gets in the habit of eating this weed, it cares for little else, and like human beings who fall victims to the opium habit, "locoed" horses become nervous wrecks, lose flesh, and eventually become so weak that they fall and can't get up, their eyes sunk in their heads, their nostrils feverish. At last they don't recognize anything and are truly a pitiable sight.

8. Spanish cowhands were fine riders, and many horse terms commonly used in the West come from the Spanish tongue: *palomino, remuda, manada,* mustang (from *mesteño*), lariat (from *la reata*), and many more. Miss Jean Beaumondy, champion trick girl roper, to whom the cowboy song, "Fightin' Mad," is credited, was the daughter of a Frenchman who had a ranch on the line of Old Mexico. He ran Old Mexican hands, than whom there are probably no greater ropers in the world—they give their children ropes about as soon as they can walk, and teach them to rope chickens, pigs, anything that walks or runs. Some of the hands on the ranch took a shine to Miss Jean when she was a tiny lass, and it was from them that she learned to rope.

9. Horses quickly adapted themselves to the kind of country they ran in, to protect themselves from falls and hurts. An ordinary loping horse in the East puts down both forefeet at once. You would never see a horse lope that way if he was raised in country undermined by gopher and rat holes. Such a horse puts down one forefoot at a time so as to be able to catch himself with the other if he should go into a hole. Again, a horse raised in the flats is not much good in the mountains. A horse whose ancestors have been running in mountains for generations tends to be mule-footed—round-hoofed; whereas those on the flats are flat-footed. A greenhorn rider on a mountain horse, on a tricky trail, is likely to try to guide him; that's the last thing to do. Such a horse knows how to take care of himself—and you. In the same situation, however, a horse raised on the flats would be timid and try to pick his way, and like the centipede when he stops and tries to think how he does it, would probably get all mixed up in his legs. Some years ago I asked Will James to make some illustrations for me, one of which was to show a rider approaching a vertical-banked arroyo at full speed on a Western horse. An artist not familiar with those horses would have depicted the rider with a tight rein. Not so Will, who had ample first-hand knowledge of cow horses and riding. His rider had perfectly loose reins, indicating his knowledge that cow horses are smart enough not to be ridden over sheer cliffs, even if their riders are fools enough to want to try it.

10. McDonald was inaugurated on January 15, 1912. When he was running, I asked him one day how he was going to make out. "Well, Jack," he said, "if half the fellows that owe me money, vote for me, I'll sure win."

11. "High salty"—the fellow who gets up and tells them where to head in; the straw boss, foreman, or *caporál*. This phrase came into common use in New Mexico, and I rather think I was the one who invented it. Years ago there was an old Scotsman in the country who had a lot of sheep and an enormous thirst. He used to drive all over the range in a little buckboard drawn by a team of yellow mules, and he was never known to be without a jug. One day we saw him come skally-hootin' across the flats, high-happy from liquor, and he was sure throwin' the buckskin into those mules, and at every bump it looked as if buckboard and Scotsman would part company for good. "Gosh!" said one of the boys, "Old Scotty's sure hittin' the salt bumps." "Yes," I said, "he's a high salty, ain't he!" The phrase caught on and spread, in the same way songs did, by being passed along from one fellow to another.

12. Fat pine could produce some strange results. On my first song-collecting trip, I headed from the Cornudas Tanks towards the reservoir at the mouth of the Sacramento River which we called the Sign Camp. There was a big earth dam here that caught the overflow waters of the Sacramento River; the tank usually held water the year round, and it was a wonderful grass country. The boys used to come down there and cut sign for lost stock, and that was how the camp got its name. There was a good big corral, and at the east end of the dam a one-room log house with a fireplace, where grub was always stored, and anybody passing could use it. I reached the cabin on this occasion an hour by the sun, and saw smoke rising, so I knew I would not have to camp alone. I rode up and whistled, and the blackest man I ever saw came to the door.

"Get down!" he invited, "Chuck's about ready."

As I went in, I noticed that everything in the cabin was as black as the man himself. Soot hung in great gobs from the ceiling and walls. It was some time before the colored man, as I supposed him to be, came to the light, and I recognized him as an old friend, Pap Logan, who worked for the Circle-Bar outfit when I did, and was still working for them. It seemed that he had been at the Sign Camp all winter looking after the company's saddle horses. The camp was a long ways from timber. The only wood Pap had for a fire was the fat pine stumps that had come down the river from the mountains during the yearly freshet. Having no mirror, he had no idea how black he was, nor that his long beard was matted with soot. Later when I got to the Circle-Bar headquarters, Bill Babers, the cook, told me that the ranch hands had nicknamed Pap "Dr. Smokey."

13. The Guadalupes, according to persistent rumor, hid other treasure than that cached by stage-coach bandits, and one of the seemingly authentic stories I heard was told me by old Manuel Torrero at his adobe cabin in the cottonwoods near La Joya on the Rio Grande. I had had a hard day's ride before my saddle horse and I espied the smoke rising from Manuel's chimney,

and we made our way to the door. I was invited in, and was soon sitting in front of a cheerful and hospitable fire. During my afternoon's ride I had seen a dead burro, and after supper I mentioned the fact to the *ranchero,* commenting on the strangeness that anything but accident could ever kill a burro. My host was then stirred to tell me his story of the Dead Burro Mine.

As a boy, Manuel said, he knew an Indian named Juan Reyes, who was considered very rich, and was believed to be the owner of a gold mine that nobody else could find. Many people had tried to follow him and learn where his gold mine was located, but in vain. When Juan wanted to elude them, he would give a *baile* and invite everybody, and while they were all enjoying themselves, he would slip away unnoticed on his famous burro, "Sal." At the end of a month he would return with plenty of money and nobody the wiser as to its source. Juan owned plenty of saddle horses, but on these disappearances he always rode "Sal," a burro as big as a Mexican mule, weighing over six hundred pounds, with speed and endurance. The probable reason for preferring this animal, it was surmised, was that the mine lay in a dry portion of the country, where a horse would suffer from lack of water, while a burro could survive and thrive on the various succulent forms of cactus. Like all *vaqueros,* Juan rode a rather gaudy saddle, with the letters J. R. outlined on the back of the cantle by silver tacks driven into the saddletree.

At that time, Manuel told me, he was a sheepherder for Don Antonio Saiz, who ran many flocks in the country east of the Rio Grande. In the rainy season, when the surface lakes were full of water, the sheep would sometimes drift as far east as the Guadalupes. One year, the rains having started, Manuel had headed his flock east to get the benefit of the new grass and water. He made camp one night at a place called La Seja de Alamo, and here he noticed the fresh tracks of a burro, evidently carrying a man or a heavy pack, headed in the same direction as the sheep. They were not the tracks of a loose burro, Manuel declared, but of one controlled by a rider. He followed the trail for more than a mile, and saw that the tracks bore directly for the point of the Guadalupes, thirty miles to the east.

Nothing more happened in the matter at this time. In the eighties, the Apache Indian raids got so bad that the different *patróns* kept their flocks of sheep close to their ranches in the Rio Grande Valley. During the disturbances, Juan Reyes seemed to bear a charmed life, going and coming as he pleased. No particular attention was paid to him. But one day somebody asked about him; and nobody could remember having seen him for more than two months —in fact, he never did return.

A few years after this unexplained disappearance, Manuel said, he accumulated some cows and quit herding sheep for his old *patrón*. Late one fall, he and his boy Giorge started for the Guadalupe Mountains to hunt. In those days the Guadalupes were alive with elk. Manuel and his son rode their horses, and drove ahead of them a bunch of burros, some loaded with water kegs, bedding, and camp outfit, and others carrying nothing, but taken along in order to bring back dried elk meat after the winter's supply had been killed and jerked. A journey of several days brought them to the point of the mountains, at the foot of the big bluff with the natural cross, where they made camp and piled their outfit into the cave known as *Cueva de Oso* (Cave of the bears), the cave which the outlaw Singleton later inhabited. Now, some distance north and west of the point of the mountains, a portion of it had split off, creating a narrow chasm, or canyon, running north and south. It was about a hundred feet wide, and half a mile long. At the head of the canyon was a deep pool of water, collected from the cliffs during the rains. The pool was accessible only to mountain goats, eagles, or a man with a rope and bucket; but it always contained water, and Manuel and his son were two of the few people who knew about its existence.

It was the presence of the pool that attracted them first to the main canyon, and that led them later into exploring a narrow side canyon—and here they found the dried remains of a man and a burro lying almost side by side. The spot where the bodies were discovered was always in the shade, hence the saddle was still in fair condition. It was identified by the initials, J. R., as belonging to the almost forgotten Juan Reyes. The dead man, who was undoubtedly Juan himself, had been scalped and shot through the head. Manual and his son buried Reyes as best they could. In the *muletas* on the saddle, they discovered a sack of very coarse gold dust and nuggets, which later proved to have a value of about twelve hundred dollars.

Manuel told me that he and his son had made yearly trips in search of the source of the gold, but he claimed they had never found it. The Dead Burro Mine is one of those phantoms of fortune still pursued by treasure hunters in New Mexico.

14. Another nervy and interesting woman who skirted the edges of the law, was "Sister" Cummings. She came of Kentucky mountain stock, and had married a distant cousin, Jim Cummings, of Breathitt County. To get away from clan hatreds, feuding, and bloodshed, they moved to the Indian Territory, which at that time was a rendezvous for outlaw bands, renegade niggers, halfbreeds, French and Spanish outlaws from the Louisiana bayou country, and outlaw Indians and breeds from the North and West. Jim Cummings went to work for a horse dealer who dealt in stolen stock, and one day while driving a bunch of horses to town for delivery, a United States deputy marshal arrested him as a thief. Jim's young wife was with him. By digging her thumbs into her horse's shoulder, she made the animal pitch, and cleverly got him between Jim and the deputy, whereupon she brought the loaded end of her riding quirt down on the officer's forearm, knocking the pistol out of his hand. Husband and wife galloped off and made their getaway in the brush. They were shrewdly tracked by a posse hastily summoned by the deputy, but by making a dangerous leap on a mountain trail which had been wiped out by a landslide, they escaped into Texas. Jim, going to a store after dark in the little town of White Rock, east of Dallas, to buy some coffee, was attacked by hoodlums, who thought he had money and meant to get it away from him. "Sister," watching from the edge of the brush, galloped to the scene, .45 in

hand, and rescued him. Indeed, her chief role as an outlaw's wife seems to have been to rescue her outlaw husband from the scrapes he got into.

The two came, after various wanderings, to Gainsville, where Jim Cummings again fell in with a wild bunch who were stealing horses and running them to the plains country, where they were sold to ranchers and cowmen. Things went from bad to worse for the young Kentuckians, and at last Jim was arrested as one of the men suspected of robbing the Gainsville Bank—a charge of which, as it happened, he was innocent. He was convicted on circumstantial evidence, and was sentenced to ten years in the penitentiary. Again his wife came to his rescue.

As a girl she had attended school for a while at a Kentucky convent. She now went to work and made a nun's habit and veil. With a rosary around her neck, she called on the local priest and represented herself as Jim Cummings' sister, in deep trouble because Jim (her alleged brother) was absolutely innocent, but there was no way to prove his innocence. The priest, convinced of the truth of her cause, took the matter up with the trial judge, who was his friend, but the latter could do nothing. Next the priest accompanied her to the state capitol at Austin, where he won permission for her to lay her case before the governor. Her plea was successful, and a pardon was granted. This was the exploit that won the nickname "Sister" for her. So far as known, the pair was not involved in any further trouble after Jim's release.

15. The derivation of the word "Pecos" is cloudy. The Spanish scholar, Mariano Velasquez de la Cadena, says it comes from the word *pecoso,* meaning full of freckles. More probably it is derived from the word *pecado,* which has the same root as the English word peccadillo, and means sin. River of Sin is the interpretation accepted by the old natives of New Mexico, on account of the many fights and murders occurring along its banks.

16. The walls of the government buildings, and some huge old cottonwoods, are about all that remain of the Post. Fort Sumner was a supply point for many of the smaller posts in New Mexico, and Colonel Francisco Chavez, who at one time was the commander here, related the following incident to illustrate the casual handling of Uncle Sam's property in those days. An enormous chain, weighing five tons, had been sent by ox team from the east coast, consigned to California. It was so heavy that the wagon broke down, the chain was left at the Fort, and more or less forgotten, and finally a dishonest quartermaster sold it to a ship chandlery in New Orleans. At an opportune time it was loaded by the buyer and taken away. Other materials or supplies were sold or stolen in similar fashion, but the policing was lax and the guilty parties were not caught. A couple of years after the selling of the five-ton chain, an adjutant with a clerk appeared in Fort Sumner and announced his intention of checking up the commissary and stores. He found the depot short of a lot of supplies.

Now, a four-mule army wagon, some time before this, loaded with supplies for Fort Stanton, had been swallowed up in the quicksands of the river. So as the adjutant read off his list of missing supplies and called for an explanation, the quartermaster each time would sing out:

"Lost in the river!"

After all the other shortages had been duly accounted for in this fashion, the matter of the five-ton chain was mentioned.

"Lost in the river!" called the quartermaster.

This was a little too stiff a dose for the adjutant. "Mr. Lane," he said, "you already have thirteen tons of merchandise listed as going down in the quicksands with that one wagon. Do you mean to tell me that this five-ton chain was on the wagon, too?"

"Yes, sir! It was a remarkably strong wagon."

17. This delightful document, which is to be taken for the most part as a picture of the mind and recollections of an uneducated but not wholly illiterate Spanish-American of New Mexico rather than as an exact account of historical events, was put down on paper at the instigation of Wesley R. Hurt, Jr., of Albuquerque, to whom I am indebted for the privilege of examining it.

18. When Theodore Roosevelt was President, he appointed Pat Garrett collector of customs at El Paso. There was considerable opposition to this appointment. People wrote to the President to say that Pat was a confirmed drunkard and an ignoramus. They said he couldn't even read or write. Pat more than once told the story of the way that Teddy tested him. He was sent for, and went in person to the White House. When he arrived, the President mentioned the stories he had been told about Pat's drunkenness, and then without a word, he handed Pat a typewritten document. It was a pledge to the effect that, if he were appointed collector of the customs, he would not drink while in office. Pat *read* it and *signed* it. And he always declared that he kept the pledge. Having known both Pat and Teddy, I think the story is undoubtedly substantially true.

19. It was sometimes surprising how fast news traveled on the range simply by being passed from one outfit to another by riding cowpunchers, at a time when there were no telephones and no other means of rapid communication. Some of the women were even pretty good at carrying the news. One of the best was old Mrs. Harris, who had a ranch on the Crow Flats west of the point of the Guadalupes, where she raised a lot of horses, and cows too. She was seventy and more, but she rode her own horses all over the range and never forgot an item of news and never failed to tell it. When I was ranching down there, one day I rode past the place of a man named McNew, who had had a herd of about three hundred steel-dust horses.

"Jack," he said, "I sold out my horses."

"Yes, I heard."

"I think you an' me could make some money," he said, "by goin' in the commission business. I could handle the El Paso end, an' you could work it out here on the range."

"Yes," I said, "but how would you know if I got an order?"

"Oh," he said, "you just tell old lady Harris, and I'll know it before night time."

20. Sometimes the men would be started out the night before for the locations from which they were to begin working. They would cram a biscuit or two in their pockets for breakfast, camp when they got to the assigned location, and start work at the crack of daylight. They would usually be in at the wagon then by noon, and branding of the calves would go forward in the afternoon.

21. Mr. John Young is probably correct when he says in his excellent book, *The Vaquero,* that the prodding and punching of the cattle to keep them on their feet in the railroad cars, is the origin of the word "cowpuncher." Mr. Young writes that in 1879 he made a shipment of cattle from the Cimmarron Cattle Company, from Las Animas, Colorado, to Kansas City. Two young Easterners wanted to go home, and asked if they could go with the cattle. Mr. Young furnished them with passes and prodpoles and told them how to use them to keep the cattle on their feet to prevent their being trampled and smothered by other cattle. "So we are now cowpunchers!" they remarked to Mr. Young. And the name stuck.

22. An unpublished letter written by a cowboy named J. O. Harshman, who worked for the Bates & Beals LX outfit, headquartered near Tascosa, in the western panhandle of Texas, about the year 1880, gives a good account of what happened to cowboys when they rode the cars to market with the cattle, and on the trail home. Harshman writes:

"As I told you Len & I started for Chicago with sixteen carload cattle. We got up to Atchison Kansas & unloaded for feed & water & rest the cattle for 24 hours. We started out to see the town but got separated & after while Len drifted back to the offices that had charge of the yards. In the meantime they had received a telegram from Mr. Beals to rush the cattle through so they loaded eight cars & started Len out with them & when I showed up several hours later they loaded the other eight cars & started me out with them. One of the steers got down & could not get up so when we got to Ottumwa, Iowa, along in the night we had the car backed to the yards & unloaded part of them before we could get it up. That caused considerable delay but we finally got started again & made the trip without further mishap. I got to the stock yards in the night. The yard men took charge & I went to a near-by hotel & stayed all night. The next morning I reported at Mr. Beals' office & found Len waiting for me. Mr. Beals payed us off & we started out to see the town. Neither of us had ever been in a big town before & we wanted to see what was just around the corner. We each drew six months pay at 45.00 per month & we had not had a chance to spend any. Talk about John D. Rockefeller being rich. He was not in the same class with us in our estimation.

"We started to walk down town but didn't get anywhere so finally took a street car. I don't know where it took us but when we got off we hunted a barber shop & got a hair cut & shave. Then we found a clothing store & got a new suit of clothes. I paid 5.00 for a broad brimmed white hat, the best I could get. When I got back to the ranch I was offered a pony for it & would not take it. Next we went to a cheap hotel some where & got a room & changed our clothing & left all our old ones. I had a boyhood friend working for Field Leiter & Co. We hunted him up. He was living in a rooming house down about where the Congress Hotel now stands, & we arranged to stay with him. We told him if he would show us around nights we would pay all expenses. There were no cars in those days so we would hire a cabby with a nice-looking outfit to drive us around town days—you know we were rich. At night my friend would show us the night life of a great city. We knew nothing about nickels or pennies & always gave a newsboy a dime for a paper. One morning we went into a fine big restaurant (at least it looked that way to us) for breakfast. Just as we got thru eating the waiter brought us a couple of finger bowls with pieces of lemon in them. Of course a finger bowl was way beyond our comprehension. Our pants legs had always been sufficient for us to wipe our fingers on. We thought it was something more to eat, so we fished out the lemons & ate them. We noticed the waiters were all watching us & grinning but we did not care. We stayed in Chicago from Wednesday to Monday. Our riches had taken wing & most of them had flown away so we said good bye & went back to our camp on the Ninescah River near Kingman Kansas. Holycott was getting ready to go back to the home ranch in Texas. . . . .

"One day one of the boys rode in town & when he came back said it was Sunday & everything closed up & suggested we all go to church. That appealed to us so that night we laid aside our guns & belts & rode in town & all attended their little church. I am sure we were of more interest to the congregation than what the preacher had to say. One afternoon just before we started on our return trip the preacher came to our camp & wanted to trade his gold watch for a pony that was broken to drive. Mr. Holycott was not there at the time but one of the boys traded him one of the ponies that had been driven down there to a cook wagon. We had plenty of ponies & the boy wanted the watch. I have often wondered what that pony done to that preacher & his covered buggy if he ever got it hitched up.

"There were six or eight of us going back. Mr. Holycott had laid in a supply of grub & a lot of things he had bought from the grangers. It was now in Sept. & the weather was fine. We had about one hundred ponies to take back & let them graze through so we were in no hurry. I have been on many camping trips but I don't believe I ever enjoyed one more than I did that one. We were over a month on the way. We soon got beyond the settlements & then it was open prairie for hundreds of miles without road or trail. We took a southwesterly course that we thought would bring us to the Canadian River some where near the ranch. We soon got down into the Indian Territory where there was considerable timber along the streams. The Indians used to take their annual hunts & the squaws would cut down a big pile of mesquite bushes & let it dry until the next year & then use it for firewood &

cut another lot for the next year. When we would find a pile we would camp for the night & set fire to the pile & soon have a nice bed of coals. Wild turkey were thick & toward evening they would go out in the open to feed. We would not waste bullets on them but would run them down with out horses. They could not fly far & we would catch them & take them into camp & eat them. We would sit up till late in the night cooking, eating & talking. Then set a watch over the horses, unroll our blankets & take a good sleep. . . . . "

23. The proper use of the *dalebuelta* was celebrated in the cowboy song, "Windy Bill." The hero was a Texas man who allowed that the steer he couldn't tie down, hadn't been born yet. The boys knew of an old outlaw that ran in the draw, and they bet the windy Texan that there was one steer he couldn't tie. He took the bet and rode after the steer with "his old maguey tied hard and fast" to the saddle horn (the maguey was a Mexican rope made from the fiber of the century plant). He landed his rope around the steer's horns all right, but from there on it was the steer's party. The cinches broke, and rope and saddle tree tailed the steer down the draw, "Windy Bill" landing in a big rock pile. The moral, according to the song, is—

> Whenever you start to tackle a steer
>   Never tie hard your maguey.
> Put on your dalebueltas,
>   'Cordin' to California law,
> And you will never see your old rim-fires
>   Driftin' down the draw.

A tied rope was a bad bargain in a pinch. But if the rope were just wrapped around the horn, it would hold the ordinary critter, but give in an ermergency.

24. Questions are often asked concerning the relation of the modern rodeo to actual work done on cow ranches. Rodeo sports are really, in part, highly specialized developments of some aspects of cow work, together with some riding and roping activities that cowboys never indulged in at all, at least in their working hours. In the days of the open range, the cowboys had roping contests, sometimes at county fairs, sometimes when two ropers of different outfits would meet on the range. The trick ropers one meets at the rodeos are seldom good range hands; they have simply fooled around with a rope and picked up one stunt after another. In their line, they are good.

Bulldogging is definitely a modern sport, having nothing to do with the cattle business as such. It was first done by a colored boy named Pickett. It takes a fast horse, and a strong, nervy man. It's the thriller of the rodeo, and makes the audience squeal. When a steer, given a good scare as he leaves the chute, is turned loose, the bulldogger races his horse and crowds the steer to the fence so he can lay alongside of his head. Gradually his horse gets abreast of the flying steer's horns. Then the bulldogger kicks free from his saddle and lands on the head of the racing steer. That takes nerve and lots of it. The steer may carry the bulldogger a hundred feet or more with both of his heels plowing up the ground till the resistance slows up and finally stops the steer. Then the bulldogger can twist the animal's neck till he gets a fall and holds up one hand for time.

The roping contests at modern rodeos are different from range practice. Now they rope calves, and when you have roped your calf you must get to it, bulldog it, and tie it, with judges keeping time on you from the passing of the deadline till you throw up your hands indicating that you have finished tying the calf. In the old days they roped full-grown steers and had to "bust" or throw them, which they did hard enough so the animal lay still, half-stunned. The roper, with his horse sitting back tight on the rope, got to the steer with his piggin' (or hoggin') string, tied him down. This took a fast man and horse. The times made then were slower than now, but they were handling animals twice and three times as heavy. Riders like Tie Randolph Reynolds, Andy McLoughlin, Clay McGonegal, Ellison Carroll, Joe Gardner, and one or two others, ran from 17 2/5 to 18 1/2 seconds.

An old-time sport of Mexican and American *vaqueros* which has no counterpart in the modern rodeo, was tailing cattle. A big steer or wild bull would be turned loose from a corral and come out a-snuffing. A *vaquero* would lay up to him with his horse, grab the bull's tail, take a couple of wraps around his saddle horn, and spur past the bull and at a little angle from him. If his horse was very fast, he'd turn the bull a somersault. The man making the fastest time throwing his animal was declared the winner. As this sport crippled so many animals, it gradually died out, like the big-steer roping.

Another old sport of American punchers and *vaqueros* of the Southwest, particularly those who worked along the Rio Grande, was the *corrida del gallo*, an old Spanish game. The sport is still kept up, especially on Mexican feast days, but has never become a rodeo feature. A rooster is buried in the ground, with only his head and neck exposed. Then one after another, the mounted contestants dash up. Leaning far over in their saddles, they reach for the rooster, and try to pull him out of the ground. The one who finally gets him is pursued by all the others, who attempt to get the bird away from him; but the rooster's neck by then has been wrung, and any pursuer who gets too close to the flying horseman is likely to get a clout on the head with the bloody fowl.

The greatest rider the Southwest ever knew was Macario Leyba. He could ride anything that came along, roll cigarettes while his horse was pitching, kick one foot out of the stirrup, then the other. He could ride without any hackamore lines, and even undress while his horse was pitching. He would use two or three horses during the performance, and as the last of his clothes came off, all the old Mexican women would scream *"Balga me, diós!"* and run for cover. One time when I was living in Santa Fe, Bugger Red and his partner, Greasewood, came to town and wanted me to get up a little rodeo so they could get some money to go on. So I got the loan of "Sky High" from Charlie

Siringo as a star attraction. This was a gentled horse, but when you flank-cinched him tight, he was a show horse and one of the hardest pitchers I ever saw. Now, Greasewood had a wooden leg and when pitchin' high, he would pull off the leg and hit the horse with it—and bring down the house.

25. Josiah Gregg, *Commerce of the Prairies*, reprint by Southwest Press, Dallas, Texas, April, 1933, p. 29.

26. A good description of this so-called food was written by Gregg in his *Commerce of the Prairies*, as follows:

"Besides the *tortilla* they make another singular kind of bread, if we may so style it, called *guayave*, a roll of which so much resembles a 'hornet's nest,' that by strangers it is often designated by this title. It is usually made of Indian corn prepared and ground as for *tortillas*, and diluted into a thin paste. I once happened to enter an Indian hut where a young girl of the family was baking *guayaves*. She was sitting by a fire, over which a large flat stone was heating, with a crock of prepared paste by her side. She thrust her hand into the paste, and then wiped it over the heated stone. What adhered to it was instantly baked and peeled off. She repeated this process at the rate of a dozen times or more per minute. Observing my curiosity, the girl handed me one of the 'sheets,' silently; for she seemed to understand but her native tongue. I found it pleasant enough to the taste; though when cold, as I have learned by experience, it is, like the cold *tortilla*, rather tough and insipid. They are even thinner than wafers." (p. 185.)

APPENDIX II

(The following brief list of rangeland words and phrases does not pretend to be exhaustive, nor are the explanations learned. These are a few of the words or phrases I remember, peculiar to the vocabulary of the Southwestern range, together with my own explanation of their meaning as I heard cowboys use them. In a few cases I have offered an explanation of the probable origin. If the reader wants a fairly exhaustive and reliable bible on this subject, I can recommend *Cowboy Lingo*, by Ramon F. Adams, published in 1936 by Houghton Mifflin Company.)

AUGER—cowboy word for gossip, talk, parley, conversation, or chin wagging of almost any kind.

BARBOQUEJO—chin-strap on a cowboy's hat, used especially in brushy country to keep the hat on the wearer's head.

BOSAL—the nose band on a hackamore.

BOTTOM—endurance, as applied to a horse.

BREAK IN TWO—the term was applied to a bronc when he quit pitching and started running.

BRONCO OR BRONC—a horse ready for riding, but not yet broken to the saddle. He may be a mustang, or he may be branded. As soon as he was broken to ride, the horse ceased to be a bronco and was known as a saddle horse. A trained saddle horse would sometimes "go bronc" with his rider, that is, act like an unbroken horse, pitching and jumping, particularly when a cold or wet saddle blanket was put on him, or if he were cinched too tight. I heard a radio singer tell how much he loved his saddle and his bronc, meaning his good old riding horse that had been his pal all these years. That singer, or the fellow who wrote his song, didn't know cow horses.

BROOMTAIL—a range mare, so called because her tail grew long; sometimes it would hang right onto the ground. All range mares were classed as "broomies." Some people called them "willows." The Spanish name for them was *llegua*.

BRUSH-POPPER—a cowhand working cattle in brushy country.

CAPORÁL—foreman.

CAVYARD (also known as the "cavvy")—the same as *remuda* (see below). Cavyard was a corruption of the Spanish *caballado*.

CHEATING—a term used in breaking horses. If, for instance, the bronc was cinched so tight that he could hardly breathe, that was called cheating. Of if the buster in staking out the horse he was breaking, never changed him to fresh grass, that also was called cheating; likewise, starving a horse till he got so weak that he could do a rider no damage, using a loaded quirt over his head if he pitched, or in fact, abusing a horse in any way. Busters of this kind were cowards, afraid of the horses they were supposed to break.

COCINERO—cook.

COTTON-PICKER—a New Mexico term for a Texas cowhand.

DALEBUELTA—a wrap of the rope around the saddle horn. Cowboys shortened the word to "dally," and you'd hear them talking of "takin' a couple o' dallies."

DOGIE—a motherless calf. Tom Livingston was the first cowhand I ever heard give the definition of dogie which later was the common property of all cowhands. My wife, Blarney, and I, soon after our marriage, had an argument about the meaning of the word, and one day when Tom was visiting us, she asked him what he understood a dogie to be. "Well, Mrs.," Tom said, "a dogie is a calf whose maw has died, an' his paw has run off with another cow."

DRAGS—the slow cattle at the rear of a trail herd.

GRULLA—a mouse-colored horse.

HIGH SALTY—the man who had the say-so with a range crew or a group of riders on the trail. (See Appendix I, note 11.)

HONDA—the loop in a rope. The word, when spelled with a final "o" instead of "a," may also mean "deep," as in Arroyo Hondo, meaning Deep Arroyo.

JAQUIMÓ (pronounced ha'-ki-mo, since the Spanish "J" is pronounced like the English "h"—a rope halter often made of pleated hair and used in breaking horses. The word is anglicized as "hackamore."

JUSGADO (transliterated by the cowboys into "hoosegow" or "jug")—the town lockup.

LICK—the range word for syrup or molasses.

LLEGUA (pronounced yeá-wa)—mare.

MALPAIS (pronounced mal-a-pie by cowhands)—loose lava rock, left by a lava flow or volcanic eruption of some sort.

MANADA—a bunch of mustangs. With the exception of the stallion and unweaned colts, all are females, the stud, or stallion, having run off all the male colts from the yearlings up.

MANSADOR—a horse breaker, also known as a bronc buster or bronc fighter.

MESTEÑERO—a wild-horse hunter. In English, *mesteño,* a wild horse, became "mustang," and *mesteñero* became "mustanger."

MORRAL—nosebag for feeding grain to the horse, generally carried on the horn of the saddle.

MOUNT—in New Mexico this word was not used to designate the particular horse that a man happened to be riding at any given time; instead, it was used to designate the bunch of horses that a cowboy commonly rode in turn when he was on the trail or working the roundup. One of the animals in his mount would be his night horse, another his favorite rope horse, a third his best cutting horse, and so on. A mount was anywhere from five to seven horses, as a rule, though upon occasion there might be more or less.

MULEY—a longhorn without horns.

MUSTANG (from the Spanish *mesteño*)—a wild horse. A mustang is a bronc, but a bronc is not necessarily a mustang.

OUTLAW—a horse that refuses to be broken to ride, or is spoiled in the breaking.

PALOMINO—a horse of a creamy dun color, with a white mane and tail.

PASEAR—journey.

PECOSED—killed. The expression came from the old Spanish custom in the Pecos Valley of weighting a murdered man's body with stones and dumping it into the convenient Pecos River.

PINTO—a "paint" pony, oddly colored, often with white spots, produced by the cross-breeding of different-colored parent strains.

POINT—the leading animals in a herd that was being trailed.

POTRANKA—filly.

POTRILLO—male colt (horse).

REMUDA—this term was commonly used in New Mexico to designate the whole bunch of saddle horses being used by the crew of men on a roundup or trail drive. The word "cavvy" or "cavyard" was also used (see above).

SCALAWAG—a steer, generally an old one, that had ideas of his own. He didn't want to be driven anywhere, especially not on the trail, and didn't mean to be if he could help it. He would make every effort to sneak away from the herd, often from the bed-ground at night, lone-wolfing it back to the home range if he made his getaway.

SOOGAN—a quilt, often made of old pieces of overall pants or other scraps patched together and filled with cotton batten, feathers, or sheepskins. Spread inside a tarpaulin seven feet wide and fourteen or more feet long, it made the cowboy's bed.

STEEL DUST—a breed of horse, usually sorrels, grays, bays, or chestnuts. The breed originated in Texas, and was the result of the mating of pure Arabians with other breeds. They were heavy-quartered, small horses, and once in a while you found one that was as fast as a ghost.

STOCK HORSES—the breeding herd on a ranch, including mares, stallions, colts, and geldings intended for saddle horses but not yet broken to ride.

STRAY MAN—on a roundup, one outfit, usually the principal user of that range, provided the chuck wagon and the main body of riders. But any other outfit that had some cattle on that range was likely to send a representative to take care of its interests. Such a representative was sometimes called a "rep," but more often, in the Southwest, a "stray man"— not because *he* had gone astray, but because his outfit's cattle had.

SWING—the sides of a trail herd when moving. The punchers at each side of the herd were said to ride "on swing."

SWITCH TAIL—a horse that had a habit of swinging his tail, the reason for it generally being that somebody had ridden him beyond his endurance. As soon as you got on his back and touched him with a spur, that tail would start and go around and around.

TRAIL (as a verb)—this word was much more commonly used in the Southwest than "drive." Also, "herd" was much more common than "band" in speaking of horses. You'd hear a cowboy say, "He carried (or trailed) a herd of horses to the Black River"—not, "He drove a band of horses."

VAQUERO—horseman.

WILLOW—see "broomtail."

INDEX